Get Creative
EMAGIC LOGIC
Composing and arranging with Emagic Logic

Keith Gemmell

PC Publishing

PC Publishing
Export House
130 Vale Road
Tonbridge
Kent TN9 1SP
UK

Tel 01732 770893
Fax 01732 770268
email info@pc-publishing.com
web site http://www.pc-publishing.com

First published 2003

© PC Publishing

ISBN 1 870775 821

All rights reserved. No part of this publication may be reproduced or transmitted in any form, including photocopying and recording, without the written permission of the copyright holder, application for which should be addressed to the Publishers. Such written permission must also be obtained before any part of this publication is stored in an information retrieval system of any nature.

Original music composed by Keith Gemmell, © 2003 Music Hot House. All rights reserved.

British Library Cataloguing in Publication Data
A catalogue record for this book is available from the British Library

Cover design by Michelle Raki

Printed in Great Britain by Bell and Bain, Glasgow

Preface

Welcome to *Get Creative with Emagic Logic*. Two questions:

1 Do you want to learn the basics of composition and arranging? The nuts and bolts as it were.
2 Do you also want to learn how to sequence, record and mix your compositions effectively within Emagic Logic?

If your answer to those questions is yes, this book will help you do both in a practical and enjoyable way. Nothing stuffy here!

There's an old proverb: *I hear and I forget, I see and I remember, I do and I understand.*

That's the essence of this book. Doing the projects and comparing your results along the way to the examples on the CD will provide you with a valuable insight into the creative process. What's more, you will be learning how to use Emagic Logic at the same time. Do and you will understand.

Two things are dealt with here:

1 The creative process, conceiving the ideas and developing them.
2 The production process, capturing, shaping and manipulating those ideas within Emagic Logic.

Both elements overlap and this book could just as easily have been entitled *Composing and Arranging with Emagic Logic*. There's no doubt that much of today's music is produced this way. The most obvious use is in the pop, techno and dance genres. However this is not the only use. Emagic Logic and similar music software production programs are used to record music for computer games, TV soundtracks, advertising jingles, radio drama and multimedia presentations to name just a few. This book is aimed at helping musicians and students interested in writing for those kind of markets with the composition process; how to get the ideas in the first place and develop, record and mix them into a satisfying whole. Everything, the sequencing, the audio recording, the effects, dynamic processing and mixing, is done within Logic itself. Of course you do not have to actually do the projects if you don't want to. The text can be followed and a great deal learned by just loading and examining the example files.

Contents

How to use this book and CD *1*
Equipment needed. The scheme of things. The CD. The projects. Logic's Environment. General MIDI. Built-in synthesizers and plug-ins.

1 MIDI sequencing: make it easy on yourself *7*
Slow it down. Break it down. Cycle record. To quantize or not to quantize. Editing – get rid of the bum notes!

Project 1 – some rock 'n' roll piano *12*

2 Get real with MIDI *17*
Listen and learn. Learn how to listen. Get a life! – play with others. Sequencing examples. Sequencing strings. Sequencing drums and percussion. Sequencing guitars. Quantization. Dynamics.

Project 2 – a rock score *28*

Project 3 – a jazz funk score *44*

Project 4 – a classical score *65*

3 Finding and developing ideas *77*
Finding new ideas. At the computer? Away from the computer? Don't doodle! Developing your ideas. Know where you are heading. Keep moving – work creates work. Repetition and variation. Keep it simple – details later. Review your work – less is more.

Project 5 – a computer game track *82*

4 A look at musical form *100*
Simple three part forms. Jazz standards. Pop song.

5 The building blocks of composition *105*
The phrase. Melody. Harmony. Rhythm.

6 Melody making *109*
Cell construction. Musical questions and answers.

7 Audio recording *112*
Recording vocals. Recording electric guitars. Recording acoustic guitars. Recording brass and woodwind. Recording strings. From microphone to audio track – the signal route.

Project 6 – a football theme *115*

8 Create illusions – a big band radio jingle *134*
Audio and MIDI tracks combined. Jitterbug Jump.

Project 7 – a TV sitcom theme *137*

9 Minimalism *153*

Project 8 – a minimalist soundtrack *156*

10 Dance music *168*
Styles and loops. Constructing a drum and bass loop.

Project 9 – Get Creative with Logic jingle *171*

11 Knowing the score *178*

Project 10 – Score clean-up *115*

12 Creative audio editing *190*

Project 11 – matching song tempo to audio *193*

Project 12 – slicing audio for tempo adjustment *195*

Project 13 – trimming regions and creating fade outs *197*

Project 14 – using Groove Machine *199*

Project 15 – audio to MIDI Groove Templates *201*

Project 16 – audio pitch shifting *203*

Project 17 – time stretching audio *205*

Appendix 1 Instrument ranges *206*

Appendix 2 Key commands for Mac *209*

Appendix 3 Key commands for PC *213*

Index *217*

Acknowledgements

Special thanks to:
David Marshall: Managing Director, Sound Technology.
Jason Byrne: Sound Technology, Senior Product Specialist, Emagic Support UK – www.soundtech.co.uk.
Keith Leblanc: www.keithleblanc.org.
Marcus Farny: Pocketfuel – www.pocketfuel.com.

How to use this book and CD

Equipment needed

All that's needed, for the projects and examples, is a Mac or PC powerful enough to run a version of Logic 5, or higher, Platinum, Gold or Audio, equipped with a suitable sound card, a large, fast hard drive and decent monitor speakers. A keyboard and MIDI interface will be needed for working through the projects. Some of these include audio recording as an option. For this you will need a microphone and possibly an external mixer.

Most projects contain MIDI tracks, and for this you will need a General MIDI sound source. This can be a keyboard with on-board GM sounds, a sound card containing a GM sound set, a software synthesizer such as Quicktime Musical Instruments or an external sound module such as a Roland Sound Canvas.

The scheme of things

The book and accompanying CD are integral parts of *Get Creative with Emagic Logic*. Much of the time you will need to use both along with a copy of Logic 5, or higher running on your computer. This is most certainly the case with the seventeen chapters containing projects. Other chapters containing general reading matter also contain references to examples on the CD but make sense away from the computer.

If you already possess a working knowledge of Logic and MIDI sequencing then you may be tempted to skip the first few chapters and projects. That's OK but there is much to be gained, from a musical standpoint, by working through them.

Where possible, for clarity, all Logic functions are referred to using the program's menus. For example the instruction 'Turn the loops into real copies' would be followed by the menu command in square brackets: [Functions > Sequence Parameter > Turn Loops to Real Copies...] (Figure 0.1). Power users can speed things up by using the many keyboard shortcuts and alternative methods available (see Appendix 2 and 3). There's usually more than one way of doing things in Logic!

> **Note**
>
> Some features in the book and on the CD will be missing from Emagic's budget version, Logic Audio (previously Logic Silver). However, the Logic Audio user will still find a great deal that's useable here. Where appropriate, three mixes are supplied on the CD, Platinum, Gold and Silver, each using slightly different plug-ins. However, should a plug-in not be found, just replace it with an equivalent included with your particular version.

Figure 0.1
Example: Loops to real copies

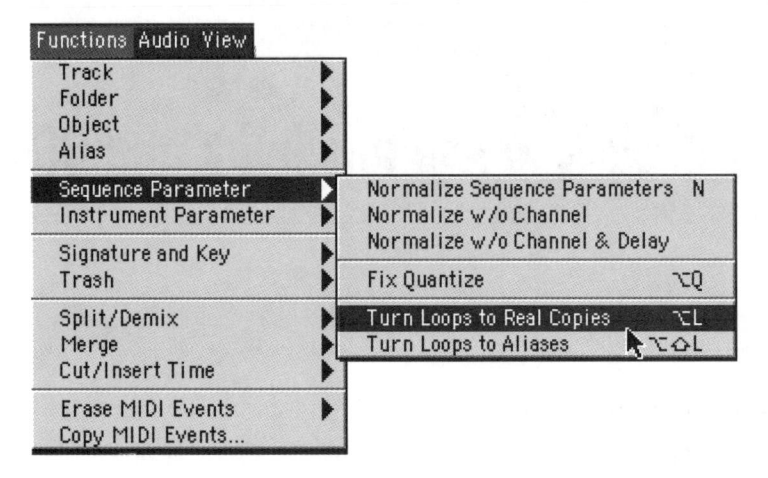

The CD

The CD is compatible with both PC and Apple Mac computers and contains:

- Audio Files supplied in AIF – Audio Interchange File – format (with the extension .aif)
- Logic Song Files (with the extension .lso)
- ReCycle files (with the extension .rex)

The CD files are arranged in folders, relevant to the project or chapter to which they relate. Most chapters refer to musical examples contained on the CD. To examine them, copy the appropriate folder across to your computer desktop or some other location. It is particularly important that all the files contained in a folder are copied across and that they remain in their respective folders, particularly the audio files. Logic 'remembers' where they are situated and if they are moved, problems are likely to arise.

The projects

The projects are a vital part of *Get Creative with Emagic Logic*. Each one builds on the techniques discussed in previous chapters and new Logic skills are progressively introduced.

- Projects 1 – 3 are concerned with MIDI sequencing skills. We record three different styles of music – a rock band, a classical ensemble and a jazz funk band.
- Projects 4 – 9 are concerned with composition and arranging. In each one we build a composition from scratch using a predetermined assignment. For example, the brief in project 5 instructs us to compose music for a soundtrack using minimalist techniques.
- Project 10 is concerned with the business of producing a readable score and parts from the Score and Layout section of Logic. Here we use a previous project, number 6, as a basis for the work.
- Projects 11 – 17 are solely concerned with the business of creative audio editing. These include such tasks as time stretching, pitch shifting and quantizing.

All the projects follow a similar pattern and begin with a list of Musical Objectives and Logic Skills. This is followed by a list of instructions headed Preparation. The first two instructions are always the same. In Project 5, for example:

1 From the CD, copy the folder named project5 to your computer. (This folder contains all the files you will need for the project).
2 On your computer, create a folder called mywork5 or something similar in which to save your work. (This is the folder where any work you create will be saved in Logic Song file format.
3 From the project5 folder, open template – templt5. (This is a specially prepared template containing the Tracks, Objects, and Logic Environment ready to work on).
4 In your new mywork5 folder, save the template as myproj5 or something similar. (Everything you do in this project from now on, will be saved here).

Next comes the assignment which contains an imaginary commission and scenario for the project. For example the assignment for Project 5 begins like this: 'OK, here's the scenario. A computer game company has commissioned you to compose the music for a scene in their latest historical title set in Elizabethan times. The piece must run for a minimum of 3 minutes.'

Each project contains a series of 'takes'. This is usually an instruction to record something in Logic. At the beginning of each take is a list of settings for the Arrange window. For example Project 5, Take 1 looks like this.

Take 1

Track 1: Nylonstr. | Guitar 1
Sequence Parameters box: Qua 1/8 – note
Instrument Parameter box: Cha 1, Prg 24
Transport Bar: (L) 1.1.1 (R) 5.1.1

The first line tells us which track or object to select and its instrument name. Next comes the Sequence Parameter box with any quantize settings needed for the recording. This is followed by the Instrument Parameter box containing the Channnel number and General MIDI program number to select. Lastly, the Transport bar information, which is usually just the Locator settings.

We then follow the text and perform the Take itself. At the completion of a Take there is always an instruction to save the work. In Project 5 it is:

- Save Song – compare with project5/5.1.

At this point you:

1 Save your work as a Song File.
2 Compare it with the example Song file, in the project 5 folder copied over from the CD. It will not sound exactly the same as yours because you will have played it differently. However, it should be something similar. If you are happy with the result then close down the example Song File and continue with the project.

Each time a take is completed follow the same procedure and save your work as a Song file. The comparison Song file will always correspond to

Tip

When loading example files containing MIDI settings its quite likely that you will initially hear the wrong sounds (very likely those from a previous project or song). Use [Options > Song Settings > Used Instrument MIDI Settings] to correct them. A faster way – quickly cursor up or down the tracks using the arrow keys on your computer keyboard.

Tip

A project invariably contains more than one song file. When opening a new song Logic presents you with a dialogue box asking 'Close current songs before opening new song?'. Choose 'Don't close'. This way all the project's songs can be found and opened from the lower section of the Windows menu (Figure 0.2).

where you are in the project. If your version has gone astray in some way, you can always continue by working on the example instead. However, to avoid confusion, if you are happy with the result of your work it is best to close down the example Song file.

Of course you do not have to actually do the projects if you don't want to. The text can be followed and much learned by just loading and examining the example files.

Logic's Environment

Yes, the dreaded Environment. It can strike fear into the hearts of even the most seasoned music tech. professional. Don't worry. Forget all that complicated virtual cabling, we don't need it here. Each example song file on the CD loads with a basic, ready to use environment based on Logic's default autoload song. It comprises the following:

- Click and Ports Layer – this will get your MIDI signals into Logic (Figure 0.3).
- MIDI Instrument Layer – containing a General MIDI Multi Instrument with its Sub-channels already set up for the project (Figure 0.4).

Figure 0.2
Windows menu

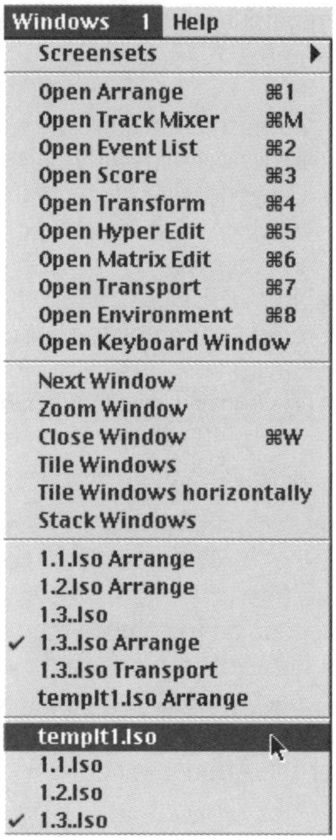

Figure 0.3
Click and Ports Layer

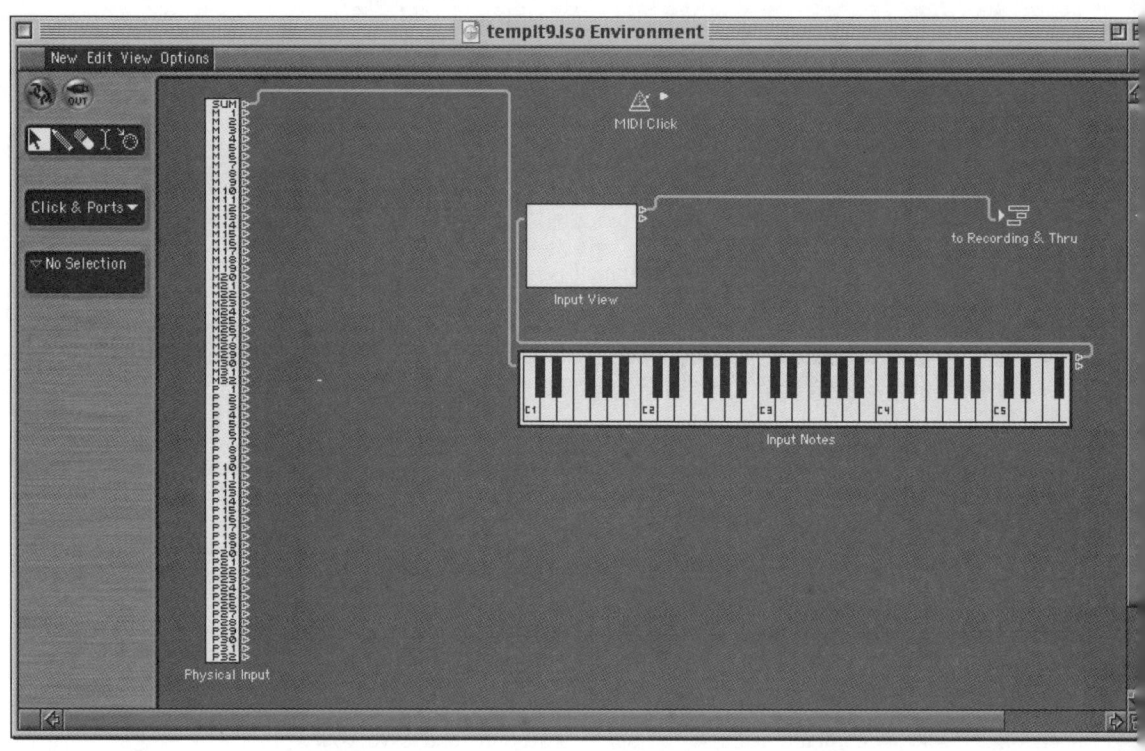

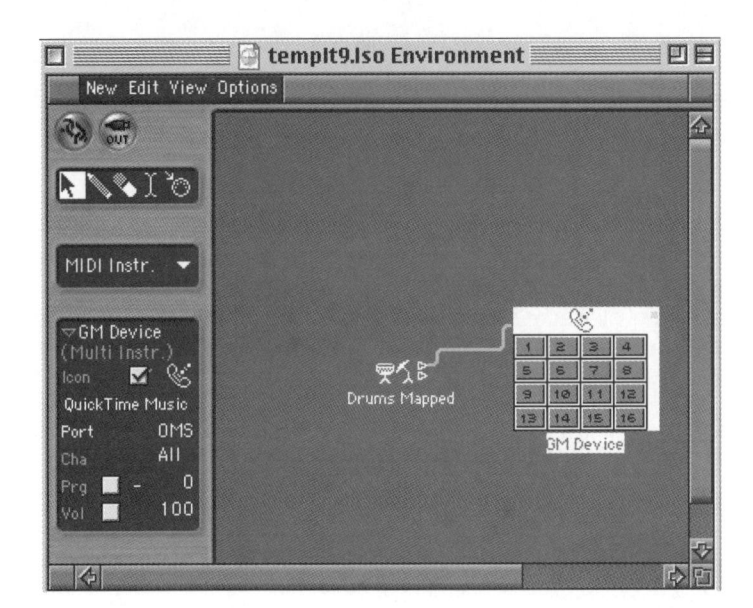

Figure 0.4
MIDI Instrument Layer

To use an internal instrument or a software GM synthesizer such as Quicktime, do the following:

1 In the Environment (MIDI Instr.), choose New > Internal > Quicktime. A Quicktime object appears.
2 Create a standard, multi, or mapped instrument.
3 Connect the output of the instrument to Quicktime. Then use the Instrument in the normal way (Figure 0.4a).

- Audio Mixer – containing the Audio Objects needed for the project (Figure 0.5).

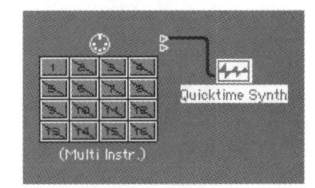

Figure 0.4a (above)
Using a Quicktime synth

Figure 0.5
Audio Mixer

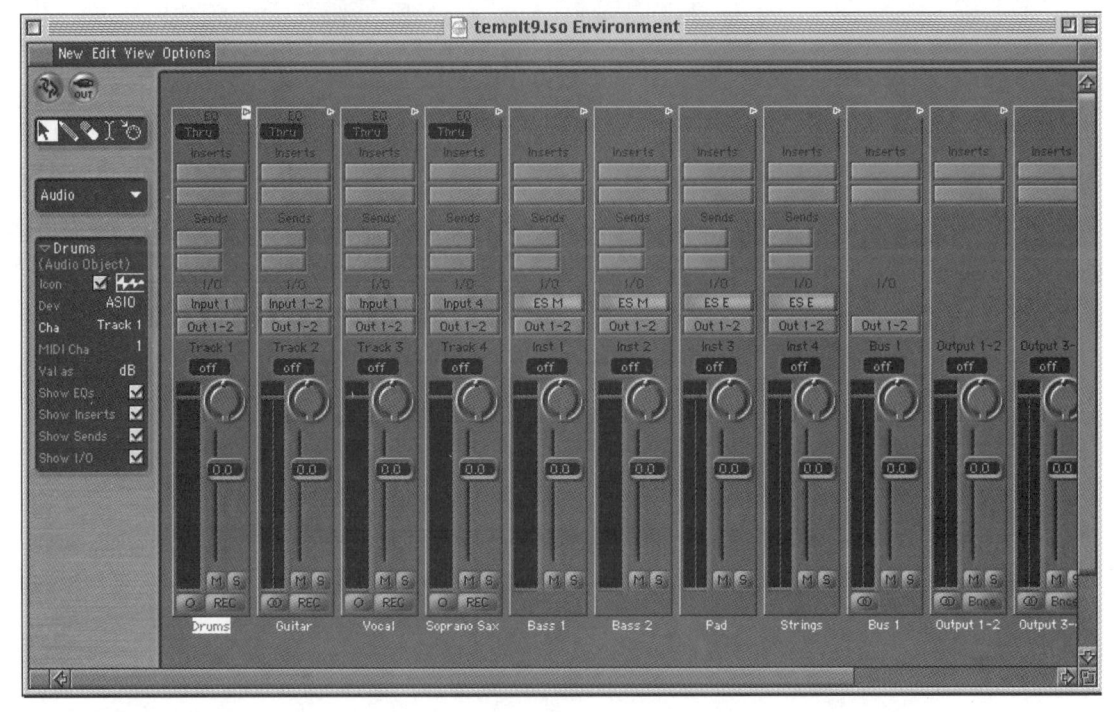

> **Tip**
>
> Ensure that the GM Multi Instrument (or indeed, any other object) is directly assigned to an output by checking that it is marked with a shaded triangle on its right side. If it's not connected the triangle will be hollow (Figure 0.6).

Figure 0.6

You will, of course, need to assign the Multi Instrument to a physical MIDI output. There's more information on this under Direct Output Assignment, MIDI Channel and Port Connection and Setting up Your MIDI Hardware in the manual.

General MIDI

General MIDI has been used for most of the MIDI content in the projects and examples. Please bear in mind that although the correct voices will be selected, sound quality and volume levels vary from one GM tone generator to another. You may have to adjust volume, chorus and reverb controls slightly for a pleasing balance.

Built-in synthesizers and plug-ins

Quite a few projects make use of Logic's built-in synthesizers; ES M, ES P, and ES E as well as various plug-ins. Because they will be used on computers with widely differing processing power, extensive use of these has been avoided. Only a few are usually operating at one time.

You can monitor the processing power being used in the System Performance window [Audio > System Performance...] (Figure 0.7) and if you experience problems, disable the least important plug-in currently in use.

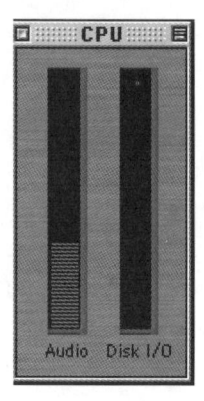

There's one other supplied software instrument called KlopfGeist (Figure 0.8). It's main use is as a metronome. It is included with each project template and inserted on channel 64.

Figure 0.7
System performance window

> **Info**
>
> A 'Klopfgeist' is the baby brother of the 'Poltergeist' but doesn't throw the furniture around! He just makes knocking and tapping sounds.

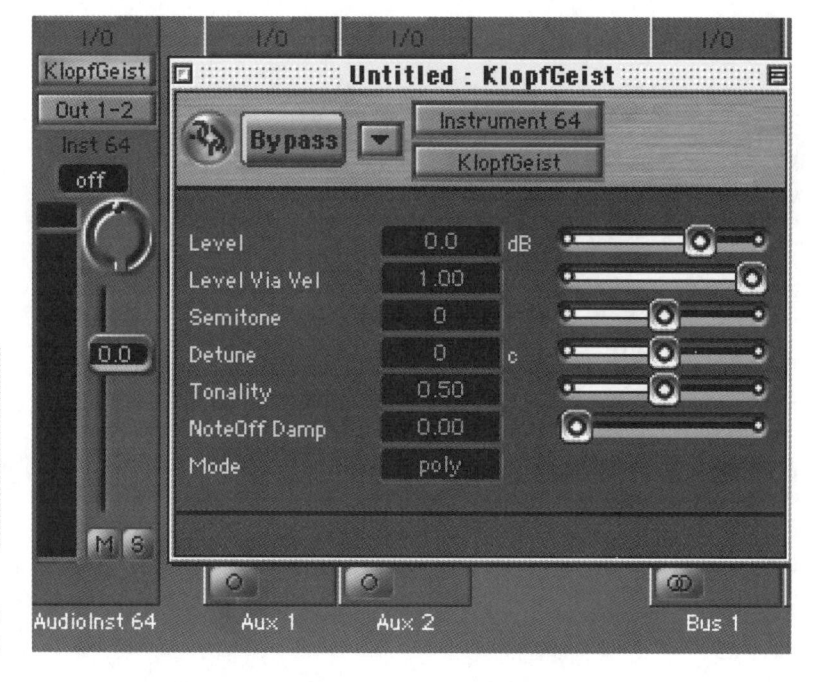

Figure 0.8
KlopfGeist

OK, that's it. Let's Get Creative.

MIDI sequencing: make it easy on yourself

Freddie is frustrated. For over an hour, as part of a college assignment, he's been slaving away on his MIDI keyboard, attempting to record a piano part into Logic Audio. Trouble is, Fred's main instrument is guitar and although he has a basic knowledge of reading music, his keyboard skills leave a lot to be desired. The piece is only eight measures long and in a simple rock style but each time he does a 'take' there is always something wrong. Sometimes it's out of time, other times it contains bum notes. 'I could be here all day', he thinks, 'and still not get it right.'

I know how he feels. It's a common myth that you have to be a good keyboard player to succeed at arranging and composing. My main instruments are clarinet and saxophone, and I too, am a 'technically challenged' piano player! However, I do manage to write a great deal of music despite my lack of technique. It was a problem until powerful sequencer programs such as Logic appeared on the scene. Now I can actually play the music I write! You can do the same. Here are a few pointers, but first an analogy.

Freddie is practising a transcribed guitar solo and encounters a difficult passage containing some awkward licks. What does he do? (no, he doesn't give up and play a 12 bar blues instead!), he slows the tempo down to a manageable speed, homes in on the nasty bits, and practises those parts repeatedly until he can play them properly. He then puts it all together again, increases the speed and performs a blistering solo. Well that's the theory anyway!

We can apply these principles to the sequencing of piano, or for that matter, any other instrument within Logic.

Slow it down

If you can't play it then slow it down. Why struggle? Computers don't make everything in life easy (the opposite is often the case) but they certainly help us dodgy piano players! However, there is a drawback to playing at a slow tempo, and that's accuracy of timing. Fortunately quantization comes to the rescue if that's a problem. More on this in a moment.

Let's suppose you are recording a piece with Logic at 120 bpm (beats per minute) and you come up against a passage that you can't play at that speed.

1 Scroll the tempo on the Transport bar to something more comfortable, 90 bpm maybe (Figure 1.1).
2 Record the tricky bit.
3 When you're done, scroll the tempo back to 120 bpm (Figure 1.2).

Figure 1.1
Slow the tempo

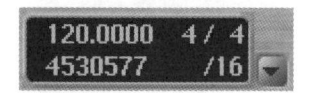

Figure 1.2
Increase the tempo

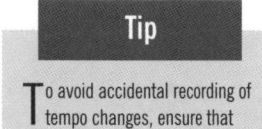

Tip

To avoid accidental recording of tempo changes, ensure that 'Allow Tempo Change Recording' in 'Recording Options' is unchecked [Options > Settings > Recording Options...] (Figure 1.3).

Figure 1.3
Uncheck 'Allow Tempo Change Recording'.

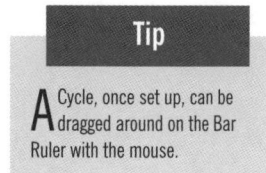

Tip

A Cycle, once set up, can be dragged around on the Bar Ruler with the mouse.

Break it down

This is very important. Why play large chunks of music and get it repeatedly wrong? Make good use of all this technology. Break the music down into manageable chunks. An eight measure section can very easily be recorded in two four measure sections or even smaller. It is important though, particularly if the material is melodic, to identify phrases, and record them intact where possible. This will help you avoid any loss of continuity and 'feel' that may be lost through recording this way.

If the music is of a rhythmic character you will probably be able to break things down into significantly smaller segments. Only where necessary of course. Don't overdo it and actually increase your working time. The main purpose of all this is to get things done quickly and easily.

Cycle record

One of the most useful things about recording in Logic is the option to cycle record. The ability to continuously repeat a tricky part and overdub piece by piece inside the cycle, adding more music on each lap is invaluable. Again this is akin to the way we practise difficult sections on our instruments. The cycle can be set up by:

1. Positioning the Left and Right Locator position.
2. Activating the Cycle button on the Transport bar. (Figure 1.4).

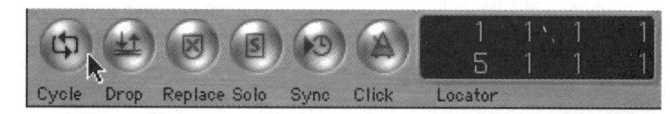

Figure 1.4
Cycle record

A quicker way is to drag the mouse over the Bar Ruler (Figure 1.5). This method will set the Locators and activate the Cycle button automatically.

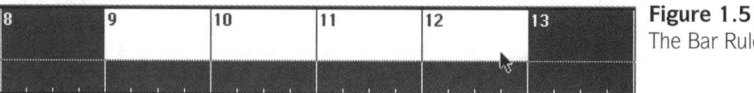

Figure 1.5
The Bar Ruler

Particularly useful is the Autodrop feature. If you've made a blunder in the middle of a certain passage, a combination of cycle and autodrop can be used. Try this:

1. Using the Bar Ruler method, set up a cycle region a bar or two either side of the 'bad' section you want to replace.
2. Activate the Autodrop button – to the right of the Cycle button on the Transport bar (Figure 1.6). The Bar Ruler will divide into two sections. The Autodrop bar appears below the cycle region (Figure 1.7).
3. Adjust the Autodrop region to capture the 'bad' section. This is done by dragging or using the new Locator window that has mysteriously replaced the word Emagic on the Transport bar!
4. Press the Record button and play along. Nothing is actually recorded before the drop-in point. When you reach it Logic will automatically 'punch in' and record your new, much improved version, and drop-out at the other end. Very handy!

Figure 1.6
The Autodrop button.

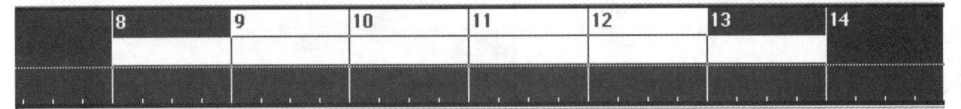

Figure 1.7
Cycle and Autodrop combined.

Info

There are various options when using Cycle Record. Click and hold the mouse over the Record button on the Transport bar and choose 'Recording Options' ... to view and edit them (Figure 1.8a and 1.8b).

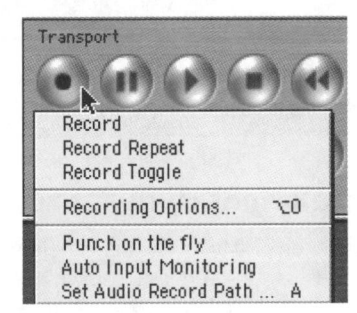

Figure 1.8a
Click and hold on Record button ...

Figure 1.8b
Recording options

> **Tip**
>
> When Cycle Recording and Quantization are used together there is a danger of double notes caused by recording events twice. These not only sound strange but can cause problems on some synthesizers. Fortunately, they can be easily erased. [Functions > Erase MIDI Events > Duplicates] (Figure 1.9)

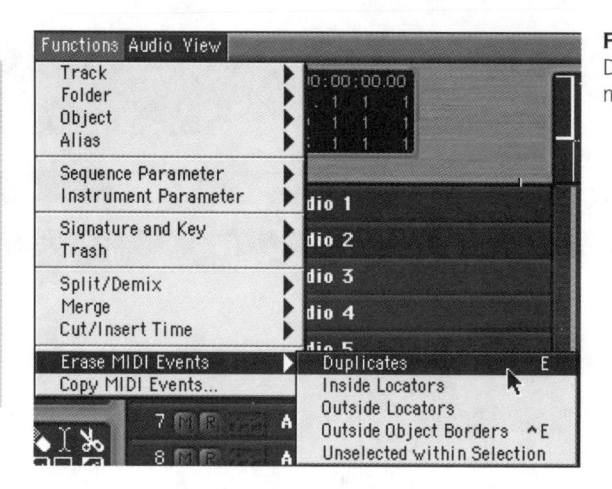

Figure 1.9
Deleting doubled notes

To quantize or not to quantize

Musicians argue endlessly over this. There's no doubt that quantization helps tremendously to tighten up loosely played performances. On the other hand it can render a beautifully expressive performance completely lifeless. So when do we resort to quantization? Well, let's suppose you are composing techno music as background music for a science documentary video. In this case quantization is probably a must. Computer music by its very nature lends itself to this kind of treatment. On the other hand, if you were working on music of a romantic nature, for a chocolate box selection advert, the music would need to 'breathe' in a rubato fashion. In this case quantization would be used sparingly, if at all.

Those are two extremes and there are many styles of music and combinations of instruments which fall in between. Choices have to be made.

Editing – get rid of the bum notes!

We all make mistakes and one of the beauties of Logic is the ability to edit any mistakes and wrong notes after recording. If you've followed the principles outlined above, hopefully, there will not be too many.

Those of you familiar with conventional music notation will find it easiest to alter, delete, and replace wrong notes in the Score. [Windows > Open Score] (Figure 1.10) Others may prefer the Matrix Edit window [Windows > Open Matrix Edit] where you will find a graphic representation of the recording with the notes placed on a grid (Figure 1.11). It's easy to determine the pitch from the virtual keyboard on the left hand side. For detailed use of these Editors, refer to your Logic manual.

OK. Enough talking. Let's do it. In the next chapter, by recording a simple rock and roll piano score we will become familiar with the basic techniques of sequencing and some of the most frequently used functions and tools within Logic.

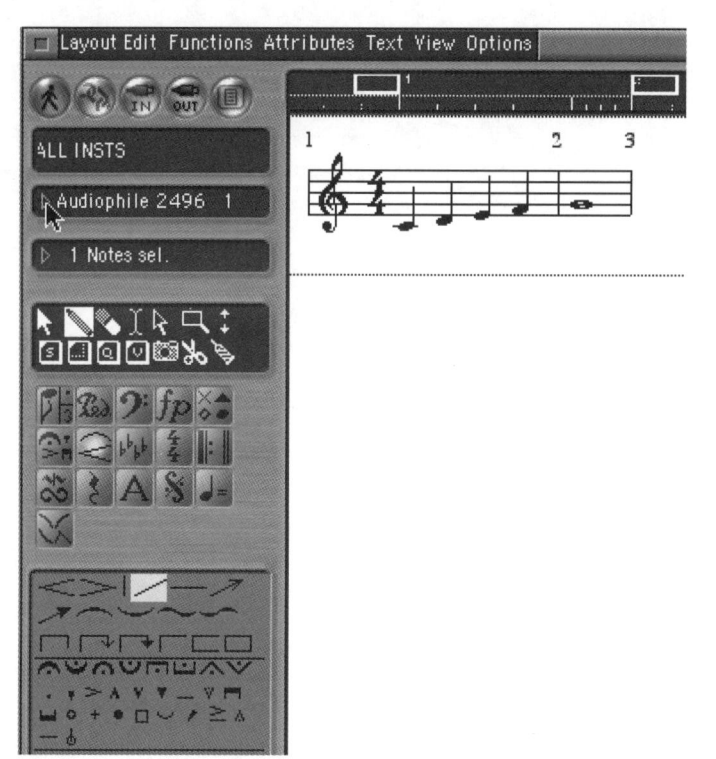

Figure 1.10
Score view

Figure 1.11
Matrix view

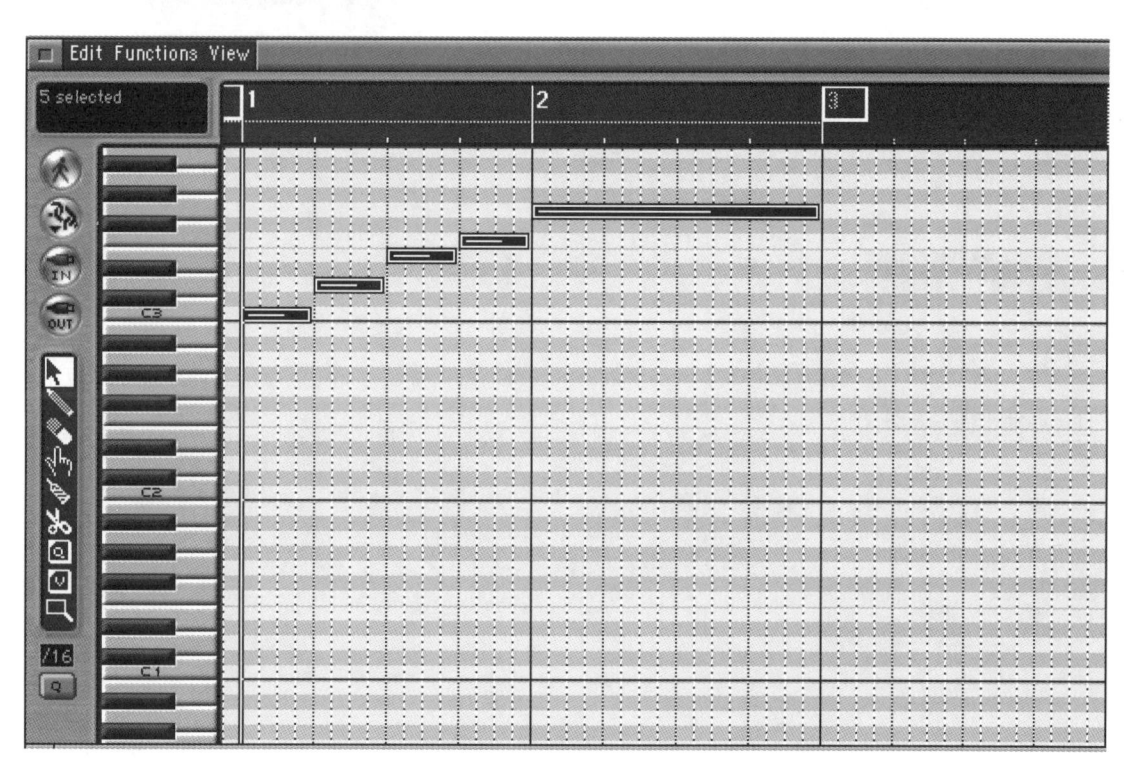

Project 1 – some rock 'n' roll piano

Musical objectives

- Record a simple rock 'n roll piano part, length eight bars.

Logic skills

- Record, cut and paste sequences in the Arrange window.
- Quantize selected objects using the Sequence Parameters box.
- Vary Q-Strength and Q-Range on selected objects using the Extended Sequence Parameters box.

Preparation

1 From the CD, copy the folder named project1 to your computer.
2 On your computer, create a folder called mywork1 or something similar in which to save your work.
3 From the project1 folder, open the template – templt1.
4 In your new mywork1 folder, re-save the template as myproj1 or something similar.

Before you start, have a listen to project1/1.3 and view the score (Figure P1.1). This will help those of you still developing your music reading skills to get the gist of it.

Take 1

Track 2: Grand Piano | Left Hand.
Sequence Parameters box: Qua off (3840).
Instrument Parameter box: Cha 1, Prg 0.
Transport Bar: (L) Left 1.1.1. (R) 5.1.1

Follow these steps:

1 Record the first four bars of the left hand part (Figure P1.2 and P1.3). You don't have to use your left hand only. This is not a piano lesson! Use both hands if it makes it easier. I do. You may prefer to load project1/1.1 first and listen through before you begin recording.

Info

The template has a time signature of 4/4 and the tempo is 100 bpm. If that's too fast for you, slow the tempo before you record.

Tip

When loading example files containing MIDI settings its quite likely that you will initially hear the wrong sounds (very likely those from a previous project or song). Use [Options > Song Settings > Used Instrument MIDI Settings] to correct them. A faster way – quickly cursor up or down the tracks using the arrow keys on your computer keyboard.

Rock 'n' Roll Piano Score

Figure P1.1
Rock 'n' Roll Piano score

Figure P1.2 (above)
The left hand piano part.

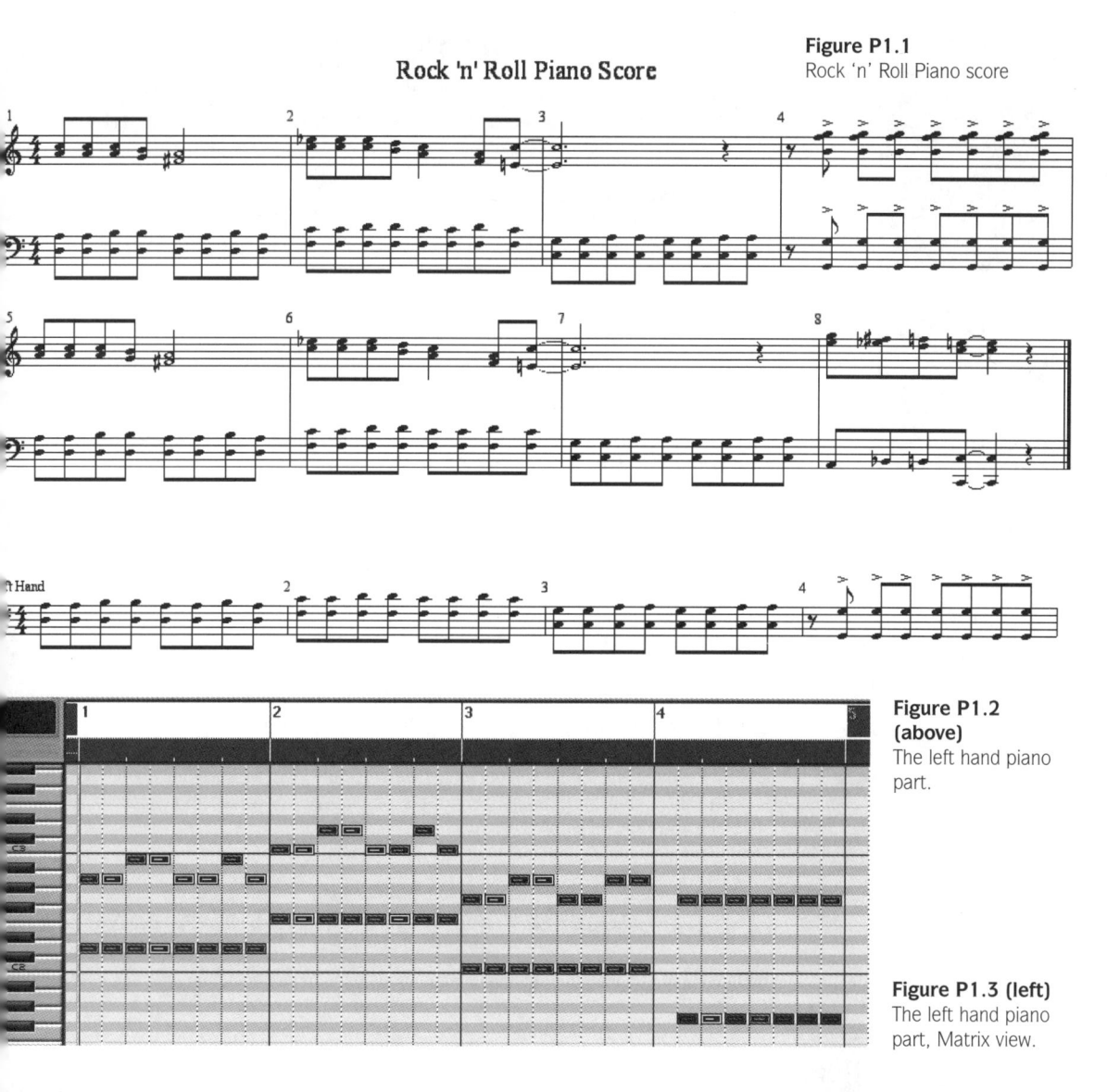

Figure P1.3 (left)
The left hand piano part, Matrix view.

2   Listen back, preferably at the correct tempo (100 bpm). The chances are – depending on your keyboard playing – that it will sound a bit ragged. Mine did! No matter. Select the recorded sequence and use the drop down menu to apply a quantize value of 1/8 – note in the Sequence Parameters box (Figure P1.4).

2   Listen back again. It should now be rock solid. Selecting a value of 1/8 – note has moved all the notes recorded to the nearest eighth note. However, rock 'n' roll piano is often just a little loose so …

3   Let's open the Extended Sequence Parameters box [Options> Extended Sequence Parameters] (Figure P1.5). Using the mouse, scroll the Q-Strength to around 75%. That'll loosen things up a bit. Experiment until it sounds right to you. Leave the Extended Sequence Parameters box open, we'll need it again.

4   Save Song – compare with project1/1.1

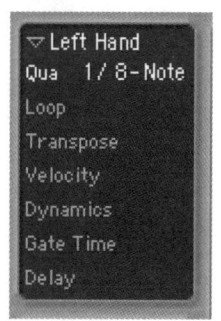

Figure P1.4
Qua 1/8 – Note in the Sequence Parameters box.

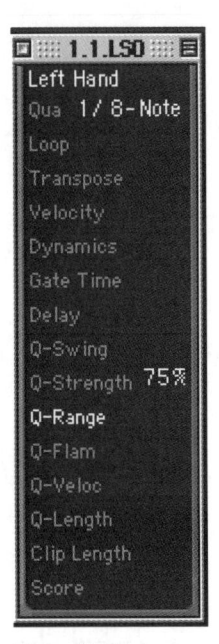

Figure P1.5
The Extended Sequence Parameters box.

> **Tip**
>
> Try running Logic and adjusting the quantize parameters in real time. You'll hear the changes as you make them.

> **Info**
>
> In the Extended Sequence Parameters box, Q – Strength determines how far notes are moved towards the quantize grid position. In my case 75% towards the nearest eighth note. Q – Range prevents notes being quantized within a set range. A negative value acts in reverse and will quantize notes outside the specified region. This is useful for tightening up sloppy playing (never use it myself of course!).

Take 2

Track 1: Grand Piano | Right Hand
Sequence Parameters box: Qua off (3840)
Instrument Parameters box: Cha 1, Prg 0.
Transport Bar: (L) Left 1.1.1. (R) 5.1.1

In Take 1 we applied our quantize parameter settings after recording a sequence. This time we will set them first.

Follow these steps:

1 Select track 1 (Right Hand) and enter 1/8 – Note in the Sequence Parameters box. In the Extended Sequence Parameters box – we left it open, remember – enter the Q – Strenngth that you found effective when applied to Take 1.
2 Now record the first four bars of the right hand piano part (Figure P1.6 and P1.7). If it is difficult to play, try playing the two harmonies separately on different passes.

Figure P1.6 The right hand piano part.

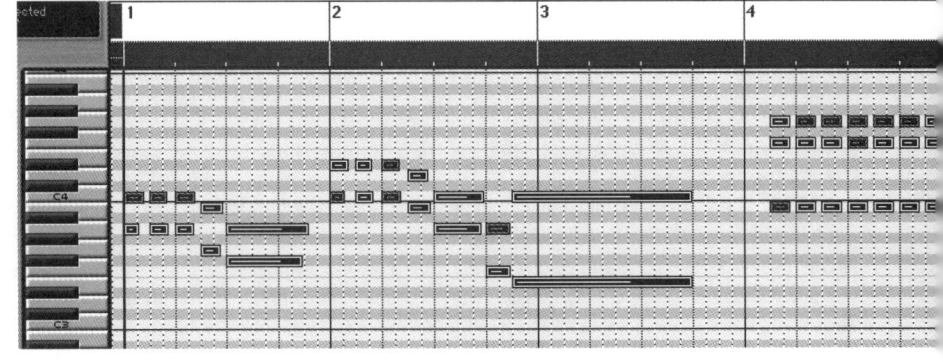

Figure P1.7
The right hand piano part, Matrix view.

Figure P1.8 Selecting Recording Options.

Figure P1.9
The Song Settings.

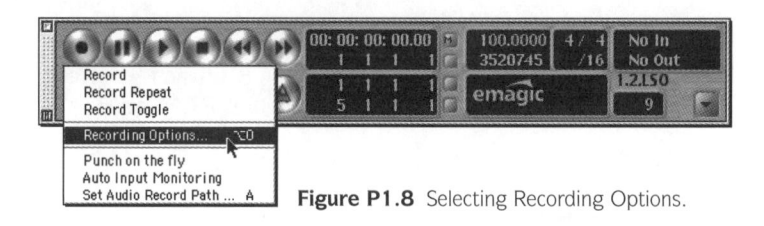

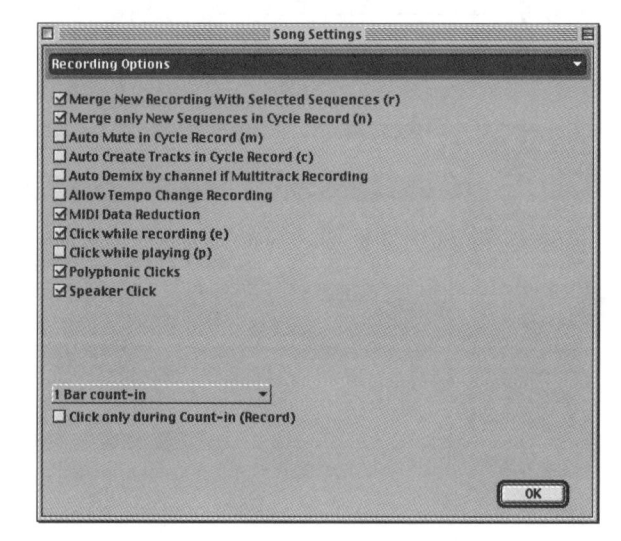

Info

Sequences recorded on different passes will be treated differently depending on how you set your Song Settings – on the Transport bar, press and hold on the record button. From the menu, choose Recording Options (Figure P1.8). The Song Settings are revealed (Figure P1.9).

3 Listen back at 100 bpm. Things should now sound pretty much as you intend them to be. If not tweak the settings in the Extended Sequence Parameters box until you're happy.

I expect you have noticed that bars 5, 6, and 7 in the left hand part are the same as bars 1, 2 and 3. To save time (and possibly high blood pressure, depending on your piano playing skills) we'll copy those bars to bar 5.

4 With the Song Position Line at 4.1.1 use the Scissors tool to split the sequence (Figure P1.10).
5 Select the first 3 bars (1-4). Copy and paste them to bar 5. Alternatively, select the first 3 bars (1-4) and duplicate a new sequence by dragging a copy to bar 5.
6 The right hand part follows the same pattern so repeat the above procedure on that part too.
7 Save Song – Compare with project 1/1.2

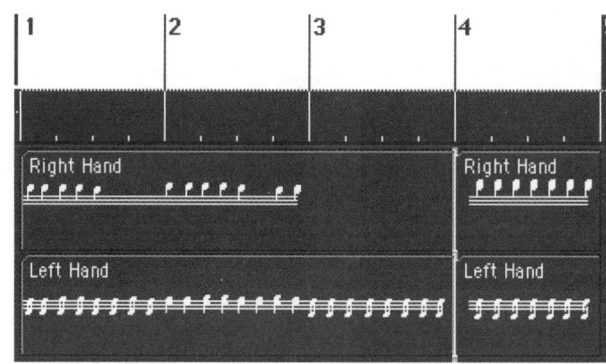

Figure P1.10
Split sequences.

Tip

When pasting a copied sequence, make sure the Song Position Line is set to the exact destination you require, otherwise it will end up somewhere else entirely. Bar 999 perhaps! It happens.

Take 3

1 Return to Track 2, set the Locators between 8.1.1 and 9.1.1 and record the last bar of the left hand piano part. (Figures P1.11 and P1.12).

Figure P1.11
The left hand piano part, bar 8.

Figure P1.12
The left hand piano part, bar 8, Matrix view.

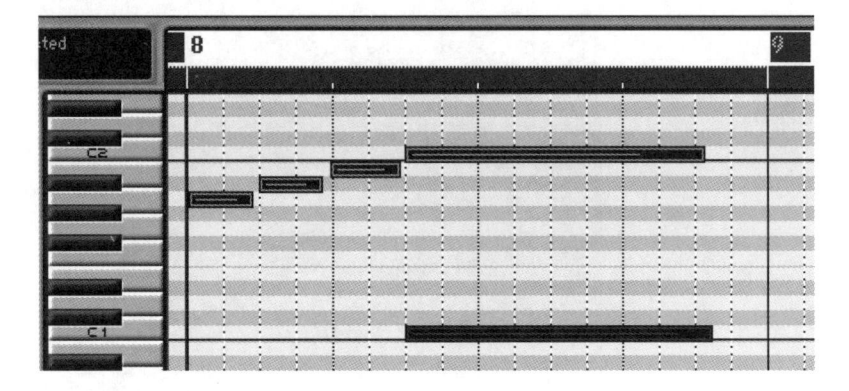

2 Switch to Track 1 and record the last bar of the right hand piano part. (Figures P1.13) and P1.14) If necessary, tweak your settings in the Sequence Parameters box and you're done.

Figure P1.13
The right hand piano part, bar 8.

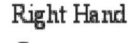

Figure P1.14
The right hand piano part, bar 8, Matrix view.

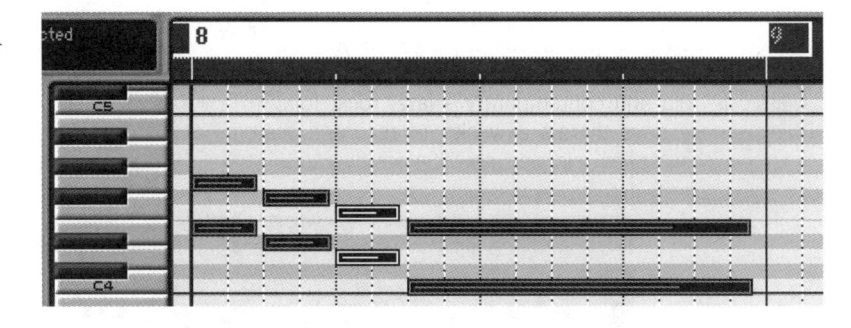

3 Save Song – compare with project1/1.3

Get real with MIDI 2

As part of a college assignment, Sara has been sequencing classical music, a string quartet, with Logic. She has played all the parts correctly from her MIDI keyboard, but for some reason, the overall result is less than convincing. The instruments just don't sound realistic.

This is a common scenario. Of course it's well nigh impossible to recreate the performance of a real violinist, or come to that, any other instrumentalist, but a pretty convincing job can be made of it if we approach things the right way. We may not be able to fool musicians but we can certainly produce something worthy enough for many a multimedia project. However, there is much to learn to achieve a good result.

So how do we transform our Logic projects into sounding like the London Philharmonic Orchestra or, for that matter, Led Zeppelin? By using our imagination, of course. Whether you have a top of the range sound module or just a humble Sound Blaster Audigy card, you'll not get far without it.

Forget the keyboard and concentrate on the virtual instrument you are recording. If it's a violin, imagine yourself actually playing it. Be that violinist. You are bowing those short rhythmic stop notes, those long flowing melodies that string sections are so good at. The same applies to any instrument. Try to get inside the mind of your virtual musician. Before you can do this confidently, you will have to spend time listening.

Listen and learn

Listen to all kinds of music. To earn a crust arrangers and composers must be able to write in just about any style. If you can afford it, get out and attend live music events and hear as much variation of style as possible. Classical – old and contemporary – jazz, rock, folk, in fact just about anything. These days there's a wealth of recorded material available on the Internet in all styles, old and new. Select the good stuff and download it. You don't have to like all this music but you should absorb it. It will all resurface when you need it.

Learn how to listen

There's not much point in listening to all this music if you haven't learned how to listen. Instead of just listening to the overall sound picture, train your ear to single out the instruments from orchestras, groups and bands. Identify the musical families they belong to.

Was that an oboe or a cor anglais solo? Is that a viola or violin playing those low notes? Is he playing a fretless bass guitar or just a regular electric bass? Are those trombones or French horns in that quiet orchestral passage? Is that a tenor or alto saxophone break in that jazz rock number?

These are the kinds of questions you should ask yourself. This is easy in a live situation, but considerably harder with recorded music. Pay particular attention to the way these instruments are played, both in a solo situation and as part of a section. It's also important to understand the comfortable playing range of the various instruments.

Get a life! – play with others

Working with Logic provides a wonderful virtual environment but unfortunately it's usually a solitary one. As well as listening, there is no substitute for actually playing live, in rock bands, jazz bands, wind bands, orchestras, folk groups and so on. The list is endless. This provides invaluable first hand experience of how real instruments are played. If you can, have a go at some of these instruments. (Ask first of course!)

Sequencing examples

I mentioned earlier how important it is to use our imagination when playing what are, after all, imaginary instruments. OK they are samples of real instruments, but lifeless unless we know how to use them. Here are some pointers.

Sequencing woodwinds and brass

The woodwinds, in the main, are split into two groups, reed instruments – clarinets, oboe, cor anglais (English horn), bassoons, saxophones – and flutes, recorders and piccolos. The brass are comprised mainly of trumpets, trombones, horns and tuba. It's important to remember that woodwind and brass players need to breathe! I've heard many a woodwind part ruined by a virtuoso keyboard player who has not thought about this. Be careful not to create overlaps when playing from the keyboard. If it happens (Figure 2.1) then clean them up, from within whichever Edit window you are using, with Functions > Note Events > Note Overlap Correction (Figure 2.2).

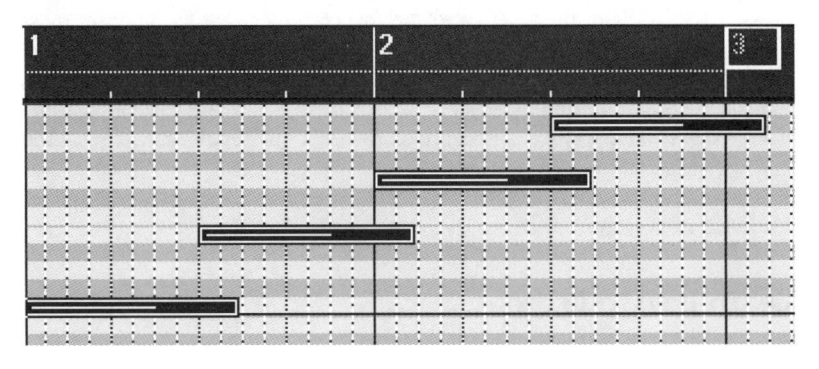

Figure 2.1
Overlapping notes.

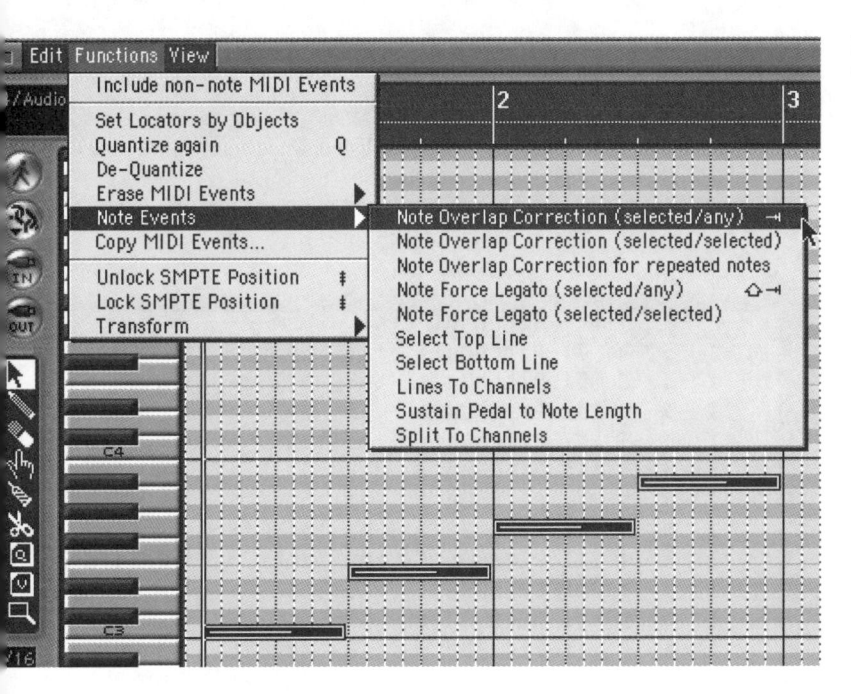

Figure 2.2
Overlapping notes fixed.

Bear in mind that 'blowers' articulate with their tongues. Unless a passage is deliberately slurred there should be small gaps between notes. This is sometimes difficult to achieve and a bit of a fiddle but it's usually a matter of keeping the best take and polishing it up afterwards, in either the Score or Matrix Edit windows. Here are two interpretations of a short flute solo (Figure 2.3).

Figure 2.3
Flute solo.

Mozart Symphony No.40 flute.arr

- Load getreal/flutes/badflt.

The flute here is badly played and ignores the breath mark (V) in the fourth measure as well as the articulation marks (slurs and staccato).

- Load getreal/flutes/goodflt.

This is clearly much better and pays heed to the articulation as well as a gap for that all important breath.

Saxophone solos will require subtle use of pitch bend to make them sound at all convincing. This is best done whilst playing, using the pitch bend controller on the MIDI keyboard. Pitch bend can be added afterwards but it's hard to beat the spontaneity of adding it live. Vibrato is sometimes used by sax players and this can be achieved with a touch of modulation. Go easy though, to avoid that 'nannny goat' sax sound!

Info

To examine the Logic Song files for this chapter, copy the folder named 'getreal' from the CD to your computer.

- Load getreal/alto/hodges.

This is a short solo in the style of the late Johnny Hodges, famed for his beautiful tone and incredible note bending. Well I can't guarantee the tone – this is a synthetic sax after all! – but I have managed to emulate his playing style with the use of pitch bend.

You can inspect the pitch bend and modulation data in the Event List window [Windows > Open Event List]. (Figure 2.4)

Figure 2.4
Pitch bend data, Event List view.

```
----------------- Start of List ---------------
POSITION         STATUS    CHA  NUM  VAL   LENGTH/INFO
1  3  2  41   PitchBd  1   113   56   =   -  911
1  3  2  91   PitchBd  1    63   37   =   - 3393
1  3  2 131   PitchBd  1    11   29   =   - 4469
1  3  3 111   PitchBd  1    94   29   =   - 4386
1  3  3 151   PitchBd  1     3   31   =   - 4221
1  3  4  71   PitchBd  1    41   32   =   - 4055
1  3  4 131   PitchBd  1    33   34   =   - 3807
1  3  4 171   PitchBd  1   108   36   =   - 3476
1  3  4 211   PitchBd  1   100   38   =   - 3228
1  4  1  11   PitchBd  1    55   39   =   - 3145
1  4  1 111   PitchBd  1    10   40   =   - 3062
1  4  1 181   PitchBd  1    47   41   =   - 2897
1  4  1 221   PitchBd  1     2   42   =   - 2814
1  4  2  41   PitchBd  1    39   43   =   - 2649
1  4  2  81   PitchBd  1   122   43   =   - 2566
1  4  2  91   Control  1     1    2  Modulation
1  4  2 106   Control  1     1    4  Modulation
1  4  2 118   Control  1     1    5  Modulation
```

Another way to view the pitch bend information is in the Matrix Edit window. Have a look [Windows > Matrix Edit]. You can't see anything other than the notes on the grid? OK, open Hyper Draw [View > Hyper Draw > Pitch Bend or Modulation]. Pitch bend and other data can be drawn and edited from here using the Pencil Tool (Figure 2.5).

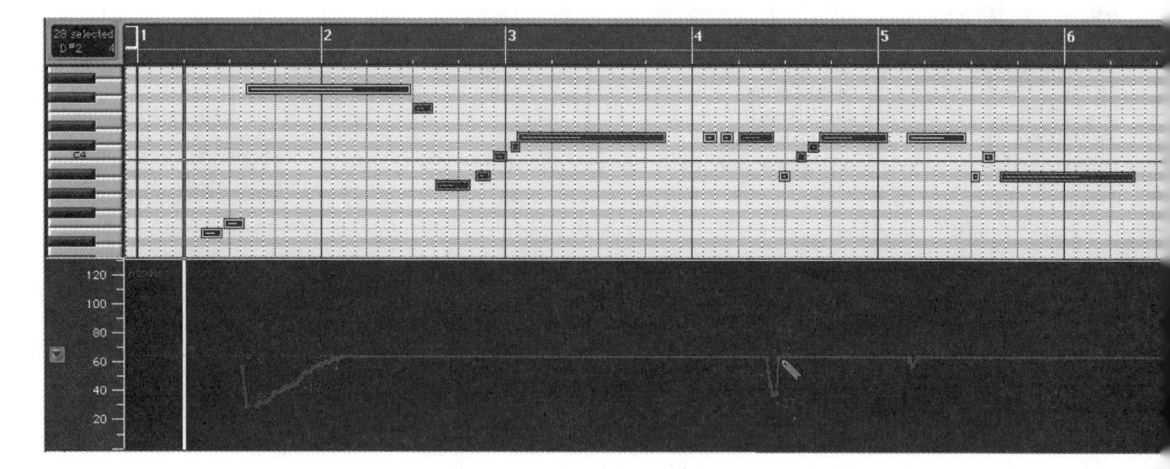

Figure 2.5
Using the Pencil Tool in Hyper Draw.

Yet another way of editing pitch bend is in the Hyper Edit window [Windows > Hyper Edit] (Figure 2.6). As with Hyper Draw, use the Pencil tool to draw in the information.

Figure 2.6
Using the Pencil tool in Hyper Edit

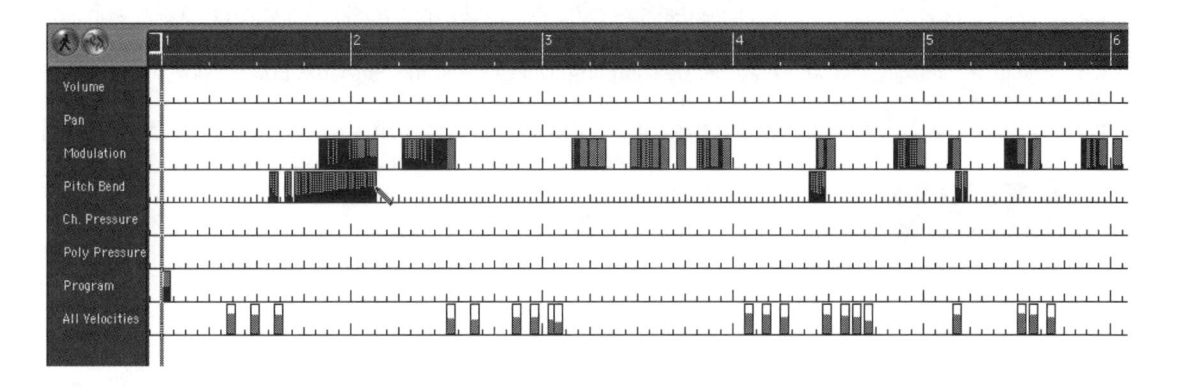

Sequencing strings

The conventional string orchestra uses four instruments. The violin, viola, cello and bass.

When emulating the instruments of the string orchestra it is important to distinguish between legato playing (long bowed sections) and individually bowed notes. As with the wind instruments, small gaps between individual notes are best, so try to adapt your playing style for this. To capture those long flowing lines it's probably best to select the notes required in the Score or Matrix Edit windows and apply Legato [Functions > Note Events > Note Force Legato] (Figure 2.7).

Figure 2.7
Applying Legato

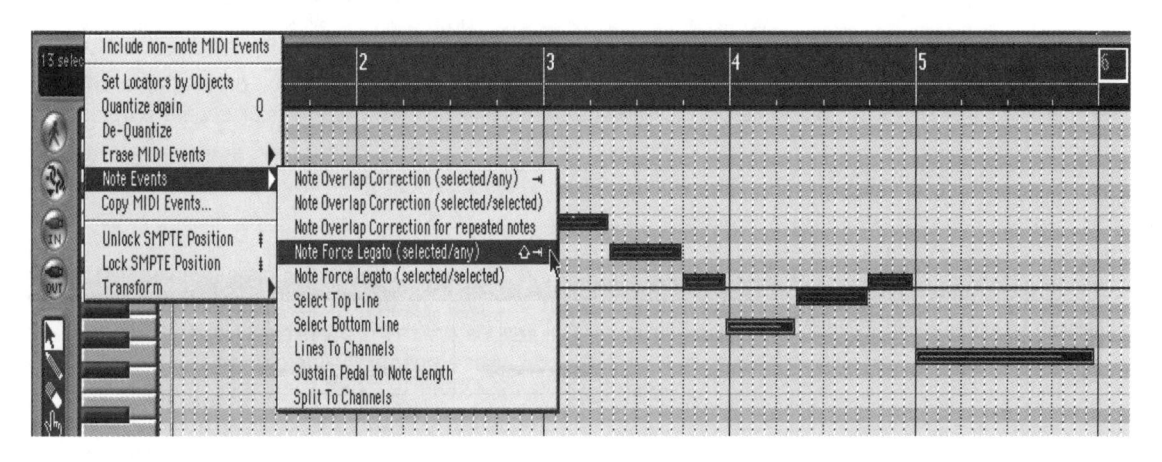

Here's an example: (Figure 2.8)

Figure 2.8
Legato strings

> **Tip**
>
> String players can play longer lines than wind players because they don't pause for breath – but their arms can ache. Give 'em a break sometimes!

> **Tip**
>
> If you are using a GM sound source use Strings 1 for general section work but consider using Strings 2 – sometimes called 'Slow Strings' – for long sustained notes and very slow moving passages.

- Load getreal/strings/okstrngs.

This sequence has been played accurately enough, but the legato phrases remain choppy.

Load getreal/strings//lgstrngs. In this version Legato has been applied. It's better, don't you think? All the notes line up end to end and the result is more authentic sounding. Check them in the Matrix Edit window.

Sequencing drums and percussion

Many Logic users prefer to sequence their drum parts by entering the beats using the Hyper Edit window configured as a drum editor. This is fine for music that relies heavily on drum loops such as dance music. Others prefer to play a 'virtual kit'. It depends on the style of music. If dynamic variation and a live feel are required it's probably best to play the part first and edit it afterwards in one of the editors. If a repetitive loop is needed, step entry may be the way to go.

For 'live style drums,' here are a few pointers:

- Another myth; 'Drums underpin the track so we have to record them first'. Not so. Unless the music is loop based – in which case they will probably be entered step by step anyway – it's often best to record some melodic material first. The advantage of this is that you will be playing with the other parts. All the dynamic variation and feel of the other parts will influence how you play the 'virtual drum kit' and will help instill feel into the music.
- If possible record in stretches of eight bars or so at a time. This helps create a natural flow and is preferable to cutting and pasting one or two bar segments.
- Drum rolls are often best sequenced by step entry. It's no easy matter to roll two fingers as fast as two drum sticks. This is usually done in the Hyper Edit window.
- On a conventional kit try playing the kick and snare drums first and overdub the hi-hats, cymbals and toms afterwards on separate tracks.

To illustrate how this might be done, I've recorded a four bar rock groove with a fill in the fourth bar. It was done in three stages.

- Load getreal/drums/groove.

1 I laid down the kick drum and snare together for three bars and left the fourth bar blank. Drums are perhaps the hardest instrument to play accurately from a MIDI keyboard – that's my excuse anyway! – so, in the Sequence Parameter box, I set a quantize value of sixteen (Qua 1/16-Note) and used the Extended Sequence Parameters box [Options > Extended Sequence Parameters...] to vary the Q-Stength, and Q-Range.
2 I moved to a different track, and added the hi-hat figure again using the Extended Sequence Parameters function.
3 I then moved to a third track and recorded the fill on toms with a cymbal crash thrown in for good measure.

Having the drums separated like this also makes it easier to carry out editing procedures.

Examine the sequences in the Score, Matrix and Hyper Edit windows. (Figures 2.9, 2.10 and 2.11) For an overall picture select track 4: Full Kit. In the Score view ensure that Style #Drums is chosen in the Display Parameter box for a standard drum notation display. In the Hyper Edit window ensure that a GM Drum Set has been created [Hyper > Create GM Drum Set] for a graphical display with velocity columns.

Figure 2.9
Drum sequences, Score view

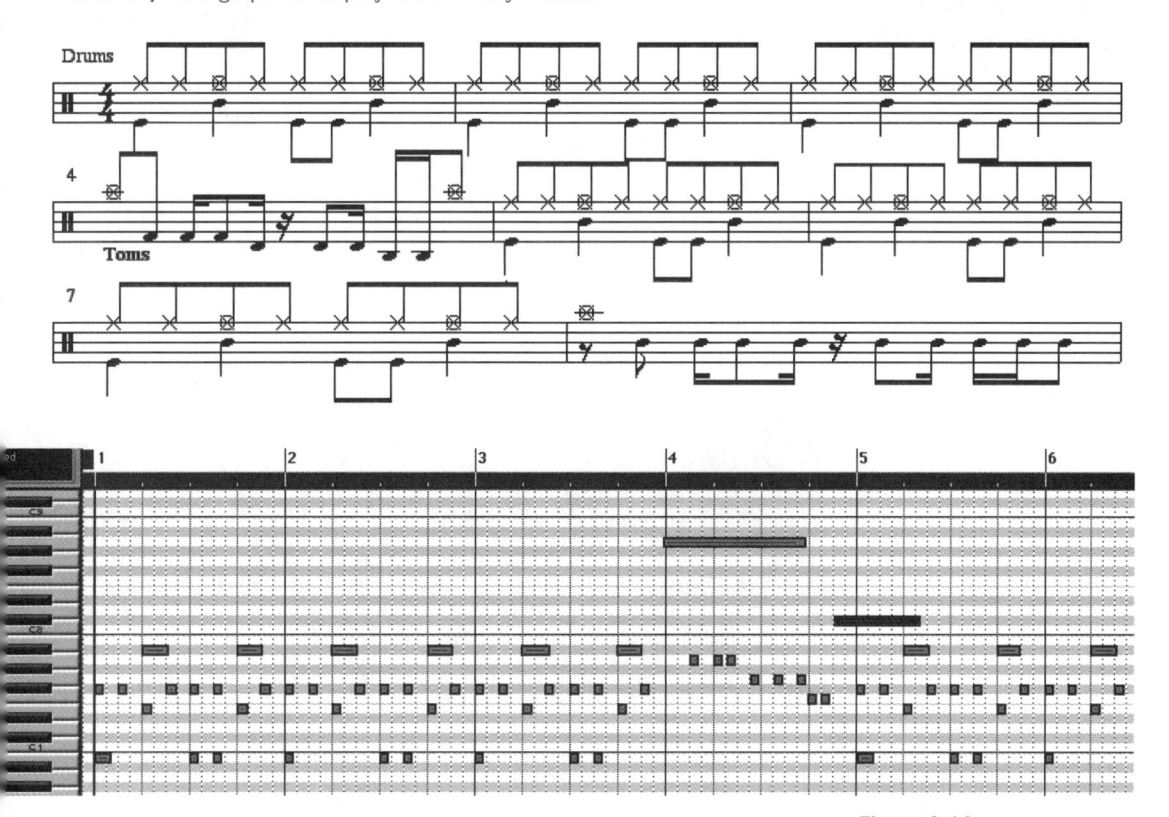

Figure 2.10
Drum sequences, Matrix view

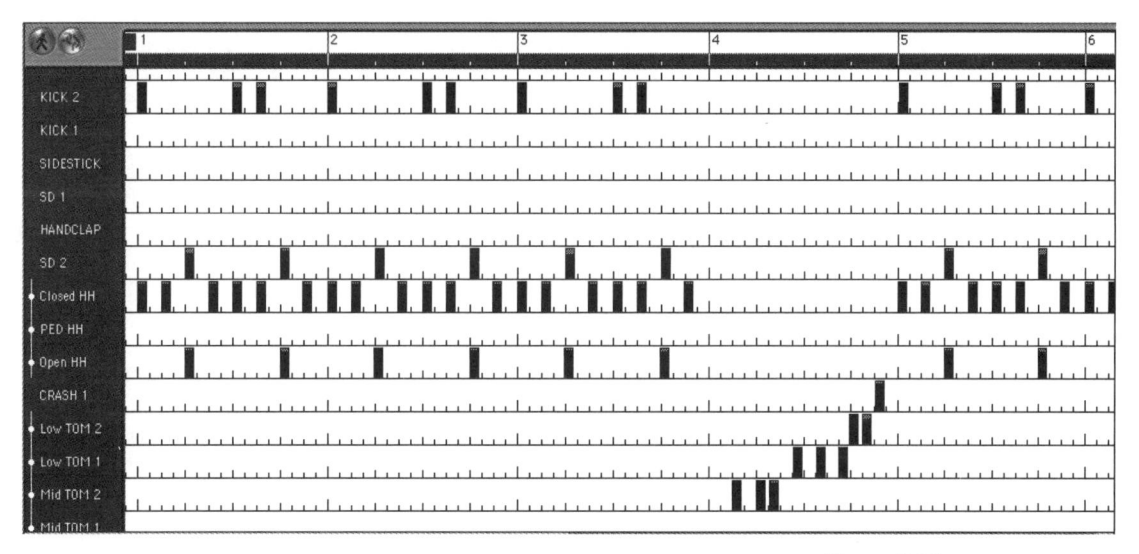

Figure 2.11
Drum sequences, Hyper view

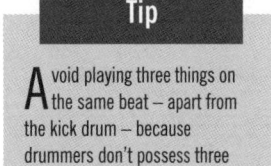

> **Tip**
>
> Avoid playing three things on the same beat – apart from the kick drum – because drummers don't possess three arms and it may sound unnatural!

Sequencing guitars

How we approach this depends on whether the instrument is acoustic or electric and whether the music is melodic or rhythmic. Straightforward melodic lines are quite easy with nylon string, steel string and jazz guitars but judicious use of pitch bend will often be needed. Rock guitar lines are harder. More pitch bend is usually required. Modulation can be added afterwards on a separate track and is one way to simulate a real players use of vibrato. Take care not to overdo it though.

- Load getreal/gtr/lick to hear a short lick recorded this way.

Use the Hyper Edit, Event List and Matrix Edit windows to examine the pitch bend and modulation information. Use Hyper Draw in the Arrange window to view the same data. Figure 2.12 shows the modulation on track 2.

Figure 2.12
Modulation on track 2

Rhythm guitars need to be approached carefully. Although a real guitar has six strings, things can get very muddy if we try to faithfully reproduce this with a synthesized MIDI guitar. We will also use up valuable polyphony and on a busy sequence this could result in the unexpected drop out of notes on other instruments.

Try using less notes in a chord. Real guitarists do not always use all six strings anyway. Often three notes are all that is needed if the guitar is used in the background. Open spacing can give the illusion of depth. For example, a chord of C major – C3, E3, G3 (Figure 2.13a and 2.13b) could be played as G2, E3, C4.

Figure 2.13a
Chord spacing

'But what about seventh chords' I hear you say. Omit the fifth or the root but be keep the third. How you move from chord to chord depends very much on voice leading and is a vast subject beyond the scope of this book.

Guitar players can of course use a special MIDI interface to play in their parts. This could be useful for playing bass, string and horn parts and other monophonic instruments but the guitar itself would be best recorded on an audio track.

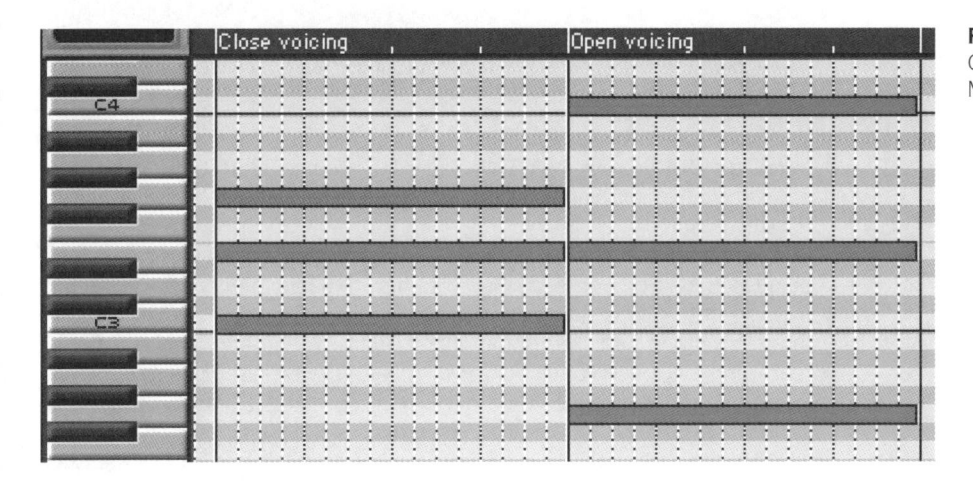

Figure 2.13b
Chord spacing, Matrix view

Quantization

Logic provides plenty of scope here. How you approach it depends mainly on the instrument you are imitating and the style of music. Choosing a quantize value in the Sequence Parameters box will move all the notes played to the nearest division of the beat. For example; selecting Qua 1/8-note will move things to the nearest eighth note, 16 to the nearest sixteenth note and so on (Figure 2.14).

Standard quantization is fine for many uses but if a less rigid result is required we can further adjust the values in the Extended Sequence Parameters dialogue box (Figure 2.15). The three most useful parameters are:

1 Q-Strength: Changing the percentage value here will enable you to determine how far notes are shifted towards the quantize grid position. A value of 100% will provide full quantization. A value of 0% leaves everything unquantized. Which percentage you choose is really determined by how acurately you played in the first place and how tight you want things to sound.

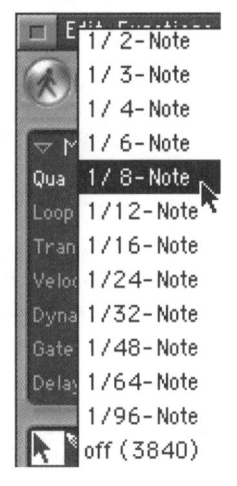

Figure 2.14 Selecting Quantize

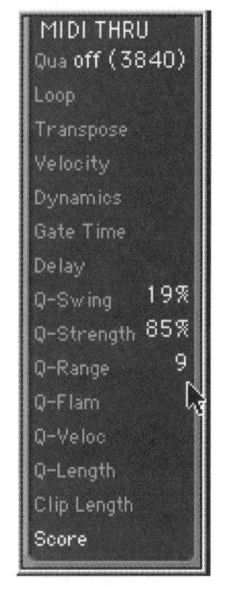

Figure 2.15
Extended Sequence Parameters box

2 Q-Range: Setting a 'capture' range here will determine which notes are quantized to the nearest quantize grid position. A tick value is used. A value of 0 will quantize the lot, a negative value will quantize only those very wayward notes outside the set range, and a positive value will quantize those notes within it. How you set this range depends mainly on how you played and what you want to hear. Confused? Don't worry. A good visual indication of what's actually going on can be seen in the Matrix Edit window. The final decision though, is down to your ears! They should be your true guide. Experiment.

3 Q-Swing: This will impose a swing feel to the music and is expressed in percentage terms. A passage of music comprised of even eighth notes can be considered to have a 50% swing value. In other words, it doesn't

swing. It can't. They're all even. Increase that value to 66% and things will begin to swing considerably. In fact they will now have a classic 'jazz quaver' feel.

If you don't want to fiddle around, Logic provides a very useful set of swing templates, 8A-8F and 16A-16F, each one stronger than the other. These are selected in the same way as standard quantization, in the Sequence Parameters box.

When and how much to quantize depends mainly on the musical material being sequenced. For example, you may be recording a flowing string melody. In this case quantization is best avoided. However if it's a rhythmic 'marcato' string part then some quantization may be appropriate. After all real string players are often behind the beat. Only joking! (Time to duck.)

Here's an example. A three piece horn section – trumpet, tenor saxophone and baritone saxophone – recorded as MIDI instruments into Logic can be very accurately played but somehow still sound imprecise when recorded without Quantization.

- Load getreal/horns/horns.

Have a listen. What do you think? Examine the sequences in the Score window and you will see that they are all played accurately enough. What do I think? OK I suppose, but I'd want better than that if was hiring them! View the sequences in the Matrix Edit window and things don't look so tight.

If quantization is used whilst recording, things are very much improved because the actual note lengths are left unchanged but they all start at exactly the same time. This retains the sense of 'realness' and is close to how a brass section actually plays. In fact we have achieved exactly what most 'real' horn sections strive for!

Listen to getreal/horns/hornsqua. Much tighter, but now they lack feeling and sound a bit mechanical. A quick way to loosen things up without spoiling the tight feel would be to randomize the notes by a few ticks in the Transform window.

A similar effect can be achieved by altering the Q-Strength in the Extended Sequence Parameters box. Depending on the percentage used, only certain notes are moved. It can be progressively applied until the required degree of tightness is heard.

Listen to getreal/horns/hornsit That's more like it. The cheques are in the post!

Dynamics

A fine musical performance, whatever the genre, usually contains a degree of dynamic variation. It goes without saying that a MIDI sequence that emulates such a performance must also contain the same dynamic ingredients; volume (loud or soft) gradual changes of volume (crescendo and diminuendo) sudden changes of volume (sforzando) and accented notes. Three MIDI controllers are used dynamically in Logic – volume, expression and velocity.

Velocity controls the volume of an individual note depending on how hard or soft a key is struck on your MIDI keyboard. Again imagination is needed. Be that percussionist. Take this timpani figure for example. (Figure 2.16)

- Load getreal/timpani/timpani

Timpani

[musical notation: Timpani figure in bass clef, 4/4 time, with dynamic marking mp crescendo to ff]

Listen and examine the sequence in the Matrix Edit window with Hyper Draw open as well (Figure 2.17). You will notice that the velocity values start at 55 and end at 125. The gradual increase in attack is not exact, nor would it be if played by a real percussionist. Although velocity values can be used to control volume and fade outs, it is wiser to use volume and expression.

Figure 2.16
Timpani figure

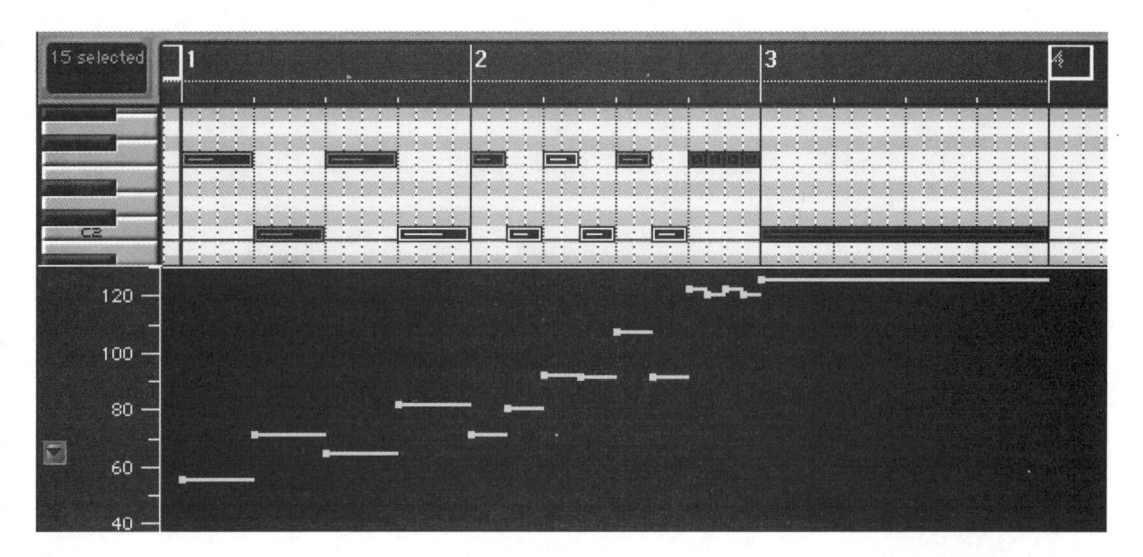

Figure 2.17
Timpani velocity in Hyper Draw

Volume (Controller No.7) and expression (Controller No.11) are essentially the same thing. They both control the volume of a sequence. However, when exporting your work as a MIDI file for use on another computer, keyboard or sound module, it is best to use volume as a master function, to control the overall picture, and expression for the dynamic changes within that picture. This allows the end user to adjust the balance of individual instruments on their equipment (what sounds loud on your gear may sound quiet on theirs) without spoiling the dynamic content of the recorded data.

A foot pedal (much like on a real piano) can be used to control these parameters in real time when playing from a keyboard. Being the imperfect keyboard player that I am, I prefer to add these changes afterwards by either using the Mixer or Hyper Draw.

Project 2 – a rock score

Musical objectives

- Sequence a rock score comprised of piano, guitar, bass and drums.
- Achieve a realistic interpretation of a live rock band.

Logic skills

- Utilize Hyper Edit as a GM Drum Editor.
- View sequences and enter beats in the Hyper Edit window.
- View GM mapped drums in the Score window
- Adjust Pan control in the Instrument Parameter box.
- Use Transposition in the Instrument Parameter box.

Preparation

1 From the CD, copy the folder named project2 to your computer.
2 On your computer, create a folder named mywork2 or something similar in which to save your work.
3 From the project2 folder, open the template – templt2.
4 In your new mywork2 folder, save the template as myproj2 or something similar.

If your music reading skills are not too hot, don't be put off by the score (Figure P2.1, P2.2, P2.3, and P2.4). Load project2/2.11 – the finished thing – and have a listen.

Info

The template has a time signature of 4/4 and the tempo is 100 bpm. If that's too fast for you, slow the tempo before you record.

Tip

When loading example files containing MIDI settings its quite likely that you will initially hear the wrong sounds (very likely those from a previous project or song). Use [Options > Song Settings > Used Instrument MIDI Settings] to correct them. A faster way – quickly cursor up or down the tracks using the arrow keys on your computer keyboard.

It's Closing Time

K.G

Figure P2.1
The score, page 1.

Figure P2.2
The score, page 2.

Play it through several times and practise reading the score one instrument at a time. When you are familiar with the tune, work through the project.

Figure P2.3 The score, page 3.

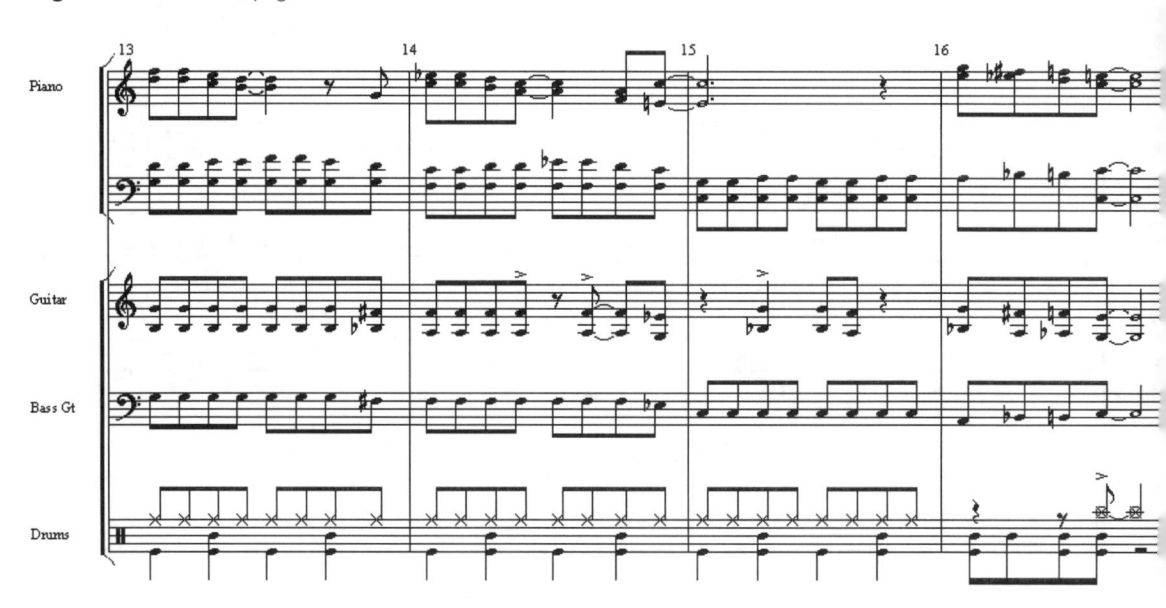

Figure P2.4 The score, page 4.

Take 1

> *Track 2:* Grand Piano | Left Hand
> *Sequence Parameters box:* Qua 1/8 – note
> *Instrument Parameter box:* Cha 1, Prg 0
> *Transport Bar:* (L) 1.1.1 (R) 5.1.1

Follow these steps:

1 Record the first four bars of the left hand piano part (Figure P2.5 and P2.6). Yes, you've guessed it. It's the same four bars used in Project 1 (Figures P1.4 and P1.5). If you want, copy and paste them over.

Figure P2.5
The left hand piano part.

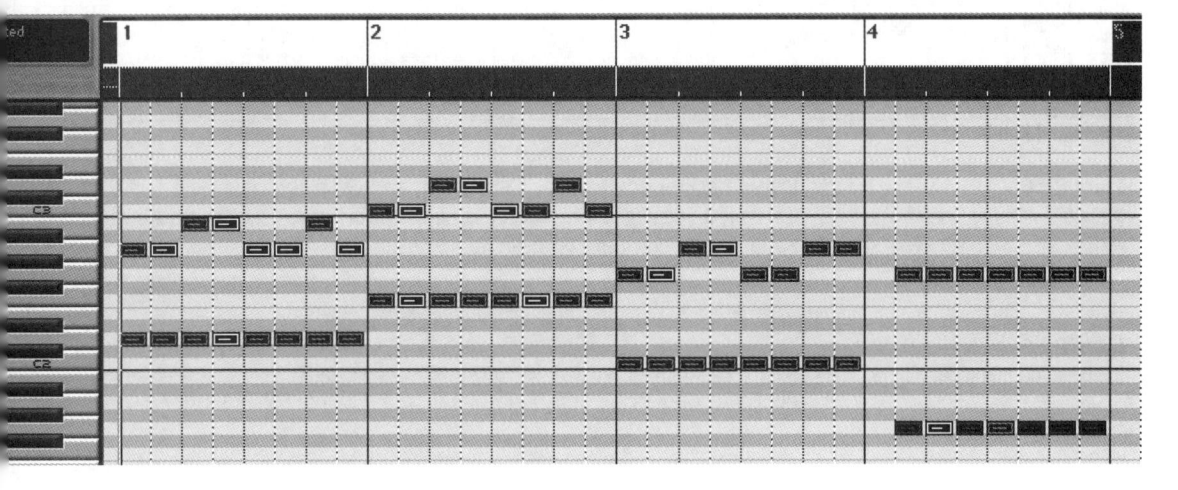

Figure P2.6
The left hand piano part, Matrix view.

2 Listen back. It should be pretty tight. Loosen things up a little using the Q- Strength and Q-Range parameters in the Extended Parameters box [Options >Extended Sequence Parameters ...]. When you're happy ...
3 Save Song – compare with project 2/2.1

Take 2

Track 1: Grand Piano | Right Hand.
Sequence Parameters box: Qua 1/8 – note.
Instrument Parameter box: Cha 1, Prog 0.
Transport Bar: (L) 1.1.1 (R) 5.1.1

Follow these steps:

1 Now record the first four bars of the right hand piano part (Figures P2.7 and P2.8). Again it's the same four bars used in Project 1 (Figures P1.8 and P1.9). If you want, copy and paste them over.

Figure P2.7
The right hand piano part.

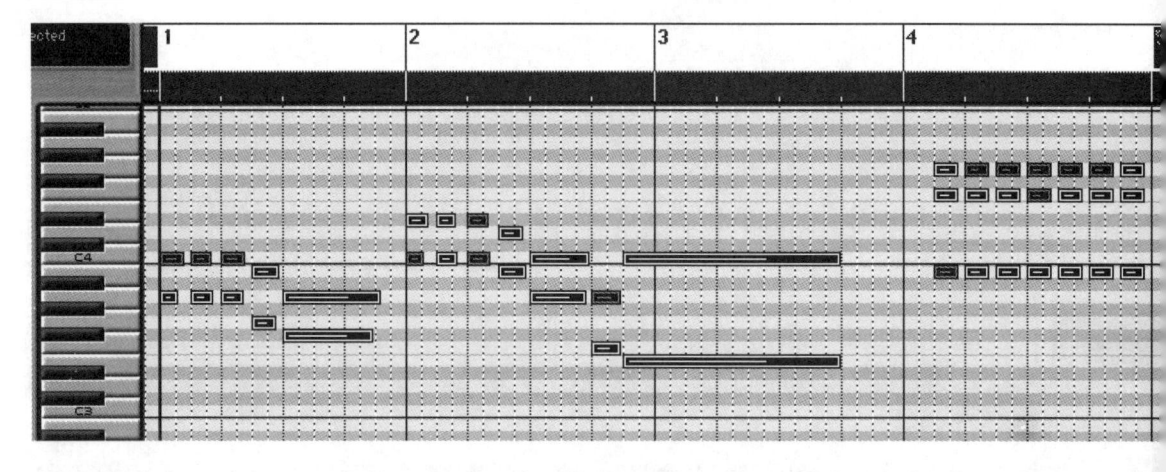

Figure P2.8
The right hand piano part, Matrix view.

2 Listen back and tweak the Q-Strength and Q-Range parameters in Extended Sequence Parameters box until you're satisfied with the result.
3 Save Song – compare with project 2/2.2.

Take 3

Figure P2.9
The left hand piano part, bars 5–9.

1 Reurn to track 2, set the Locators to (L) 5.1.1 (R) 9.1.1 and record the next four bars of the left hand piano part (Figures P2.9 and P2.10).

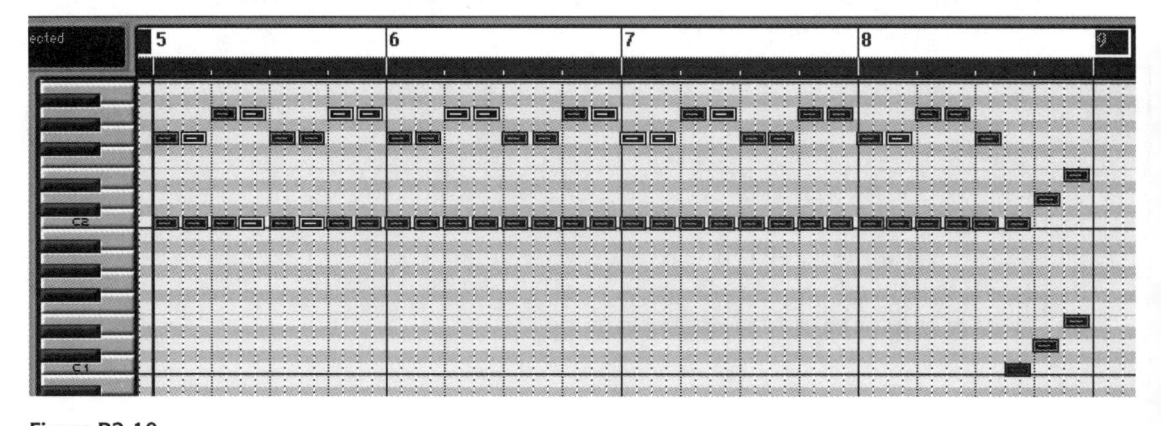

Figure P2.10
The left hand piano part, bars 5–9, Matrix view.

2 Switch to track 1 and record the right hand piano part between the same Locator set up (Figures P2.11 and P2.12).
3 Listen back and as before, tweak the quantize parameters until happy.
4 Save Song – compare with project2/2.3

Figure P2.11 (above)
The right hand piano part, bars 5–9.

Figure P2.12 (below)
The right hand piano part, bars 5–9, Matrix view.

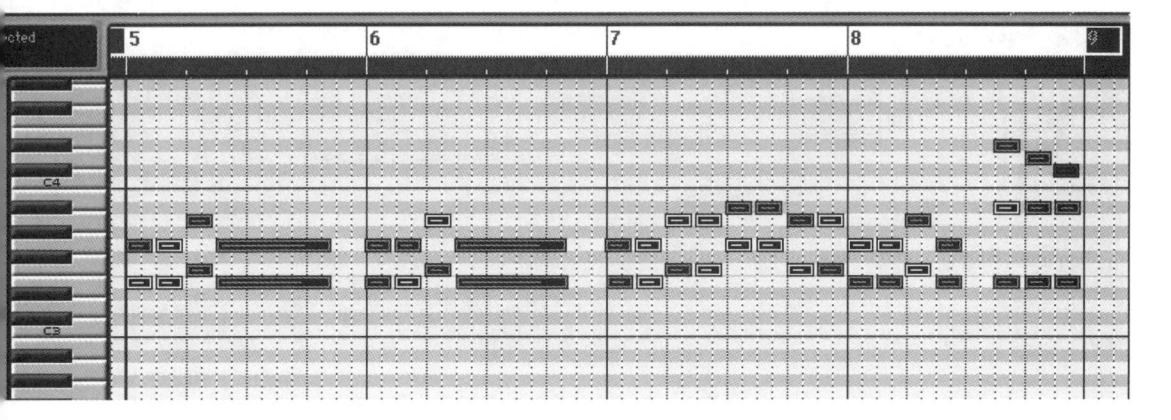

Take 4

1 Return to track 2, set the Locators at (L) 9.1.1 (R) 13.1.1 and record the next four bars of the left hand piano part (Figures P2.13 and P2.14).

Figure P2.13
The left hand piano part, bars 9–13.

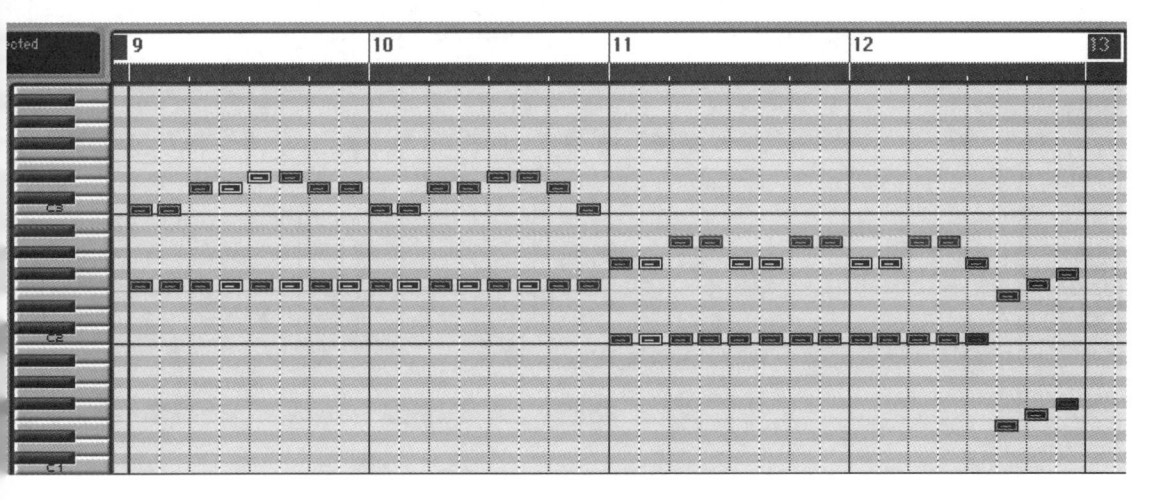

2 Switch to track1 and record the right hand piano part between the same Locator set up (Figures P2.15 and P2.16).

Figure P2.14
The left hand piano part, bars 9–13, Matrix view.

Figure P2.15 (above)
The right hand piano part, bars 9–13.

Figure P2.16 (below)
The right hand piano part, bars 9–13, Matrix view.

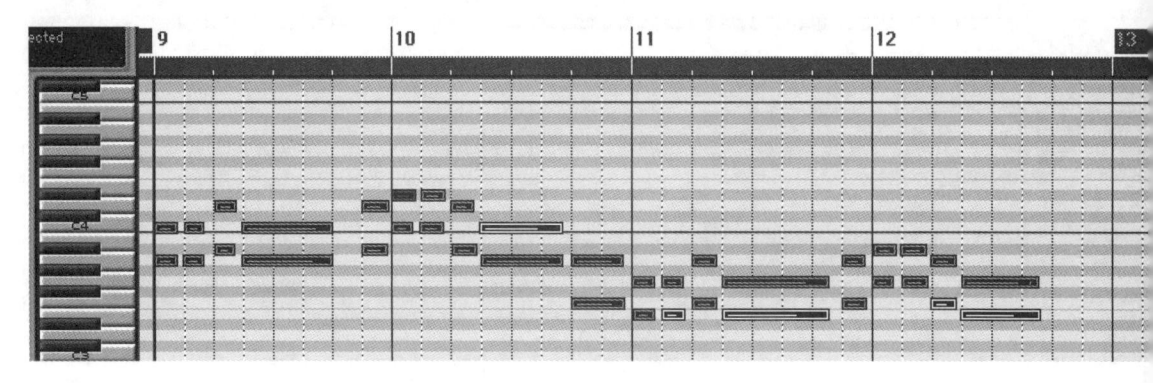

3 Listen back and once again, tweak those quantize parameters for all you're worth, on both sequences.
4 Save Song – compare with project2/2.4

Take 5

Figure P2.17
The left hand piano part, bars 13–17.

1 Return to track 2, set the Locators to (L) 13.1.1 (R) 17.1.1 and record the next four bars of the left hand part (Figures P2.17 and P2.18).

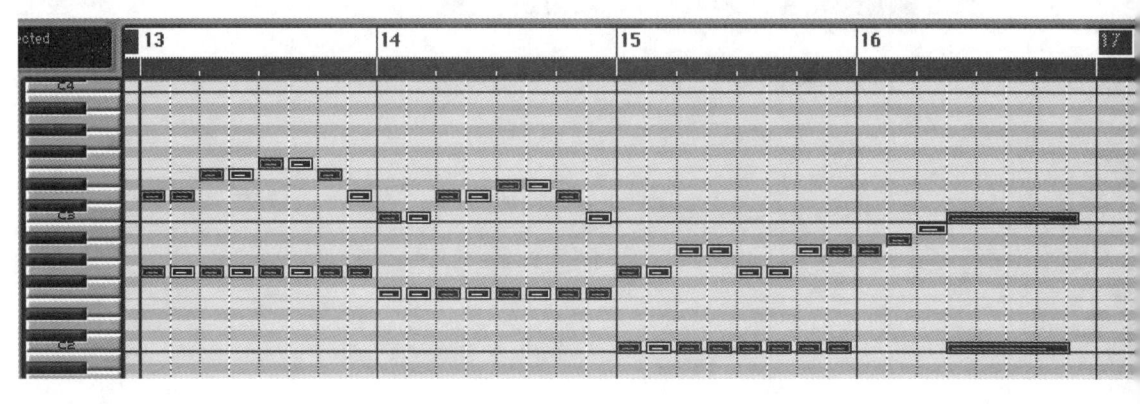

Figure P2.18
The left hand piano part, bars 13–17, Matrix view.

2 Switch to track 1 and record the right hand piano part between the same Locator set up (Figures P2.19 and P2.20).
3 Listen back and tweak the quantize parameters for both sequences.
4 Save Song – compare with project 2/2.5

Figure P2.19 (above)
The right hand piano part, bars 13–17.

Figure P2.20 (below)
The right hand piano part, bars 13–17, Matrix view.

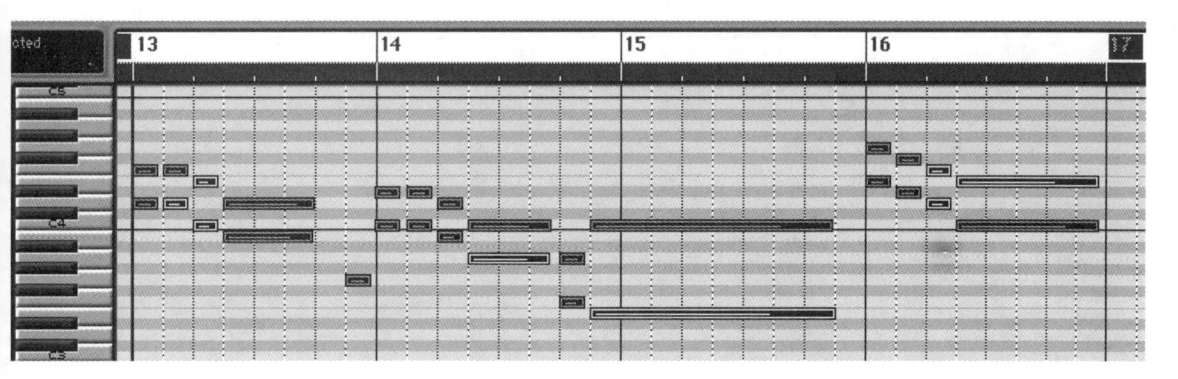

OK, that's the piano out of the way. Now for the guitar. Take a look at the guitar part on the score (Figures P2.2, P2.3 and P2.4). You'll notice that it's in two part harmony. No doubt a real guitarist would have played a few more notes, but for our purposes it's fine. I chose the GM MIDI preset 30, Distortion Guitar for extra bite.

Take 6

Track 3: Distortion Guitar.
Sequence Parameters box: Qua 1/8 – note.
Instrument Parameter box: Cha 2, Prog 30.
Transport Bar: (L) 5.1.1. (R) 9.1.1

Follow these steps:

1 Record the fours bars between the Locators (Figures P2.21 and P2.22).

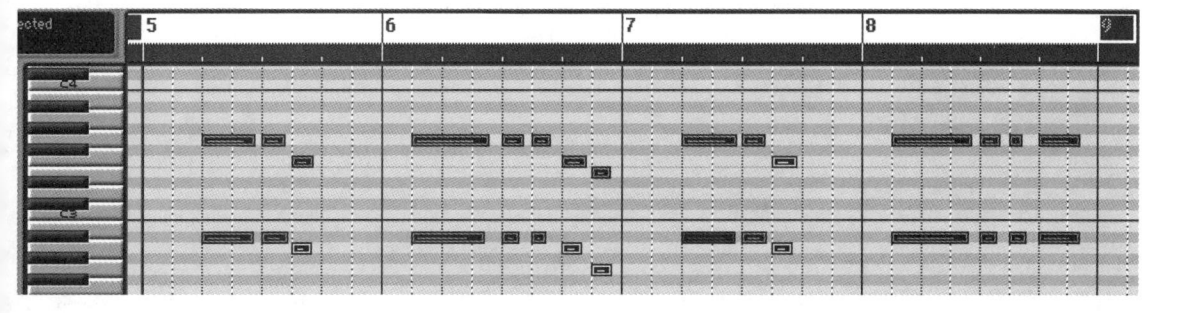

Figure P2.21 (top)
The guitar part, bars 5–9.

Figure P2.22 (bottom)
The guitar part, bars 5–9, Matrix view.

Figure P2.23
The guitar part, 9–13.

2 Record the next four bars, 9–13 (Figures P2.23 and P2.24).

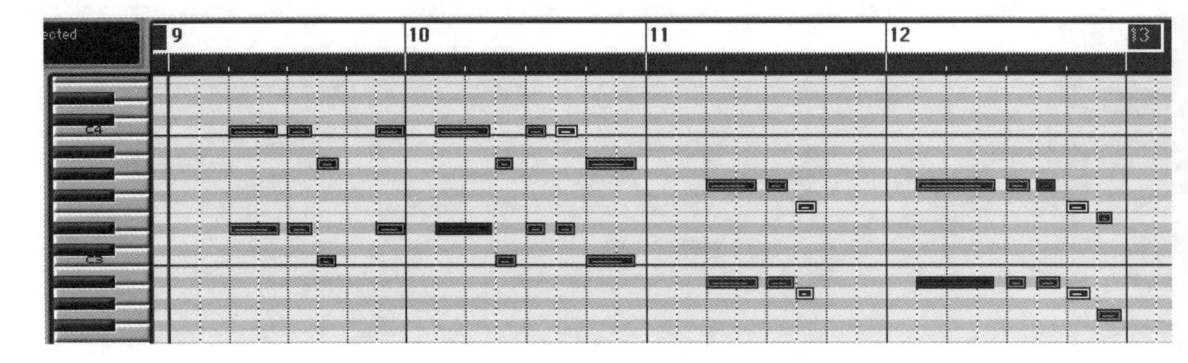

Figure P2.24
The guitar part, 9–13, Matrix view.

3 Record another four bars, 13–17 (Figures P2.25 and P2.26).
4 Listen back and tweak the quantize parameters for all three sequences until you are happy with the result.

Figure P2.25
The guitar part, bars 13–17.

Figure P2.26
The guitar part, bars 13–17, Matrix view.

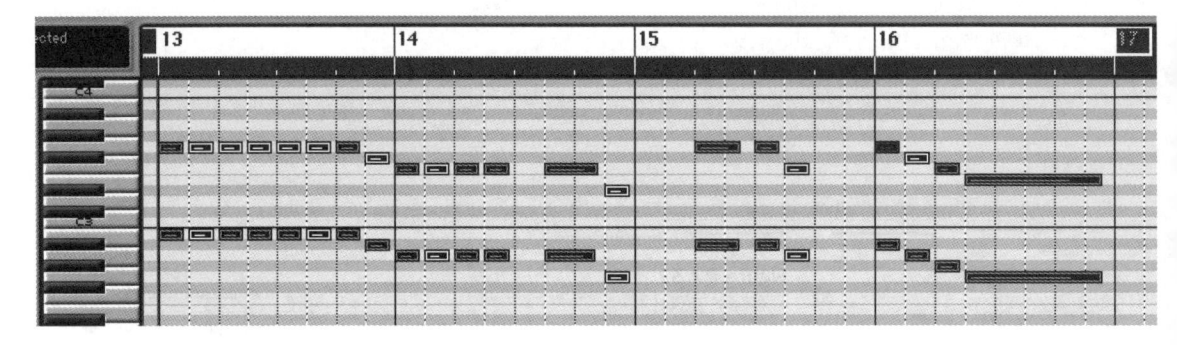

5 Save Song – compare with project 2/2.6

Take 7

> **Info**
>
> Note the transposition of -12 in the Instrument Parameter box for Take 7. The reason for this? – bass guitar is notated one octave higher than it actually sounds.

Track 4: Picked bass
Sequence Parameters box: Qua 1/8 – note
Instrument Parameter box: Cha 3, Prog 34, Transpose –12
Transport Bar: (L) 5.1.1 (R) 9.1.1

Follow these steps:

1 Record the four bars between the Locators (Figures P2.27 and P2.28).

Figure P2.27
The bass guitar part, bars 5–9.

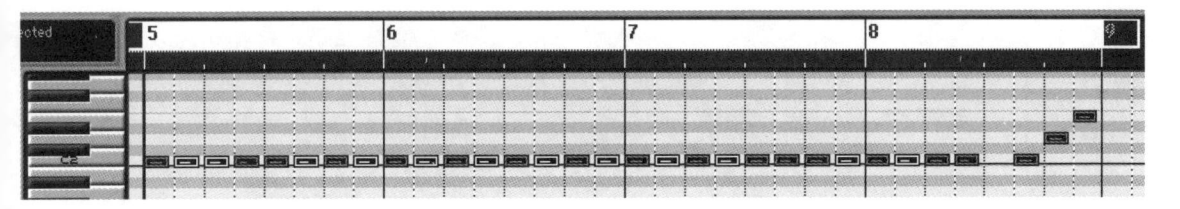

Figure P2.28
The bass guitar part, bars 5–9, Matrix view.

2 Record the next four bars, 9–13 (Figures P2.29 and P2.30).

Figure P2.29 (above)
The bass guitar part, bars 9–13.

Figure P2.30 (below)
The bass guitar part, bars 9–13, Matrix view.

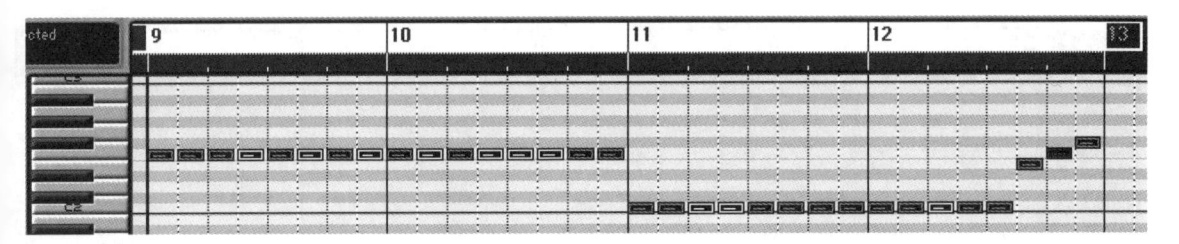

3 Record another 4 bars, 13-17 (Figures P2.31 and P2.32).

Figure P2.31
The bass guitar part, bars 13–17.

Figure P2.32
The bass guitar part, bars 13–17, Matrix view.

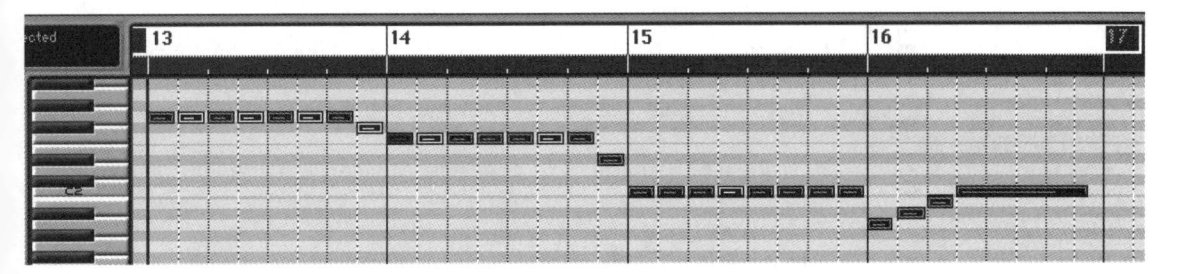

4 Listen back and tweak the quantize parameters for all three sequences until you are happy with the result.
5 Save Song – compare with project2/2.7.

Right, now the drums.

Take 8

Track 5: Standard drums | Kick/Snare
Sequence Parameter box: Qua 1/8 – note
Instrument Parameter box: Cha 10, Prg 0
Transport Bar: (L) 5.1.1 (R) 9.1.1

Follow these steps:

1 Play and record the kick and snare drums together (C1 & E1) between the Locators (Figures P2.33 and P2.34).

Figure P2.33
The kick and snare drums, bars 5–9.

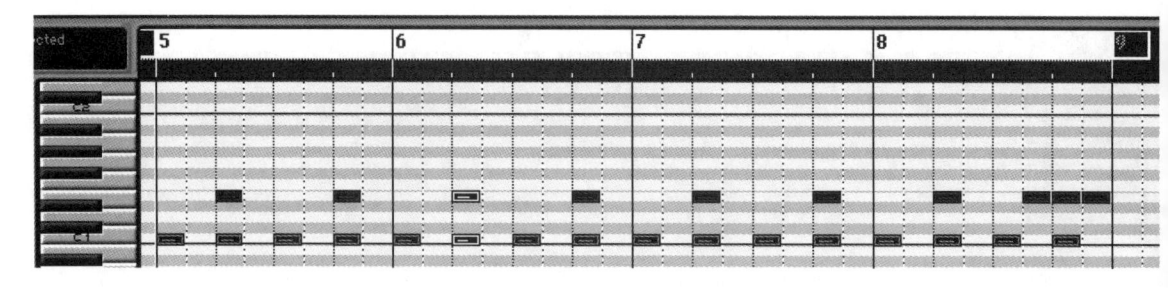

Figure P2.34
The kick and snare drums, bars 5–9, Matrix view.

2 Listen back and tweak the quantize parameters until a nice rock feel is achieved. If you find it difficult to play kick and snare together record them separately.
3 Save Song – compare with project2/2.8a.

Another way to create this simple drum pattern is to use the Hyper Edit menu. When Hyper Edit is configured as a drum editor the beats can be entered manually, with the mouse. Do it this way:

1 Select track 5 – Kick/Snare, and with the Pencil tool create an empty sequence between the Locators.
2 Open the Hyper Edit window [Windows >Open Hyper Edit] (Figure P2.35).
3 'It doesn't look much like a drum editor to me' I can hear you mutter. Nope, we're not quite there yet. From within the Hyper Edit window use the Hyper menu to create a GM drum editor [Hyper >Create GM Drum Set] (Figure P2.36).

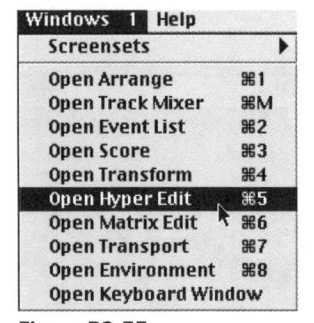

Figure P2.35
Open Hyper Edit

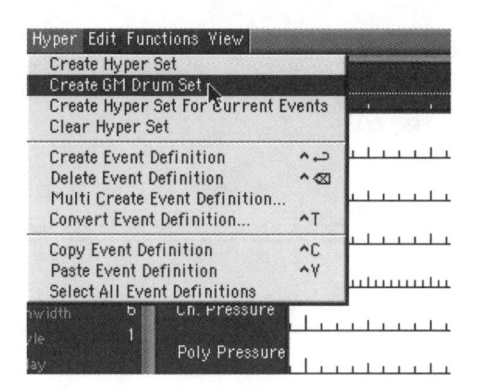

Figure P2.36
Create a GM Drum Set.

4 The Hyper Edit window will change to a drum editor (Figure P2.37). In the Parameter box, choose a Grid value of 1/8 – note from the drop down menu (Figure P2.38) and use the Pencil tool to enter the beats on the grid corresponding to the Kick 1 and SD2 event definitions (Figure P2.39). Vary the velocities by altering the shading in the columns.

Figure P2.37
The Hyper Edit GM Drum Set.

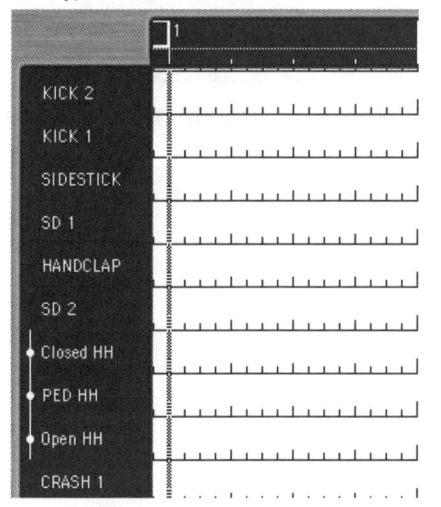

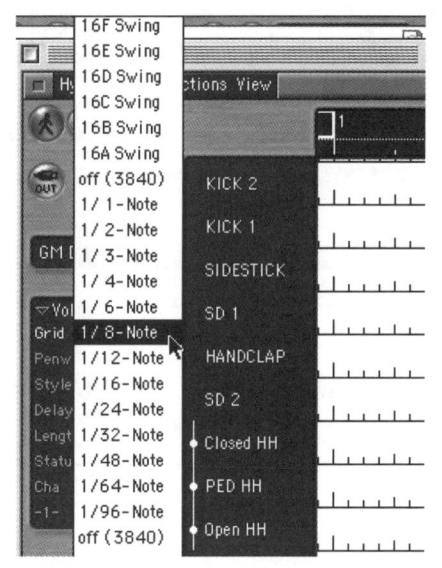

Figure P2.38
A Grid value of 1/8 – note.

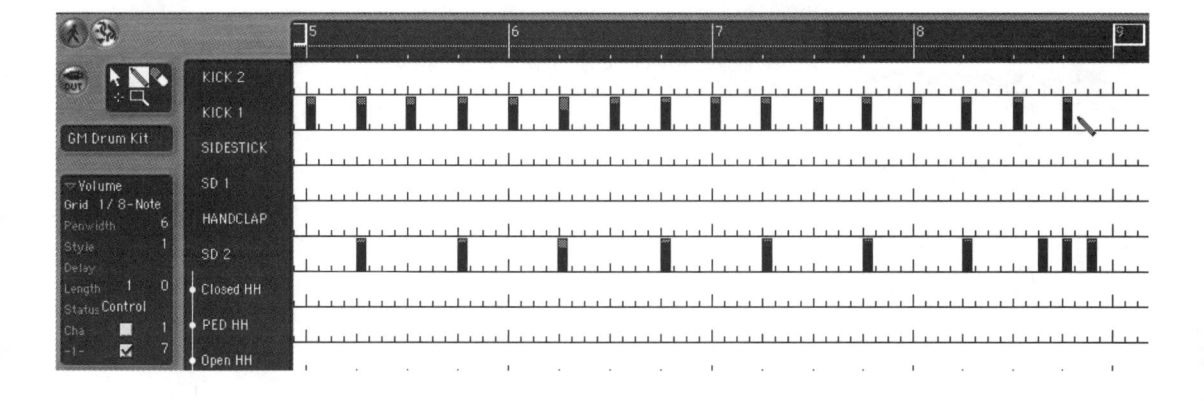

Figure P2.39 (below)
Enter beats.

Tip

Remember, if you decide to enter the drum beats manually in the Hyper Edit window, all the events will be hard quantized. Tweak the Quantize parameters in the Extended Sequence Parameters box afterwards to loosen things up a bit.

5 The next four bars, 9 – 13, are the same. You can either record or enter them again or do it the easy way and duplicate the previous sequence.

6 Play and record, or enter manually, the last four bars, 13 – 17 (Figures P2.40, P2.41 and P2.42).

Figure P2.40 (above)
The kick and snare drums, bars 13–17.

Figure P2.41 (below)
The kick and snare drums, bars 13–17, Matrix view.

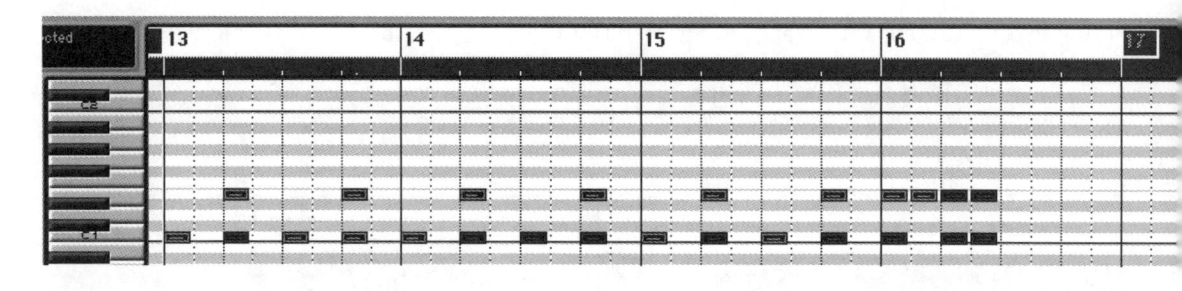

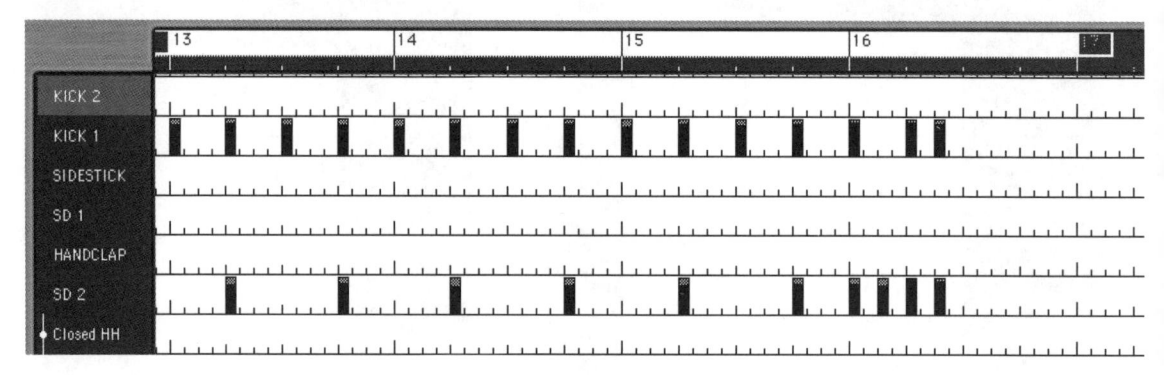

Figure P2.42
The kick and snare drums, bars 13–17, Hyper view.

7 Tweak the quantize parameters.
8 Save Song – compare with project2/2.8b.

Regardless of the method you used to create the drum sequences in Take 8, why not take a look at the results in all three Edit windows.

- The Hyper Edit window will provide a graphical display and corresponding drum names – remember to create a GM Drum Set.
- The Matrix Edit view will provide a graphical display that corresponds to the notes actually played on the keyboard.
- The Score Edit view will present the sequences as standard drum notation on a special drum staff. If you played it correctly, it should look the same as our score. Choose #Drums in the Display Parameters box (Figure P2.43).

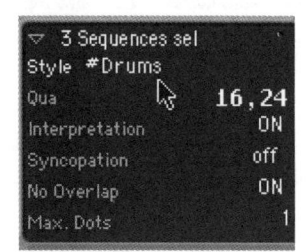

Figure P2.43
The Display Parameters box: Style #Drums.

Take 9

Track 6: Standard drums | Hi – Hat
Sequence Parameters box: Qua 1/8 – note
Instrument Parameter box: Cha 10, Prg 0
Transport Bar: (L) 5.1.1 (R) 9.1.1

Follow these steps:

1 Record or manually enter the hi-hat (F#1) between the Locators (Figures P2.44, P2.45 and P2.46).

Figure P2.44
The closed hi-hat, bars 5 – 9.

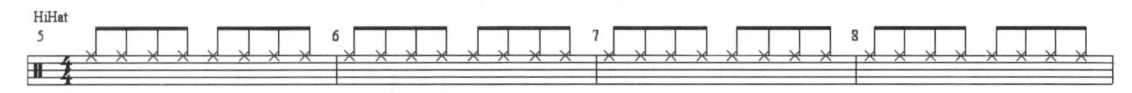

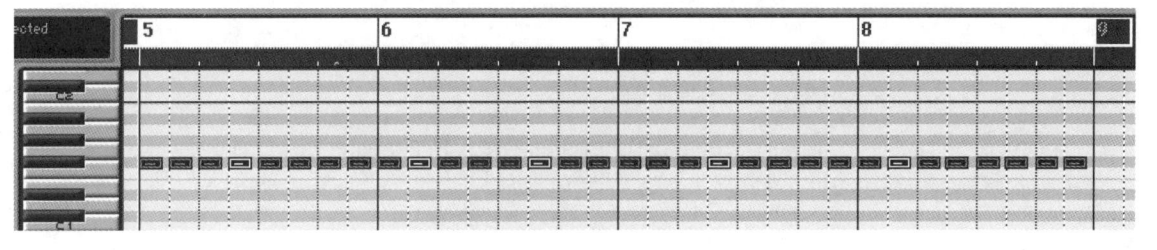

Figure P2.45 (above)
The closed hi-hat, bars 5 – 9, Matrix view.

Figure P2.46 (below)
The closed hi-hat, bars 5 – 9, Hyper view.

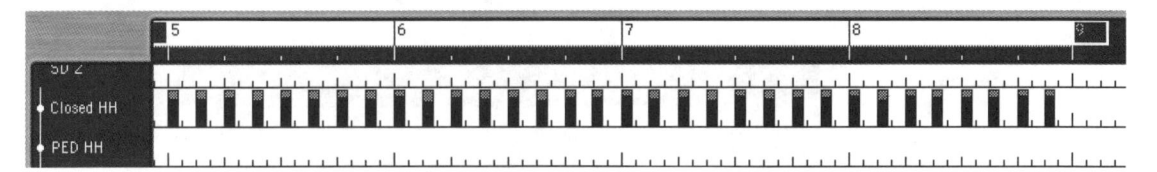

2 Listen back and maybe tweak the quantize parameters.
3 The next four bars, 9 – 13, are the same. You can either record or enter them again or do it the easy way and duplicate the previous sequence.
4 Record or enter the hi-hat, bars 13 – 17 (Figure P2.47, P2.48 and P2.49).

Figure P2.47 (top)
The closed hi-hat, bars 13–17.

Figure P2.48 (bottom)
The closed hi-hat, bars 13–17, Matrix view.

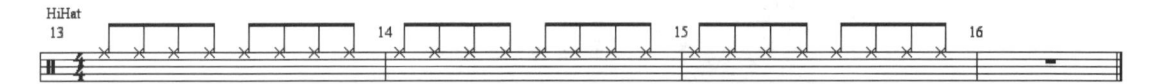

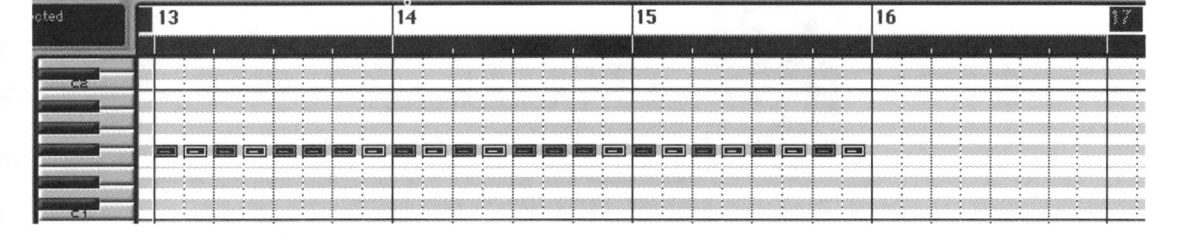

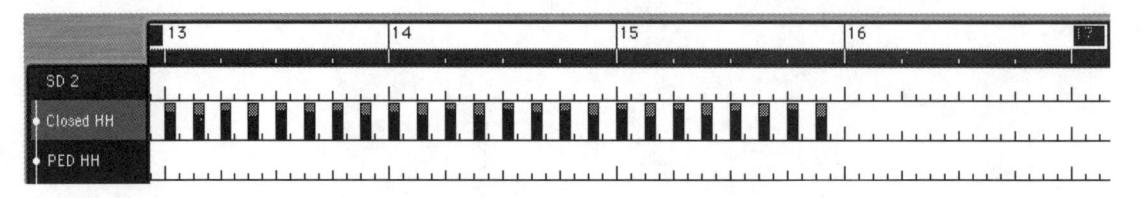

Figure P2.49
The closed hi-hat, bars 13–17, Hyper view.

5 Listen back and maybe tweak the quantize parameters.
6 Save Song – compare with project 2/2.9.

Take 10

Track 7: Standard drums | Toms
Sequence Parameters box: Qua 1/8 – note
Instrument Parameters box: Cha 10, Prg 0
Transport Bar: (L) 4.1.1 (R) 5.1.1

Follow these steps:

1 Record both toms together (C2 & F1) or enter them manually in the Hyper Edit Edit window using the GM Drum Set (Figures P2.50, P2.51 and P2.52).

Figure P2.50
The toms.

Figure P2.51
The toms, Matrix view.

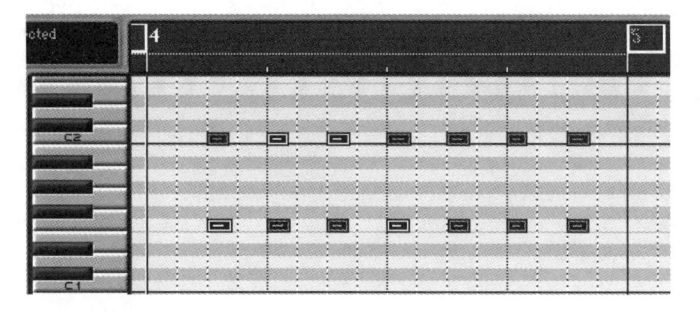

Figure P2.52
The toms, Hyper view.

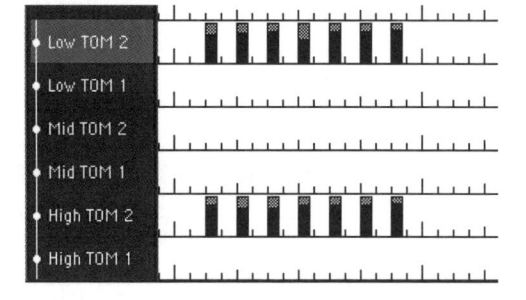

2 Listen back and tweak the quantize parameters.
3 Save Song – compare with project2/2.10.

Take 11

Track 8: Standard drums | Crash Cymbal
Sequence Parameters box: Qua 1/8 – note
Instrument Parameter box: Cha 10, Prg 10
Transport Bar: (L) 5.1.1 (R) 17.1.1

Follow these steps:

1 They're not marked on the score, but, as a finishing touch, why not record the odd crash cymbal (C#2). On the first beat of bar 5 maybe. I also placed one at the beginning of bar 9 and another on the fourth 1/8th note in bar 16 (Figures P2.53, P2.54 and P2.55).

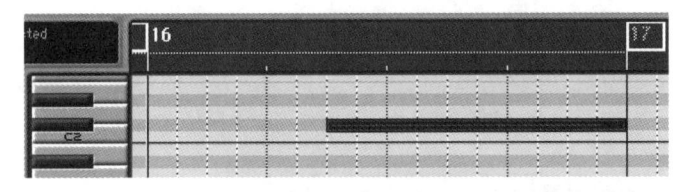

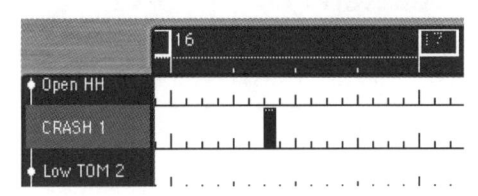

Figure P2.53
The cymbal crashes.

Figure P2.54
The cymbal crashes, Matrix view.

Figure P2.55
The cymbal crashes, Hyper view.

2 Listen back and maybe tweak the quantize parameters.
3 Save Song – compare with project2/2.11.

Project 3 – a jazz funk score

Musical objectives

- Achieve a realistic interpretation of a short jazz funk score comprising rhythm and 'horns' – trumpet, tenor sax and trombone.
- Improvise one-bar breaks in the horn parts using a blues scale.
- Achieve a satisactory mix – volume balance and stereo picture.

Logic skills

- Use a preset swing groove.
- Use the Track Mixer.
- Use Transform to humanize selected sequences.

Preparation

1 From the CD, copy the folder named project3 to your computer.
2 On your computer, create a folder named mywork3 or something similar in which to save your work.
3 From the project3 folder, open the template – templt3 in Logic.
4 In your new mywork3 folder, re-save the template as myproj3 or something similar.

OK, let's take a look at the score (Figures P3.1, P3.2, P3.3 and P3.4). Ouch! It looks complicated, right? Don't be put off. This kind of music looks horrendous written down. Once you hear it things make more sense.

Load project3/3.mix and have a good listen. Play it several times and follow the score. Sounds easier than it looks, doesn't it? Mute and solo tracks to hear individual tracks and sequences. The 'groove' is important here, and it is probably best to start this one with drums and bass.

> **Info**
>
> The template has a time signature of 4/4 and the tempo is 95 bpm. If that's too fast for you, slow the tempo before you record.

> **Tip**
>
> When loading example files containing MIDI settings its quite likely that you will initially hear the wrong sounds (very likely those from a previous project or song). Use [Options > Song Settings > Used Instrument MIDI Settings] to correct them. A faster way – quickly cursor up or down the tracks using the arrow keys on your computer keyboard.

Figure P3.1
Jazz Funk score, page 1.

Figure P3.2
Jazz Funk score, page 2.

Figure P3.3 (above)
Jazz Funk score, page 3.

Figure P3.4 (below)
Jazz Funk score, page 4.

Take 1

Track 7: Standard drums | Kick/Snare
Sequence Parameters box: Qua 1/8 – note
Instrument Parameter box: Cha 10, Prg 0
Transport Bar: (L) 1.1.1 (R) 5.1..1.1

Project 3 – a jazz funk score 47

Follow these steps:

1 Record (or enter manually in the Hyper Edit window: GM Drum Set) four bars of kick (C1) and snare (D1) drums (Figure P3.5, P3.6 and P3.7).

Figure P3.5
Kick and snare drums.

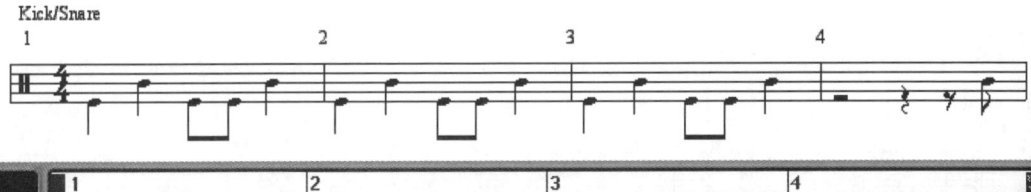

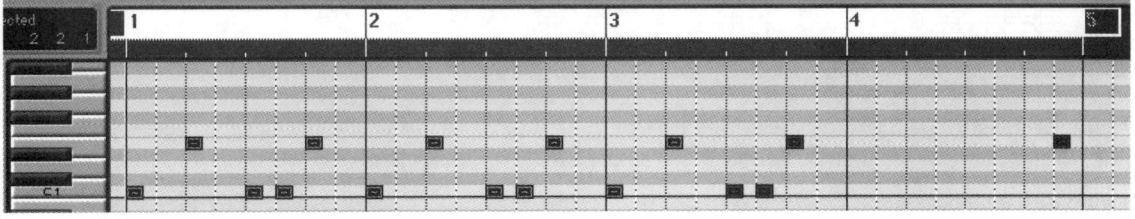

Figure P3.6 (above)
Kick and snare drums, Matrix view.

Figure P3.7
Kick and snare drums, Hyper view.

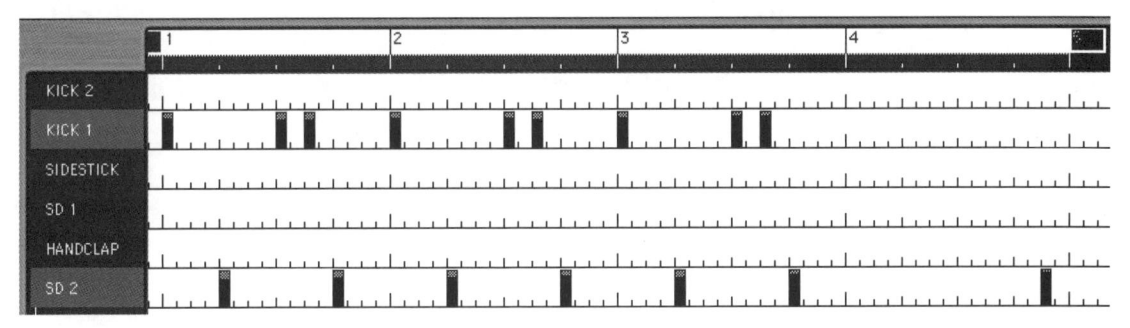

2 Select the newly recorded sequence and copy it to bar 5 [Functions >Object >Repeat Objects... x1] (Figure P3.8), We now have eight bars of drums (1 – 9).
3 Save Song – compare with project3/3.1

Figure P3.8
Repeat objects

Take 2

Track 6: Slap Bass 2
Sequence Parameters box: Qua 1/8 – note
Instrument Parameter box: Cha 6, Prg 37, Transpose –12
Transport Bar: (L) 1.1.1 (R) 5.1.1

Follow these steps:

1 Record four bars of slap bass guitar (Figure P3.9 and 3.10)

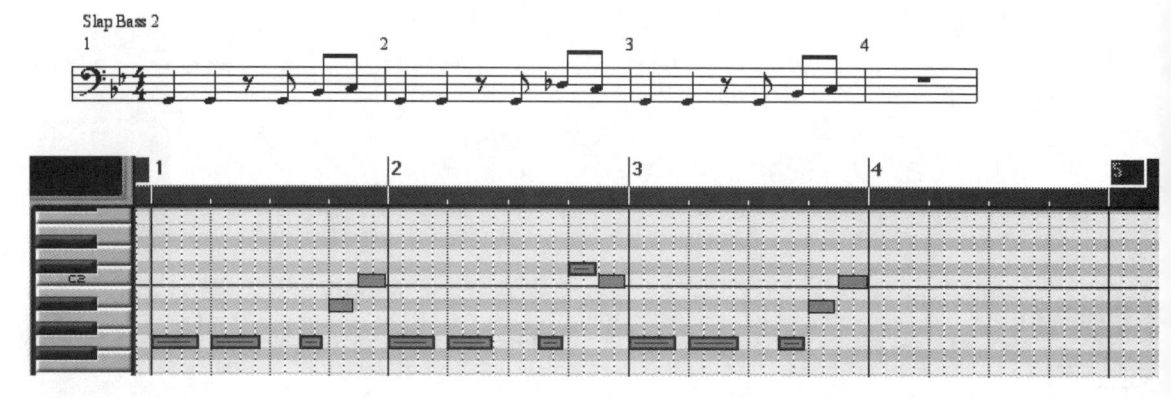

Figure P3.9 (top)
Slap bass guitar

Figure P3.10 (above)
Slap bass guitar, Matrix view

2 Select the newly recorded sequence and copy it to bar 5.
3 Save Song – compare with project3/3.2.

That's a basic drum and bass pattern established. Now for the horns. Trumpet first.

Take 3

> *Track 1:* Trumpet
> *Sequence Parameters box:* Qua 16B Swing
> *Instrument Parameter box:* Cha 1, Prg 56
> *Transport Bar* (L) 1.1.1 (R) 5.1.1

Follow these steps:

Figure P3.11 (top)
Trumpet

Figure P3.12 (bottom)
Trumpet, Matrix view

1 Record the trumpet between the Locators, bars 1 – 5. Note bar 4 is blank (Figure P3.11 and 3.12). I have chosen 16B Swing as my quantize value (Figure P3.13). You may prefer another setting. 16C and 16D work quite well but anything beyond that becomes too 'swingy' for the funk background.

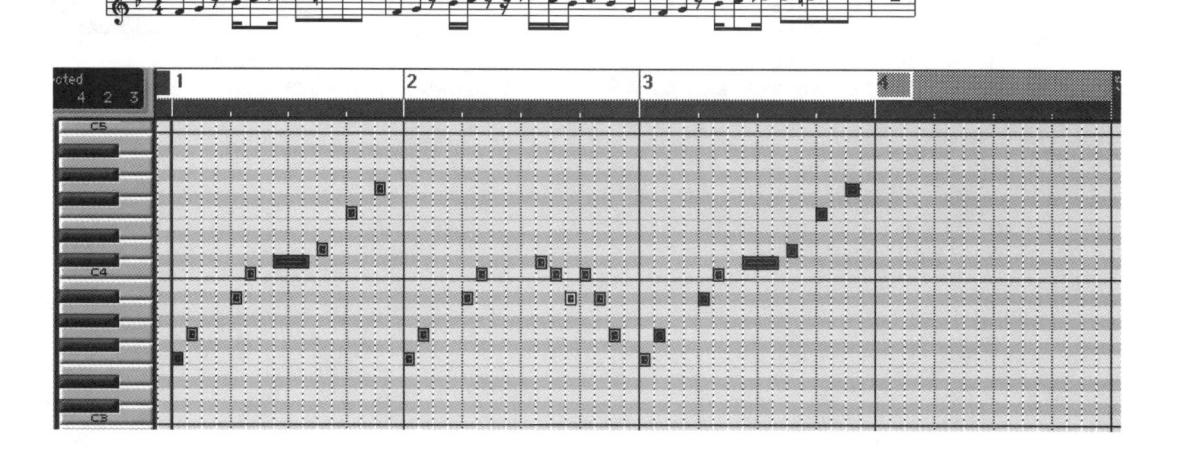

Project 3 – a jazz funk score   49

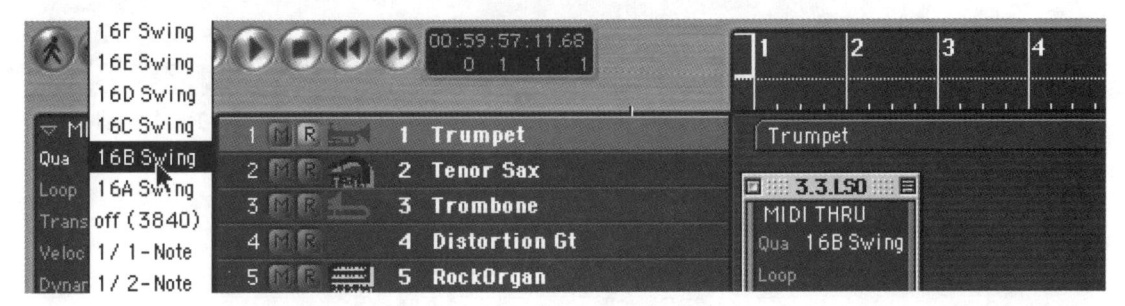

2 Copy the new trumpet sequence to bar 5.
3 Save Song – compare with project 3/3.3

Figure P3.13
A quantize value of 16B Swing

```
POSITION         STATUS    CHA   NUM  VAL  LENGTH/INFO
-------------- Start of List --------------
 0  4  4 235    Note        1    F3   113   _  _  _ 159
 1  1  2  13    Note        1    G3   102   _  _  _ 198
 1  1  4 222    Note        1    A#3  110   _  _  _ 155
 1  2  1 220    Note        1    C4   105   _  _  _ 184
 1  2  4  36    Note        1    C#4  119   _  _  2 133
 1  3  2 227    Note        1    D4   102   _  _  _ 196
 1  3  4 213    Note        1    F4   107   _  _  _ 216
 1  4  2 231    Note        1    G4   107   _  _  _ 194
 2  1  1  58    Note        1    F3   110   _  _  _ 155
 2  1  2  15    Note        1    G3   102   _  _  _ 191
 2  1  4 216    Note        1    A#3  110   _  _  _ 157
 2  2  2   4    Note        1    C4   105   _  _  _ 160
 2  3  2  48    Note        1    C#4  105   _  _  _ 139
 2  3  3  47    Note        1    C4   100   _  _  _ 134
 2  3  4  76    Note        1    A#3   91   _  _  _ 128
 2  4  1  68    Note        1    C4   107   _  _  _ 167
 2  4  2  78    Note        1    A#3  100   _  _  _ 137
 2  4  3  55    Note        1    G3    98   _  _  _ 158
```

Info

A very useful set of pre-defined swing templates are supplied with Logic. They've been there since the Atari days when the program was called Notator and I find them invaluable. Figure P3.14 shows bar 1 of the unquantized trumpet part displayed in the List Edit window. Compare these positions after 16B Swing has been applied (Figure P3.15).

Figure P3.14
The trumpet before quantization

```
POSITION         STATUS    CHA   NUM  VAL  LENGTH/INFO
-------------- Start of List --------------
 1  1  1   1    Note        1    F3   113   _  _  _ 159
 1  1  2  21    Note        1    G3   102   _  _  _ 198
 1  2  1   1    Note        1    A#3  110   _  _  _ 155
 1  2  2  21    Note        1    C4   105   _  _  _ 184
 1  2  4  21    Note        1    C#4  119   _  _  2 133
 1  3  3   1    Note        1    D4   102   _  _  _ 196
 1  4  1   1    Note        1    F4   107   _  _  _ 216
 1  4  3   1    Note        1    G4   107   _  _  _ 194
 2  1  1   1    Note        1    F3   110   _  _  _ 155
 2  1  2  21    Note        1    G3   102   _  _  _ 191
 2  2  1   1    Note        1    A#3  110   _  _  _ 157
 2  2  2  21    Note        1    C4   105   _  _  _ 160
 2  3  2  21    Note        1    C#4  105   _  _  _ 139
 2  3  3   1    Note        1    C4   100   _  _  _ 134
 2  3  4  21    Note        1    A#3   91   _  _  _ 128
 2  4  1   1    Note        1    C4   107   _  _  _ 167
 2  4  2  21    Note        1    A#3  100   _  _  _ 137
 2  4  3   1    Note        1    G3    98   _  _  _ 158
```

Figure P3.15
The trumpet after 16B Swing quantization

You may be wondering why we are not tweaking the values in the Extended Quantize Parameter box. We did so much of it in Project 2 after all! Well hang on a bit. We are going to humanize things a different way at the end of this project. Logic is a very flexible program and there is usually more than one way of doing things.

Take 4

Track 2: Tenor Sax
Sequence Parameters box: Qua 16B Swing
Instrument Parameters box: Cha 2, Prg 66, Transpose –12
Transport Bar: (L) 1.1.1 (R) 5.1.1

Follow these steps:

1 Record the tenor sax between the Locators. Note bar 4 is blank (Figure P3.16 and P3.17). Again I have chosen a 16B Swing for a quantize value. If you chose another on Take 1, choose it again here otherwise the horns may sound sloppy!

Figure P3.16
Tenor sax.

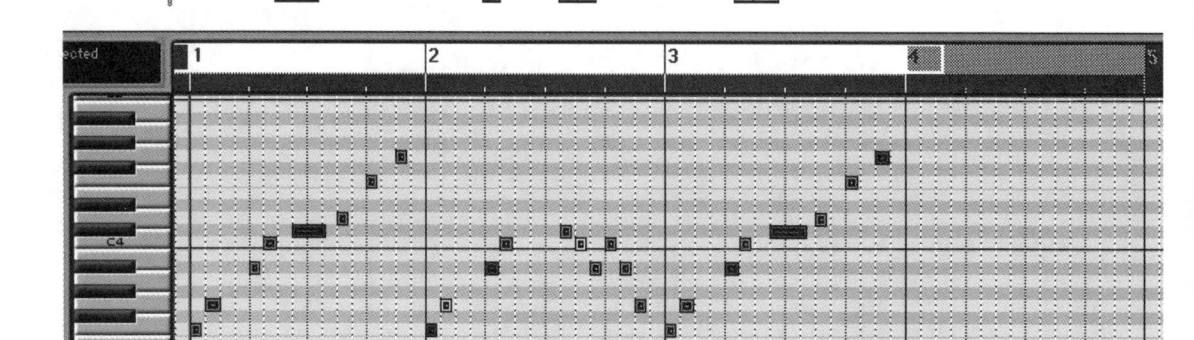

Figure P3.17
Tenor sax, Matrix view.

Figure P3.18
Treble clef with figure 8.

Info

You may have noticed the figure eight just below the treble clef sign at the beginning of the tenor sax staff (Figure P3.18). This tells us that the tenor sax is notated one octave higher on the score than it actually sounds. That's why we have –12 entered in the Instrument Parameter box for this take.

2 Copy the new tenor sax sequence to bar 5.
3 Save Song – compare with project3/3.4

Take 5

Track 3: Trombone
Sequence Parameters box: Qua 16B Swing
Instrument Parameter box: Cha 3, Prg 57
Transport Bar: (L) 1.1.1 (R) 4.1.1

Follow these steps:

1 Record the trombone part between the Locators (Figures P3.19 and P3.20).
2 Copy the new trombone sequence to bar 5.
3 Save Song – compare to project3/3.5.

Figure P3.19
Trombone.

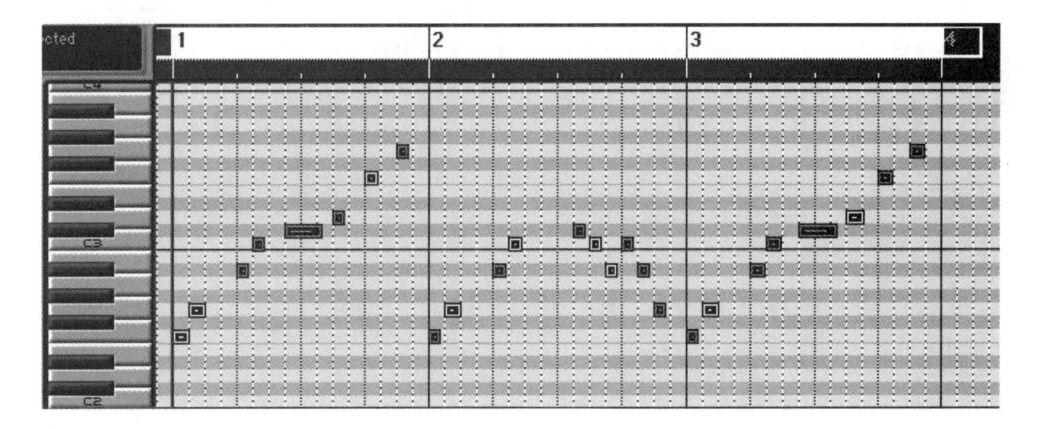

Figure P3.20
Trombone, Matrix view.

'Hang on a minute,' I hear you say, 'what about the notes in bar 4? We've left them out!' True, but that's a 'Solo Break' and we'll record it separately. All in good time!

Take 6

Track 7: Standard drum | Kick/Snare
Sequence Parameters box: Qua 1/8 – note
Transport Bar: (L) 9.1.1 (R) 13.1.1

Follow these steps:

1 Record, or enter in the Hyper editor, the drum pattern between the Locators (Figure P3.21, P3.22 and P3.23).
2 Save Song – compare with project3/3.6.

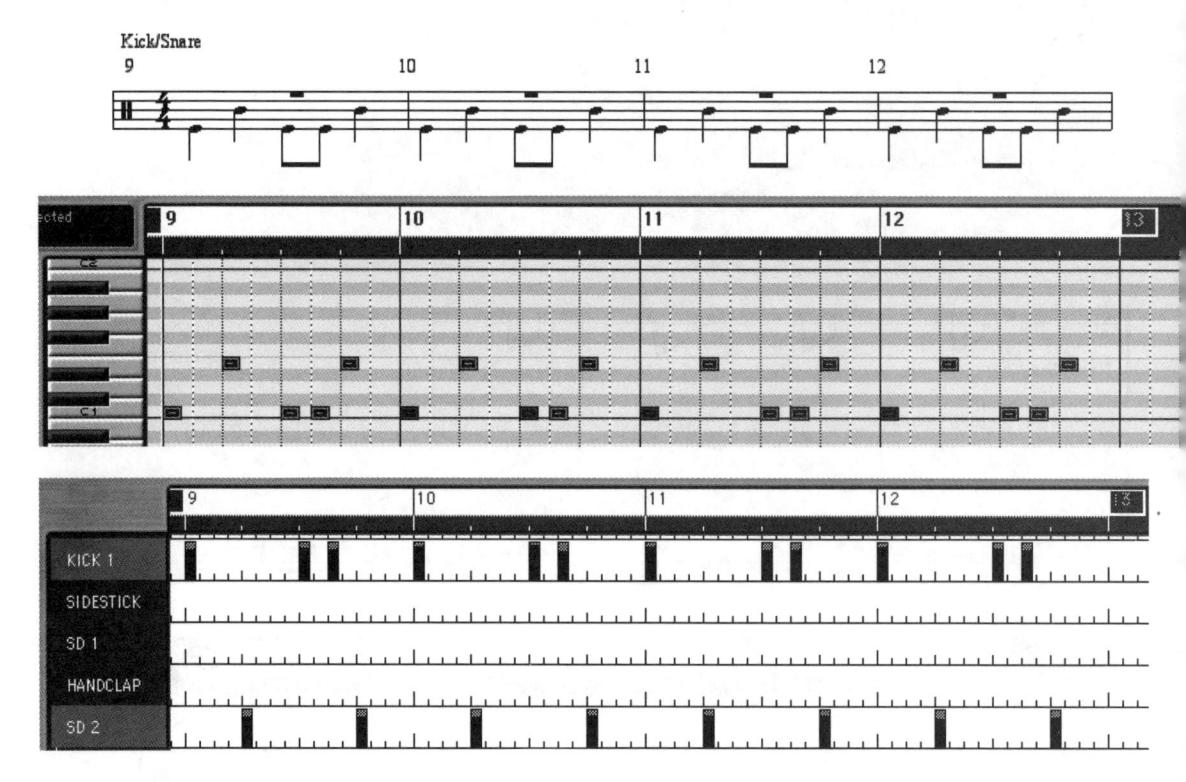

Figure P3.21 (top)
Drums

Figure P3.22 (centre)
Drums, Matrix view

Figure P3.23 (bottom)
Drums, Hyper edit view

Take 7

Track 6: Slap Bass 2
Sequence Parameters box: Qua 1/8 – note
Transport Bar: (L) 9.1.1 (R) 13.1 1

Follow these steps:

1 Record the slap bass between the Locators (Figure P3.24 and P3.25).
2 Save Song – compare with project3/3.7

Figure P3.24 (above) Slap bass   **Figure P3.25** (below) Slap bass, Matrix view

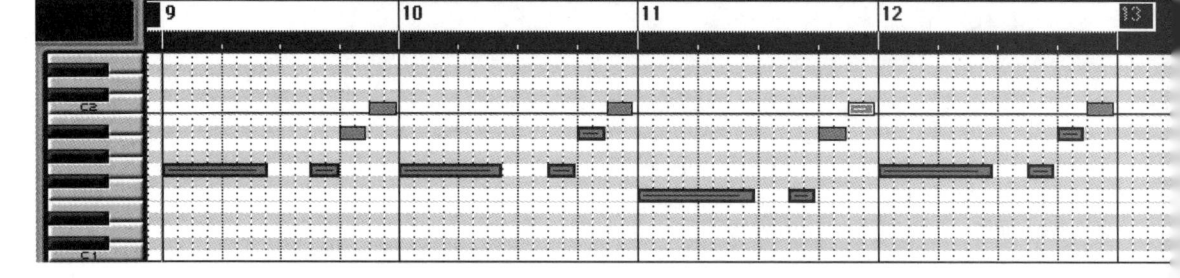

Take 8

1 With the Locators at (L) 9.1 1 (R) 13.1 1, record the trumpet, tenor and trombone on their respective tracks (Figure P3.26, P3.27, P3.28 and 3.29). As before, be consistent with the quantization. Mine is 16B Swing.
2 Save Song – compare with project3/3.8.

Figure P3.26
Trumpet, tenor sax and trombone.

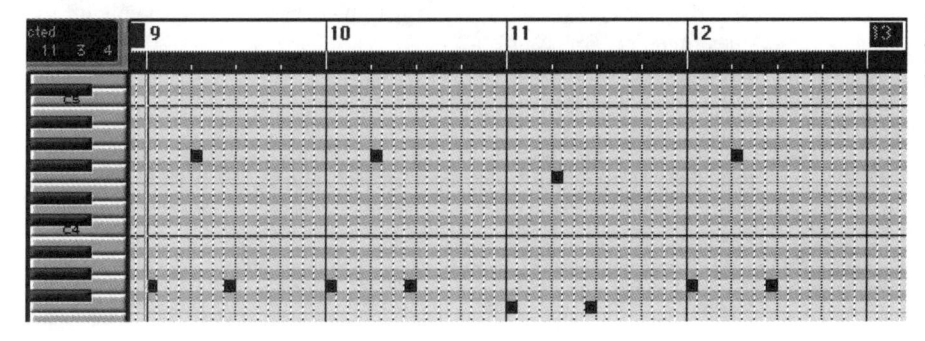

Figure P3.27
Trumpet, Matrix view.

Take 9

1 With the Locators at (L) 13.1 1 (R) 17.1 1, record the last four bars of drums and slap bass on their respective tracks (Figures P3.28 – P3.31). Use 1/8 – note quantization.

Figure P3.28
Drums and slap bass

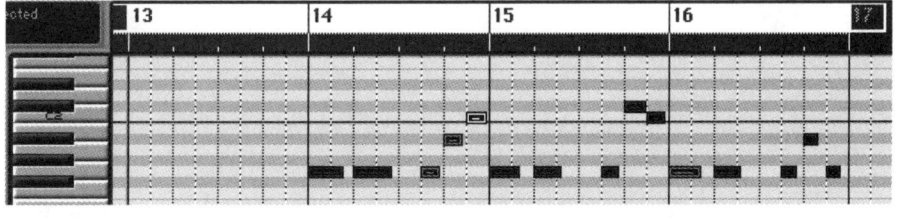

Figure P3.29
Slap bass, Matrix view

Figure P3.30
Drums, Matrix view

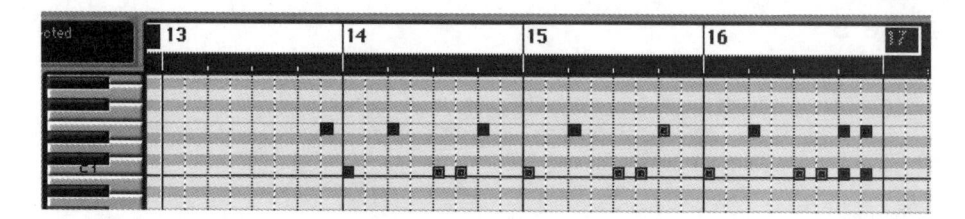

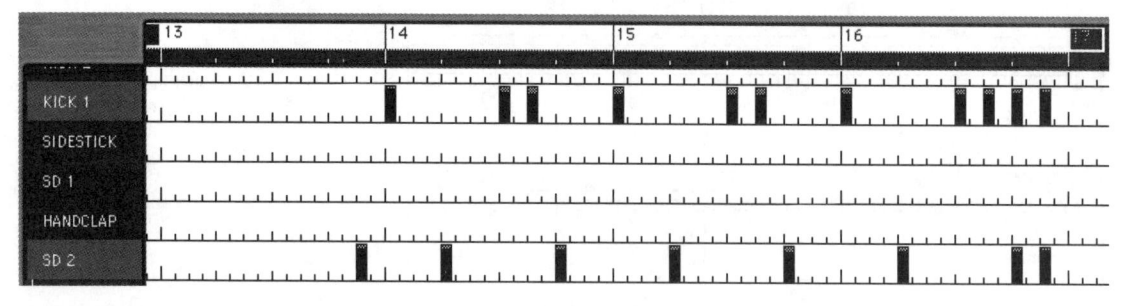

Figure P3.31
Drums, Hyper edit view

2 Save Song
3 Record the last four bars of trumpet, tenor sax and trombone on their respective tracks (Figure P3.32). Again, be consistent with the quantize values (mine is 16B Swing).
4 Save Song – compare with project 3/3.9

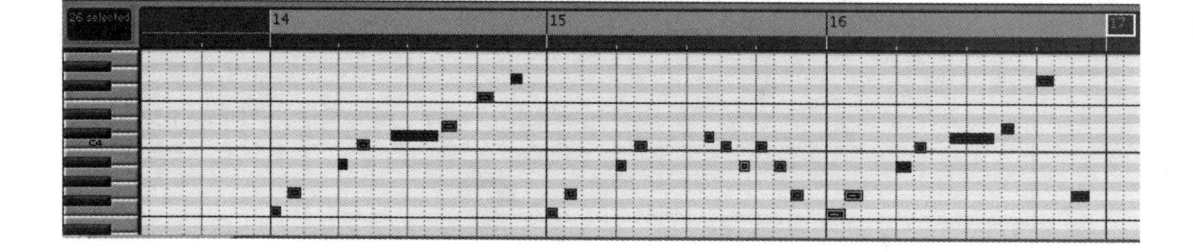

Figure P3.32
Trumpet, tenor sax and trombone

Figure P3.33
Trumpet, Matrix view

Take 10

Track 4: Distortion Guitar
Sequence Parameters box: Qua 16B Swing
Instrument Parameters box: Cha 4, Prg 30
Transport Bar: (L) 1.1.1 (R) 5.1.1

Guitar parts are usually written one octave higher than they actually sound, even on a concert score. In this case, as we are playing a keyboard, it has been left at concert pitch. Play exactly as written, nice and choppy. Short notes.

Follow these steps:

1 Record the guitar between the Locators (Figure P3.34 and P3.35). If you have problems playing against the horn parts, mute them.

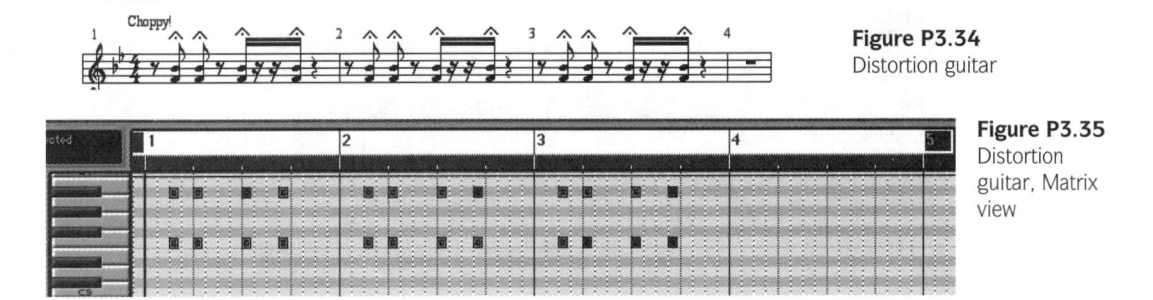

Figure P3.34
Distortion guitar

Figure P3.35
Distortion guitar, Matrix view

2 Copy the new sequence to bars 5 (5 – 8) and 14 (14 – 17).
3 Set the Locators at (L) 9.1.1 (R) 13.1 1 and record the middle section (Figures P3.36 and P3.37).
4 Save Song – compare with project3/3.10

Figure P3.36 (top)
More distortion guitar

Figure P3.37
More distortion guitar, Matrix view

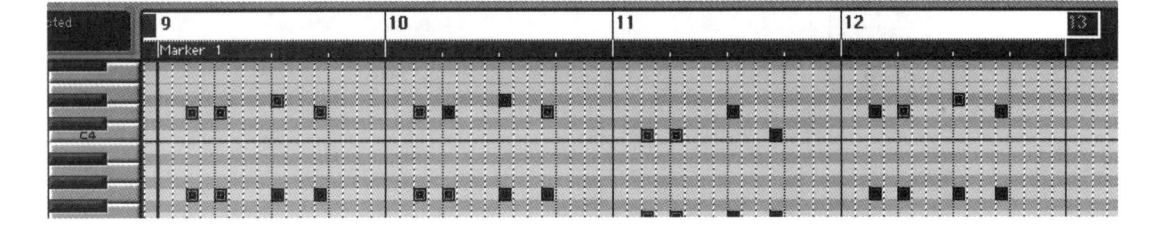

Take 11

Track 5: Rock Organ
Sequence Parameters box: Qua 1/8 – note
Instrument Parameter box: Cha 5, Prg 18
Transport Bar: (L) 1.1.1 (R) 5.1.1

Follow these steps:

1 Record the organ between the Locators (Figures P3.38 and P3.39). Play it quietly, it's only a supporting part. Reducing the velocity value in the Instrument Parameter box will help achieve this.

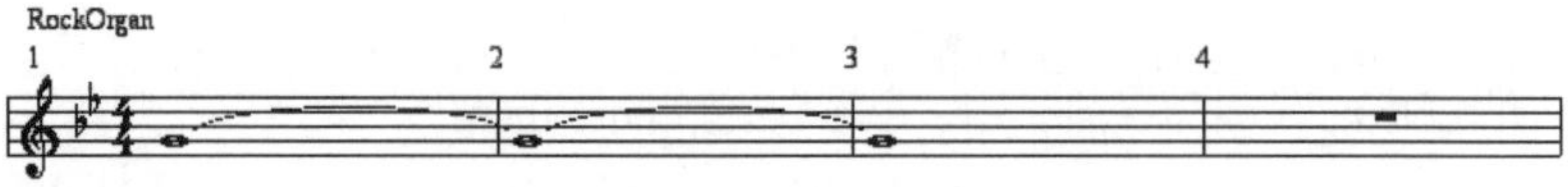

Figure P3.38
Rock organ

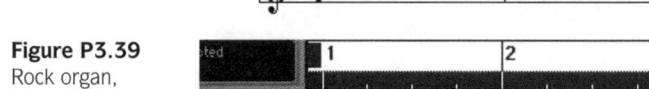

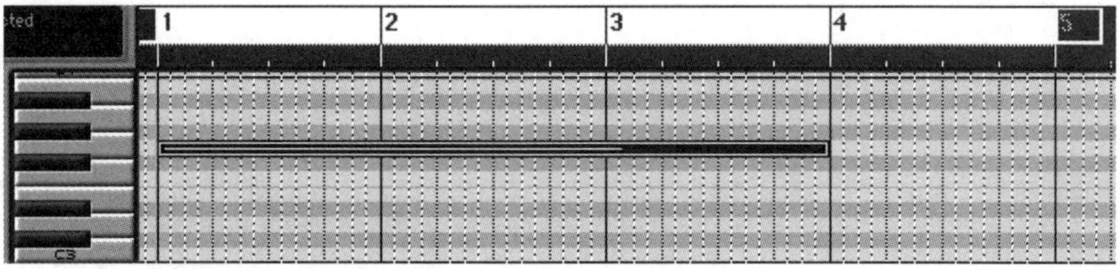

Figure P3.39
Rock organ, Matrix view

2 Copy the sequence to bars 5 (5 – 8) and 14 (14 – 17).
3 Change the Locators to (L) 9.1.1 (R) 13.1 1 and record the middle section (Figure P3.40 and P3.41).
4 Save Song – compare with project3/3.11.

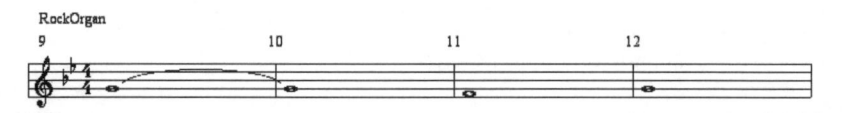

Figure P3.40
More rock organ.

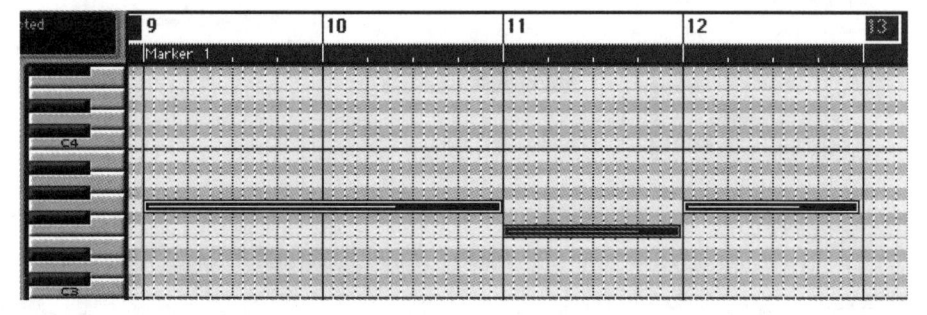

Figure P3.41
More rock organ, Matrix view.

Project 3 – a jazz funk score   57

Tip

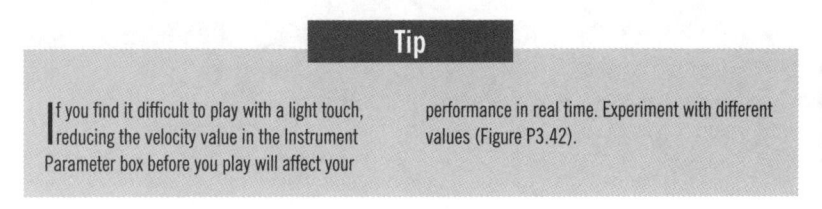

If you find it difficult to play with a light touch, reducing the velocity value in the Instrument Parameter box before you play will affect your performance in real time. Experiment with different values (Figure P3.42).

Take 12

Track 3: Trombone
Sequence Parameters box: Qua off (3840)
Transport Bar: (L) 4.1.1 (R) 5.1.1

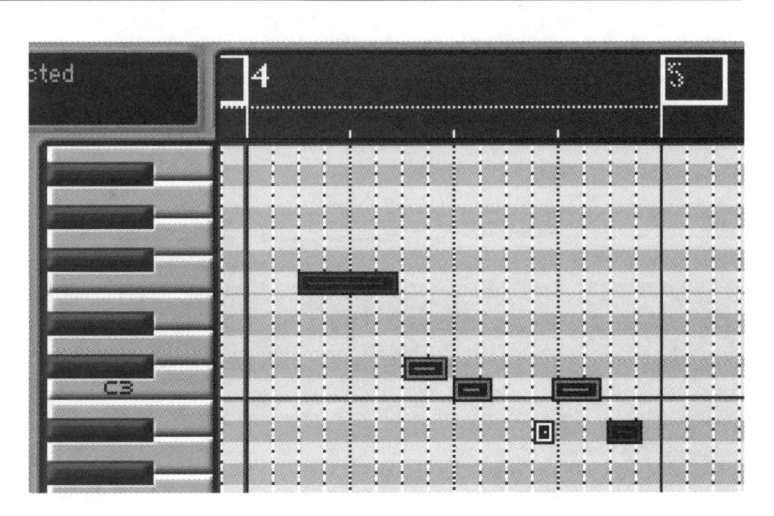

Figure P3.42
Reducing velocity.

OK, it's time to add those 'solo breaks'. You can copy the score or invent your own. You may have noticed that most of the parts are made up from the 'blues scale' beginning on G (G Bb C C# D F G). Try using it for your improvised breaks.

Follow these steps:

1 Ensure that 'Qua off' is selected. This will give us a more realistic performance.
2 Either record my trombone break (Figures P3.43 and P3.44), or better still, invent your own. Rule of thumb? – keep it simple!

Figure P3.43
Trombone break.

Figure P3.44
Trombone break, Matrix view.

3 Record a tenor sax break (Figures P3.45 and P3.46).

> *Track:* 2 Tenor Sax
> *Sequence Parameters box:* Qua off (3840)
> *Transport Bar:* (L) 8.1.1 (R) 9.1.1

Figure P3.45
Tenor sax break.

Figure P3.46
Tenor sax break, Matrix view.

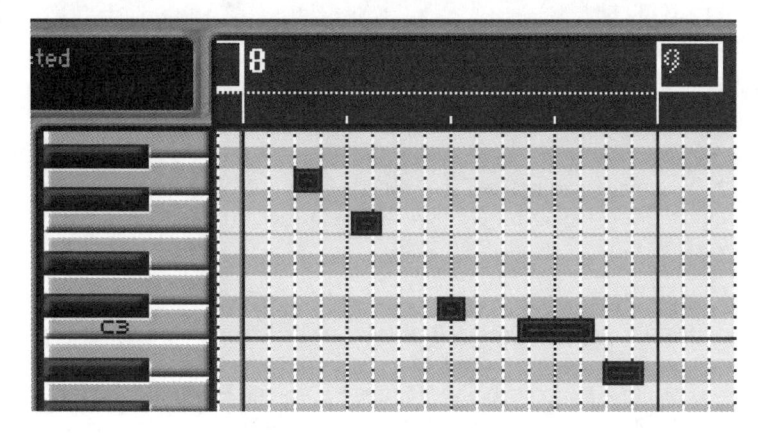

4 Record a trumpet break (Figure P3.47 and P3.48)

> *Track 1:* Trumpet
> *Sequence Parameters box:* Qua off (3840)
> *Transport Bar:* (L) 13.1 1 (R) 14.1 1

Figure P3.47
Trumpet break.

Figure P3.48
Trumpet break, Matrix view.

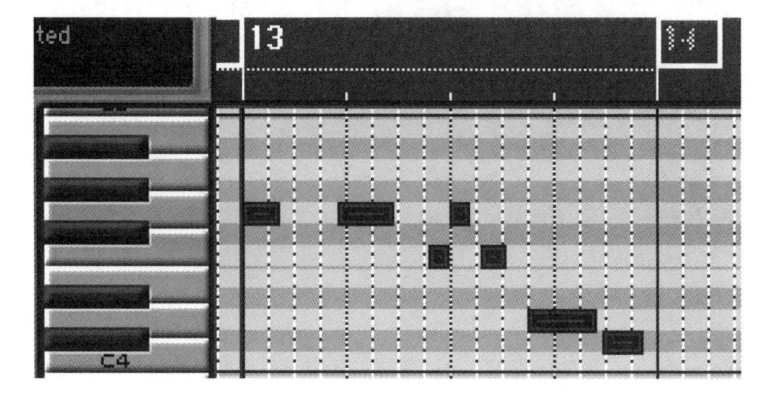

Project 3 – a jazz funk score

5 Save Song – compare with project3/3.12.

Figure P3.49
Pitch bend data, Event List view.

```
POSITION        STATUS   CHA   NUM  VAL   LENGTH/INFO
-------------- Start of List --------------
  4  1  3   9  Note     1   F3   119   _  _  3  228
  4  2  2  87  PitchBd  1   52    61   =  -     332
  4  2  2 126  PitchBd  1   91    51   =  -    1573
  4  2  2 147  PitchBd  1   39    43   =  -    2649
  4  2  2 167  PitchBd  1    3    31   =  -    4221
  4  2  2 187  PitchBd  1   42    21   =  -    5462
  4  2  2 209  PitchBd  1   20    16   =  -    6124
  4  2  2 230  PitchBd  1   73    13   =  -    6455
  4  2  3  32  Note     1   C#3  110   _  _  1  192
  4  2  3  97  PitchBd  1    0    64   =  -       0
  4  3  1  24  Note     1   C3    98   _  _  1  127
  4  3  4  30  Note     1   A#2   89   _  _  _  189
  4  3  4 216  Note     1   C3   107   _  _  1  232
  4  4  2 228  Note     1   A#2  122   _  _  1  111
-------------- End of List ----------------
```

Figure P3.50 (below)
Pitch bend data, Hyper view.

Tip

Try adding some pitch bend data from your keyboard as you play the breaks. A trombonist will typically use his 'slide' for glissando effects in solos.

Info

View the pitch bend data in the Event List window (Figure P3.49) or Hyper Draw – in the Arrange window, zoom in on a sequence (Figure P3.50).

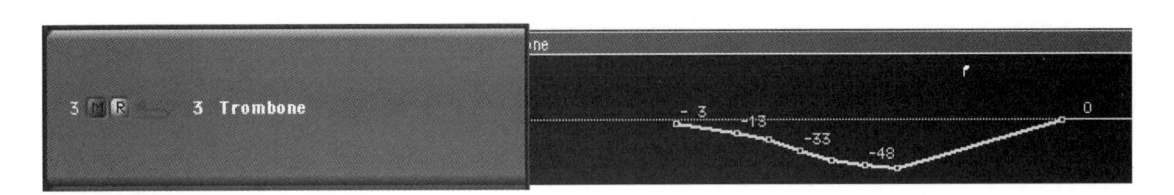

Take 13

Track 8: Standard drums | Hi – Hat
Sequence Parameters box: Qua 16B Swing
Instrument Parameter box: Cha 10, Prg 0
Transport Bar: (L) 9.1.1 (R) 13.1 1

Follow these steps:

1 Record the hi-hat between the Locators (Figures P3.51, P3.52 and P3.53) closed (F#1).
2 Save Song – compare with project3/3.13.

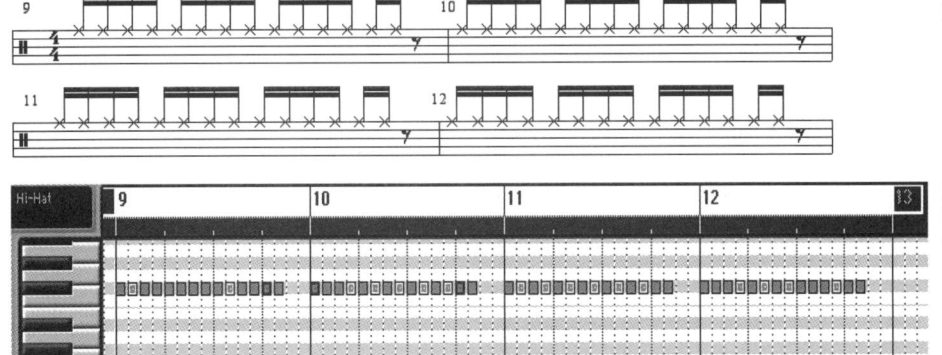

Figure P3.51
Hi-hat.

Figure P3.52
Hi-hat, Matrix view.

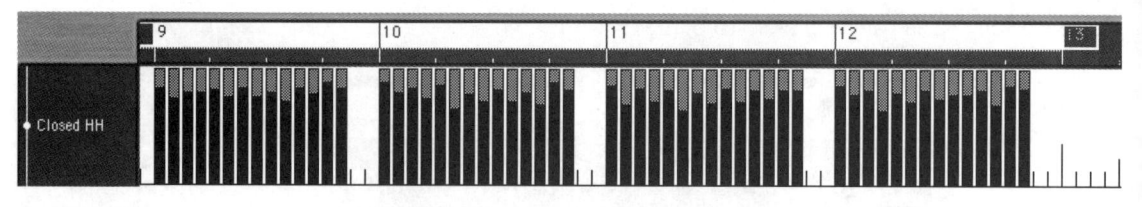

Figure P3.53
Hi-hat, Hyper view.

Last, but not least, add the crash cymbal.

Take 14

> *Track 9:* Standard drums | Crash Cymbal
> *Sequence Parameters box:* Qua 1/8 – note
> *Instrument Parameter box:* Cha 10, Prg 0
> *Transport Bar:* (L) 9.1 1 (R) 13.1 1

Follow these steps:

1 Record the cymbal crashes – A2 or C#2 (Figures P3.54 and P3.55).
2 Save Song – compare with project3/3.14.

Figure P3.54
Cymbal crashes.

Figure P3.55
Cymbal crashes, Matrix view.

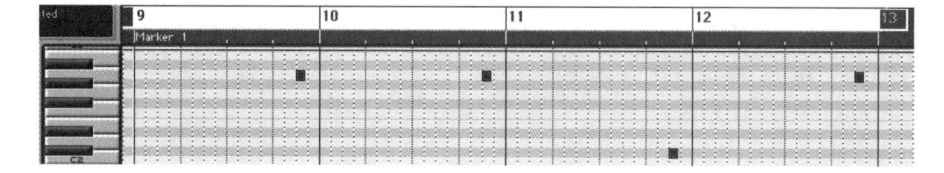

The Mix

We can change the pan settings in the Instrument Parameter box from the Arrange window. We can also control volume from there. However, there is a more intuitive method.

1 Open the Track Mixer [Windows >Open Track Mixer]. A virtual mixing console appears with a channel strip for each GM device we are using (Figure P3.56).
2 Use the faders to balance volume and the pan control knobs – immediately above – to create a stereo picture.
3 Above the pan control knobs you'll see three rows of knobs which can be assigned to different MIDI controllers via the drop-down menus on the left (Figure P3.57). Experiment by applying reverb and chorus to the various instruments.

Figure P3.56
The Track Mixer.

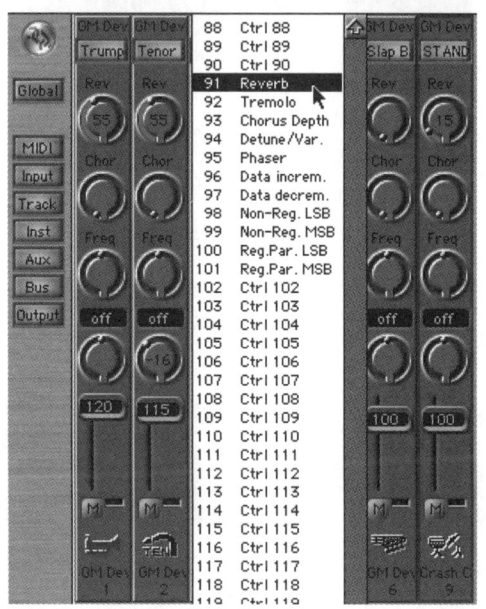

Figure P3.57
Assigning MIDI controllers.

These were my settings:

	Trumpet	Tenor Sax	Trombone	Dist. Gtr.	Rock Organ	Slap Bass	Drums
Vol.	120	115	115	85	85	100	100
Pan	64	48	80	32	96	64	64

> **Tip**
>
> For those of you who have not used reverberation before, beware! – use sparingly. Too much will muddy the mix.

A finishing touch: the brass section sounds real tight! Too tight maybe. Let's humanize it.

1 In the Arrange window, select all five objects on Track 1 (trumpet) and with the glue tool, join them together by clicking on the first object. You should now have one long sequence for Track 1.

2 Open the Event List window [Window > Open Event List]. The sequence was quantized using a value of 16B Swing and should look something like Figure P3.58 This is fine but all three horns are playing exactly the same thing, in unison. Had they been in three part harmony things would be a little better but as it is, only their note lengths are different.

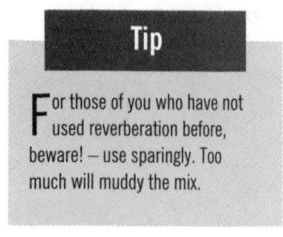

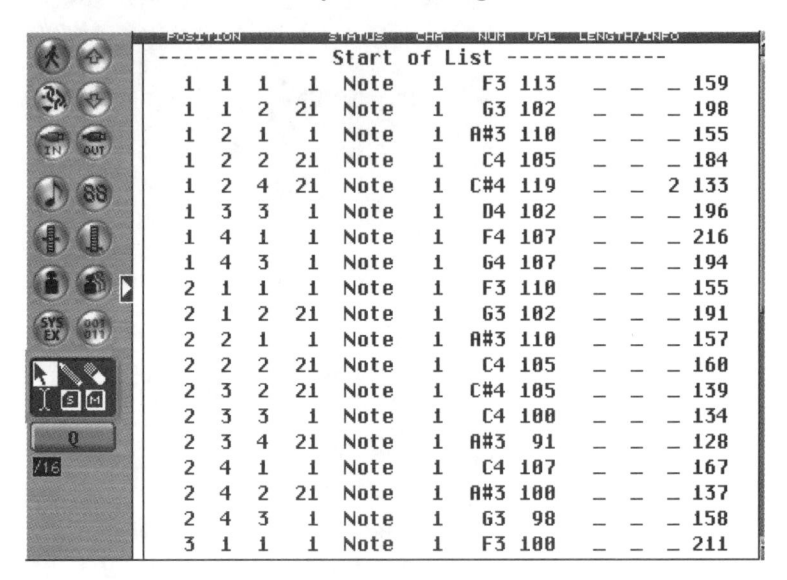

Figure P3.58
Trumpet quantized with 16B Swing, Event List view.

POSITION				STATUS	CHA	NUM	VAL	LENGTH/INFO
-------------- Start of List --------------
1	1	1	1	Note	1	F3	113	_ _ _ 159
1	1	2	21	Note	1	G3	102	_ _ _ 198
1	2	1	1	Note	1	A#3	110	_ _ _ 155
1	2	2	21	Note	1	C4	105	_ _ _ 184
1	2	4	21	Note	1	C#4	119	_ _ 2 133
1	3	3	1	Note	1	D4	102	_ _ _ 196
1	4	1	1	Note	1	F4	107	_ _ _ 216
1	4	3	1	Note	1	G4	107	_ _ _ 194
2	1	1	1	Note	1	F3	110	_ _ _ 155
2	1	2	21	Note	1	G3	102	_ _ _ 191
2	2	1	1	Note	1	A#3	110	_ _ _ 157
2	2	2	21	Note	1	C4	105	_ _ _ 160
2	3	2	21	Note	1	C#4	105	_ _ _ 139
2	3	3	1	Note	1	C4	100	_ _ _ 134
2	3	4	21	Note	1	A#3	91	_ _ _ 128
2	4	1	1	Note	1	C4	107	_ _ _ 167
2	4	2	21	Note	1	A#3	100	_ _ _ 137
2	4	3	1	Note	1	G3	98	_ _ _ 158
3	1	1	1	Note	1	F3	100	_ _ _ 211

3 From here (the Event List window) choose [Functions >Transform >Humanize]. The Transform window will open complete with the Humanize preset.

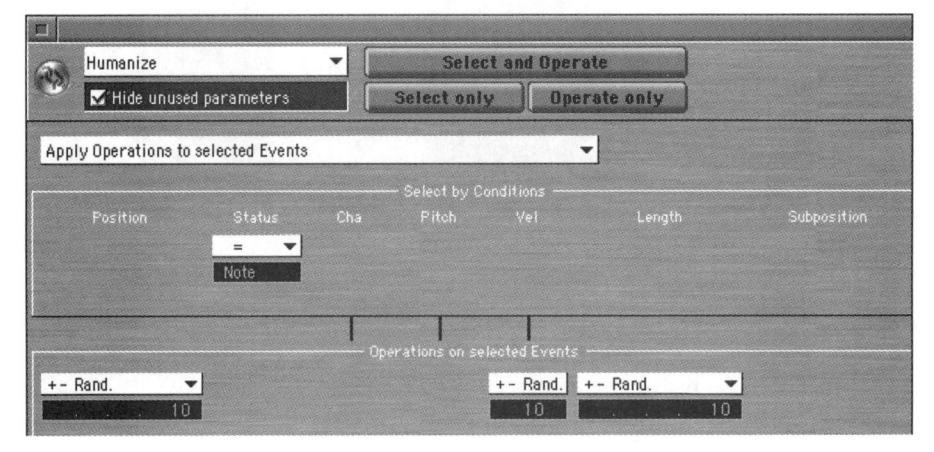

Figure P3.59
The Transform window – 'Humanize' preset

Project 3 – a jazz funk score

We are going to Randomize all the notes by plus or minus five ticks.

1 In the 'Select by Conditions' section you'll see [Status = Note]. Leave it.
2 In the 'Operations on selected Events' section, from left to right, you'll see [Position + – Rand 10]. Scroll this value to 5.
3 The other two boxes in the Operations on selected Events section show a value of 10. Scroll them both to 0. We don't want to randomize the trumpet velocities or note lengths.

The Transform window should now look like Figure P3.60

Info

Just about anything can be done with MIDI from the Transform window. To get an idea, take a look at some of the presets using the drop-down menu in the top left corner.

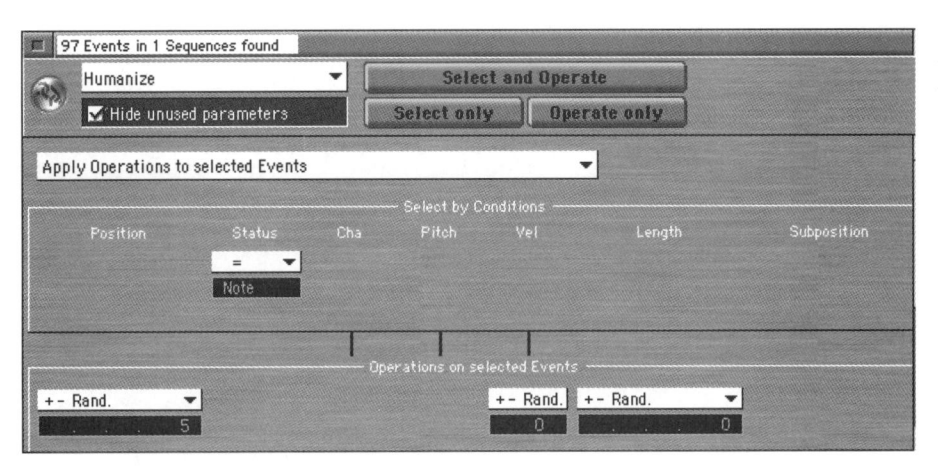

Figure P3.60
The altered Transform window.

4 Perform the transformation by pressing the 'Select and Operate' button at the top of the window. The events selected and transformed – in this case 97 – are now shown in the title bar.
5 Close the Transform window and return to the Event List window. All the trumpet note events are now shown as selected and randomized within plus or minus five ticks from their previous position. (Figure P3.61).

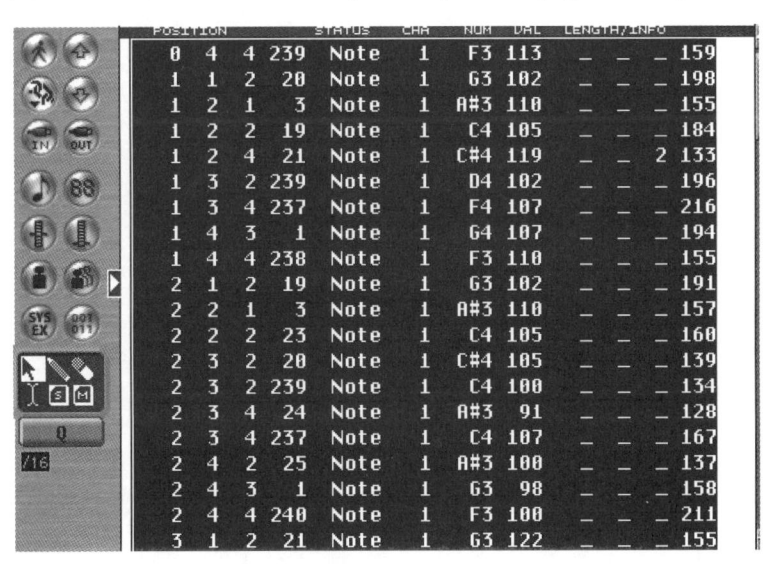

Figure P3.61
The Event List after randomization.

POSITION				STATUS	CHA	NUM	VAL	LENGTH/INFO			
0	4	4	239	Note	1	F3	113	–	–	–	159
1	1	2	20	Note	1	G3	102	–	–	–	198
1	2	1	3	Note	1	A#3	110	–	–	–	155
1	2	2	19	Note	1	C4	105	–	–	–	184
1	2	4	21	Note	1	C#4	119	–	–	2	133
1	3	2	239	Note	1	D4	102	–	–	–	196
1	3	4	237	Note	1	F4	107	–	–	–	216
1	4	3	1	Note	1	G4	107	–	–	–	194
1	4	4	238	Note	1	F3	110	–	–	–	155
2	1	2	19	Note	1	G3	102	–	–	–	191
2	2	1	3	Note	1	A#3	110	–	–	–	157
2	2	2	23	Note	1	C4	105	–	–	–	160
2	3	2	20	Note	1	C#4	105	–	–	–	139
2	3	2	239	Note	1	C4	100	–	–	–	134
2	3	4	24	Note	1	A#3	91	–	–	–	128
2	3	4	237	Note	1	C4	107	–	–	–	167
2	4	2	25	Note	1	A#3	100	–	–	–	137
2	4	3	1	Note	1	G3	98	–	–	–	158
2	4	4	240	Note	1	F3	100	–	–	–	211
3	1	2	21	Note	1	G3	122	–	–	–	155

> **Tip**
>
> After randomization it's quite likely that the very first trumpet note will be pushed just ahead of the beat, 0. 4. 4. 239 maybe. Change it back to 1. 1. 1. 0 or you will not hear it!

6 Repeat this operation on the tenor sax and trombone tracks. The result will still be very tight but just that little bit more realistic sounding.

The process can also be applied to the rhythm section. I've used a randomize value of 10 on the slap bass. Go too far though and the band will sound like they've been at the bar too long before the gig!

7 Save Song – compare with project3/3.mix.

Project 4 – a classical score

Musical objectives

- Sequence a short extract from Mozart's Clarinet Concerto.
- Achieve a convincing interpretation of a string orchestra and solo clarinet.
- Position the instruments in a realistic stereo picture.

Logic skills

- Use Transposition in the Instrument Parameter box.
- Apply compression using Dynamics in the Sequence Parameters box.
- Apply Legato to slurred notes using either the Matrix Edit or Score.
- Automate the Track Mixer and create a Track Mix.

Preparation

1 From the CD, copy the folder named project4 to your computer.
2 On your computer, create a folder named mywork4 or something similar in which to save your work.
3 From the project4 folder, open the template – templt4.
4 In your new mywork4 folder, re-save the template as myproj4 or something similar.

OK this is Mozart. Don't be scared. It's not difficult. It's slow for a start!
   To begin with, load project4/automix and have a listen as you view the score. Play it through several times until it becomes familiar. The clarinet solo is in from bar 1, so let's get that down and take it from there.

Take 1

> *Track 1:* Clarinet
> *Sequence Parameters box:* Qua 1/8 – note, Dynamics 75%.
> *Instrument Parameter box:* Cha 1, Prg 71, Transpose -2
> *Transport Bar:* (L) 1.1.1 (R) 5.1.1

Take a look at the score (Figures P4.1, P4.2, P4.3 and P4.4).

> **Info**
>
> The template has a time signature of 3/4 and the tempo is 65 bpm.

> **Tip**
>
> When loading example files containing MIDI settings its quite likely that you will initially hear the wrong sounds (very likely those from a previous project or song). Use [Options > Song Settings > Used Instrument MIDI Settings] to correct them. A faster way – quickly cursor up or down the tracks using the arrow keys on your computer keyboard.

Figures P4.1 and **P4.2**
Clarinet concerto score, pages 1 and 2.

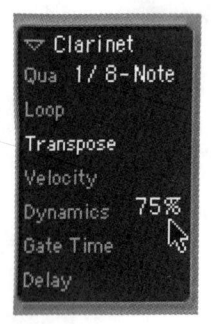

Figure P4.5
Applying compression.

The strings are written in Eb (three flats) and the clarinet in F (one flat). This is because clarinets are pitched in Bb. When Bb is played on the piano a clarinet plays the note C. Wiithout getting into the complexities of a thorough explanation, what this means is we read and play the score as written and transpose it down a tone. To achieve this it is necessary to enter –2 in the Sequence Parameters box.

In order to achieve a nice smooth classical clarinet sound we also need to apply 75% compression using Dynamics, also in the Sequence Parameters box (Figure P4.5). This will raise the velocity values of notes played too lightly and reduce those played too hard. It's preferable in this case to reducing the velocities as a whole.

Follow these steps:

Figures P4.3 and **P4.4**
Clarinet concerto score, pages 3 and 4.

1 Record the first four bars of clarinet (Figures P4.6 and P4.7). Play in a nice legato style. Any overlapping notes can be cleaned up afterwards.
2 In the Sequence Parameters box, change the quantize value to 1/16 – note. This is to take account of the sixteenth note in bar 8. Set the Locators to cycle between 5.1.1 and 9.1.1 and record the next four bars (Figure P4.8 and P4.9). Join the two resulting sequences together with the Glue Tool (select them both and click on the first) to make a sequence eight bars long.
3 Listen back. I mentioned earlier about woodwind players articulating with their tongues. Where a slur joins a group of notes only the first note is slurred. Some editing is necessary to achieve this effect.
4 From within either the Score or Matrix Edit windows, select all the notes under each slur, except the last, and apply Legato. [Functions >Note Events >Note Force Legato (selected/any)]

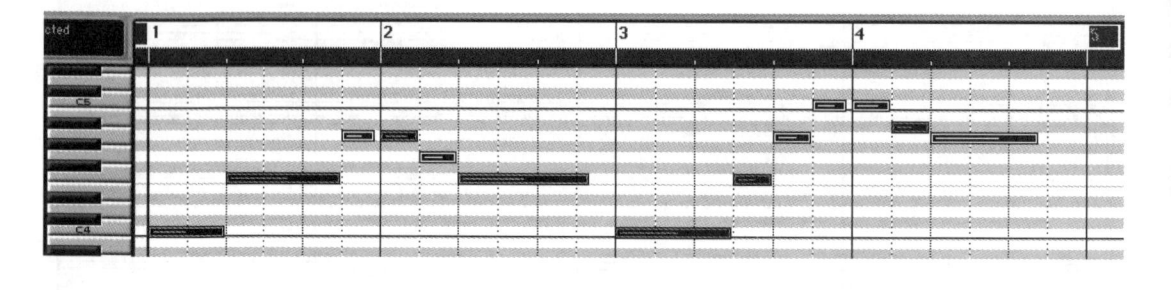

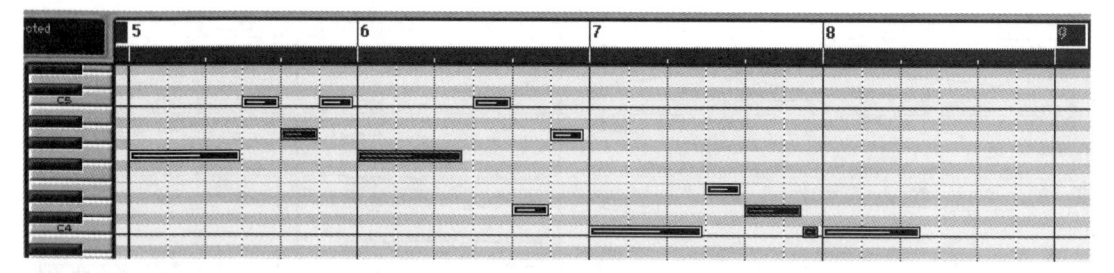

Figures P4.6 – P4.9
Clarinet parts in Score and Matrix views

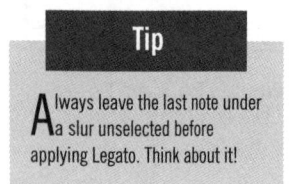

> **Tip**
>
> Always leave the last note under a slur unselected before applying Legato. Think about it!

5 The following eight bars are an exact repetition of the first so copy the new sequence (bars 1 – 9) to bar 9 [Functions >Object >Repeat Objects... x1]. We now have 16 bars. Clean up any overlapping notes – impossible on a clarinet! – by viewing the sequences in the Matrix Edit window, selecting all the events, and applying [Functions >Note Events >Note Overlap Correction (selected any)] and [Note Overlap Correction for repeated notes].

6 Save Song – compare with project4/4.1.

Take 2

> *Track 2:* Strings | Violin 1
> *Sequence Parameters box:* 1/8 – note, Dynamics 75%
> *Instrument Parameter box:* Cha 2, Prg 48
> *Transport Bar:* (L) 1.1.1 (R) 9.1.1

We are simulating a small string orchestra here so we use Program 48 – Strings – and not an individual instrument. You can of course use single instruments if you wish, but the effect will be somewhat thinner. The nature of this concerto, I think, benefits from a rather more lush background.

Follow these steps:

1 Record the first eight bars of the violin 1 part (Figures P4.10 and P4.11). Break it down into smaller sections if necessary. Again I have applied 75% compression for smoothness.

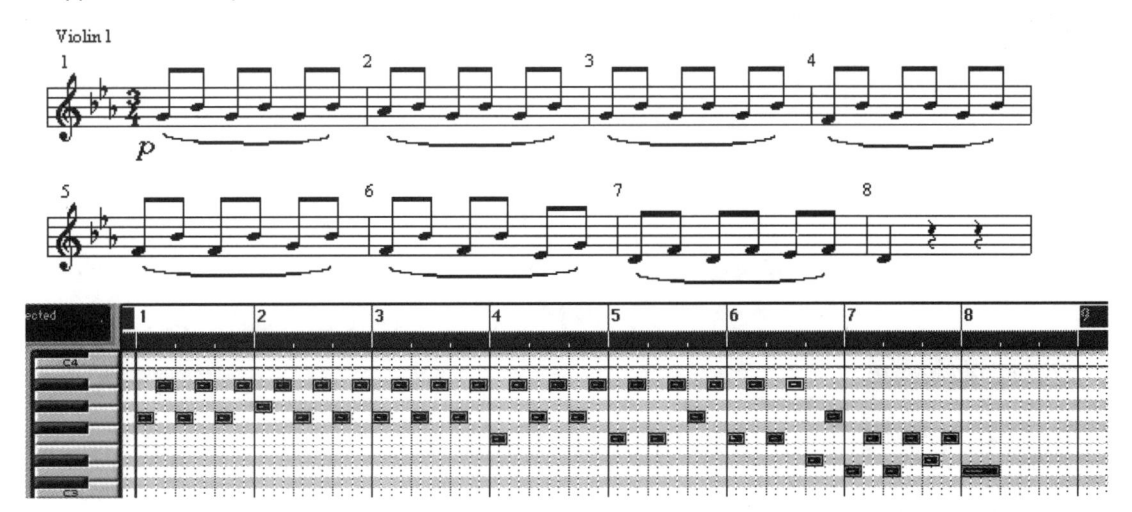

2 Listen back, and as with the clarinet part, apply Legato to the slurred notes and clean up with the Note Overlap Correction functions.
3 Save Song – compare with project4/4.2.

Figures P4.10 and **4.11**
Violin 1, Score and Matrix view.

Take 3

Track 3: Strings - Violin 2
Sequence Parameters box: Qua 1/8 – note, Dynamics 75%
Instrument Parameter box: Cha 3, Prg 48
Transport Bar: (L) 1.1.1 (R) 9.1.1

Follow these steps:

1 Record the first eight bars of violin 2 (Figures P4.12 and P4.13). Apply Legato and clean up as in Take 2.
2 Save Song – compare with project4/4.3.

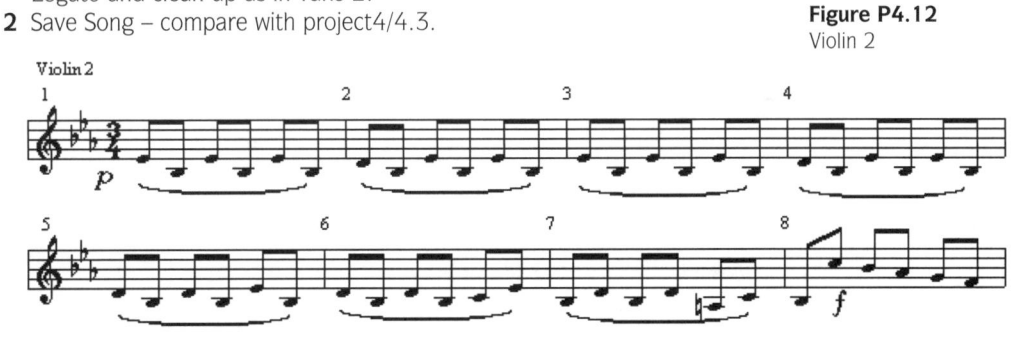

Figure P4.12
Violin 2

Figure P4.13
Violin 2, Matrix view

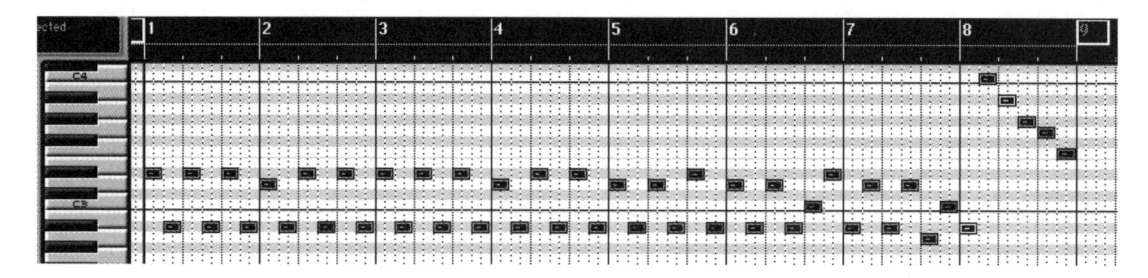

Take 4

Track 4: Strings – Viola
Sequence Parameters box: Qua 1/8 – note, Dynamics 75%
Instrument Parameter box: Cha 4, Prg 48
Transport Bar: (L) 1.1.1 (R) 9.1.1

Tip

An easy way to read and play from the Alto clef: in the Instrument Parameter box, enter a Transpose value of –10 and play the part as if reading from the Treble clef.

Follow these steps:

1 Record the first eight bars of Viola (Figures P4.14 and P4.15). Viola parts are written in Alto Clef. Middle C is on the middle line of the staff. As with the violins, apply Legato and clean up where necessary.
2 Save Song – compare with project4/4.4.

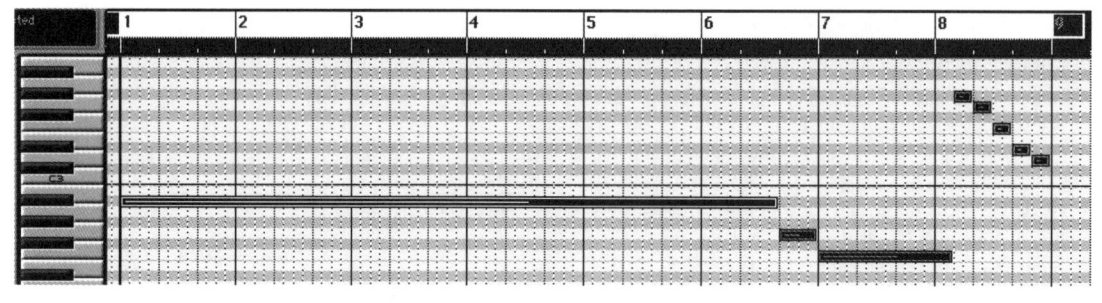

Figures P4.14 and P4.15
Viola, Score and Matrix view

Take 5

Track 5: Strings | Cello
Sequence Parameters box: Qua 1/8 – note, Dynamics 75%.
Instrument Parameter box: Cha 5, Prg 48.
Transport Bar: (L) 1.1.1 (R) 9.1.1

Project 4 – a classical score

Follow these steps:

1 Record the first eight bars of cello (Figures P4.16 and P4.17). If you play it carefully, Legato need not be applied. However you may have to use the Note Overlap Correction functions. I did!
2 Save Song – compare with project4/4.5

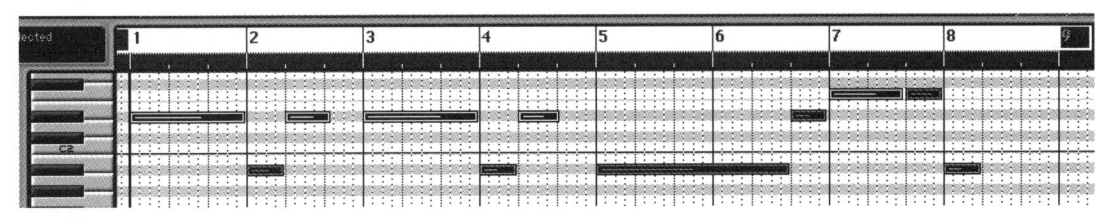

Figures P4.16 and **P4.17**
Cello, Score and Matrix view

Take 6

Track 2: Strings – Violin 1
Sequence Parameters box: Qua 1/16 – note, Dynamics 75%
Instrument Parameter box: Cha 1, Prg 48
Transport Bar: (L) 9.1.1 (R) 17.1.1

Follow these steps:

1 Record the remaining eight bars of violin 1 (Figures P4.18 and P4.19) (note: Quantize Value is now 1/16 – note). Break it down into four bar sections if you wish. Apply Legato and clean up note lengths.

Figures P4.18 and **P4.19**
Violin 1, Score and Matrix view

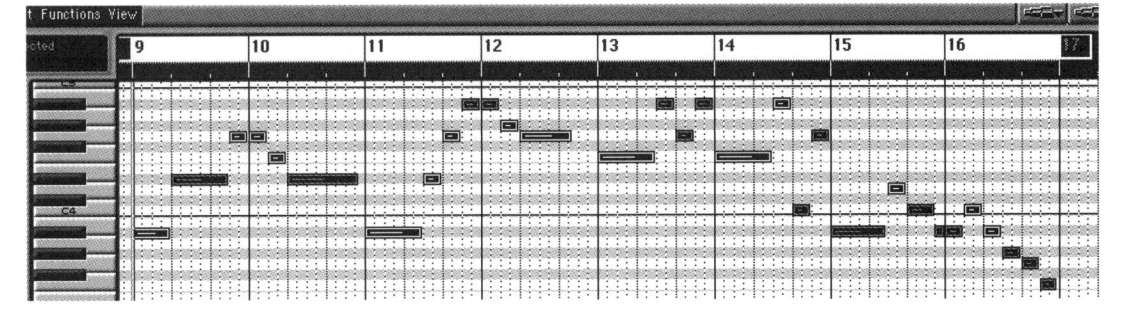

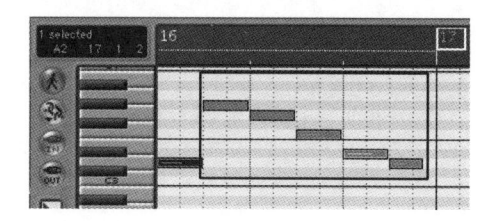

Figures P4.20 and **P4.21**
Violin 2, five more notes in Score and Matrix view

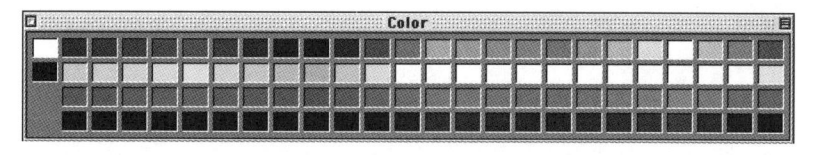

Figure P4.22
Changing object colours

Info

It's often a good idea to organize tracks and sequences by colour. Select a track or object and use [View >Object Colors] to open a colour palette. Choose your favourite colours from Figure P4.22.

Figure P4.23
Deleting notes.

Take a look at the score again. Bars 9 – 17 of violin 2 are almost the same as bars 1 – 9 of violin 1. No point in making extra work!

2 Select the violin 1 (bars 1 – 9) sequence and drag a copy over to bar 9 on track 3 (violin 2).

3 There are of course five notes to add to this new sequence in bar 16 (Figures P4.20 and P4.21). Return to track 3 – violin 2, set the Locators at (L) 16.1.1 (R) 17.1.1 and overdub them. Apply Legato and clean up any over-lapped notes.

4 To avoid confusion, it's a good idea to glue the new violin 2 sequences (9 – 17) together and re-name the resulting single sequence 'Violin 2'. It is also a good idea to change the colour accordingly. Selecting the objects on track 3 – violin 1 and using [View >Instrument Colors to Objects] will do the trick.

Another glance at the score also tells us that the viola part between bars 9 and 17 is also a duplication of the violin 2 part between bars 1 and 9.

5 Select the violin 2 sequence (bars 1 – 9) and drag a copy over to bar 9 on track 4 – viola.

6 This time there are five notes to delete in bar 16 (Figure P4.23). Selecting them in either the Matrix Edit or Score window and pressing the delete key on your computer keyboard is probably the easiest method of doing this. You may well need to lengthen the remaining note in this bar. Selecting it in the Matrix Edit window and resizing with the pencil tool is probably the simplest way of doing this.

7 Again, it's a good idea to re-name the sequence 'Viola' and change the colour accordingly.

8 Save Song – compare with project4/4.6.

Take 7

Track 5: Strings | Cello
Sequence Parameters box: Qua 1/8 – note, Dynamics 75%.
Instrument Parameter box: Cha 5, Prg 48.
Transport Bar: (L) 9.1.1 (R) 17.1.1

Follow these steps:

1 Record the cello between the Locators (Figures 4.24 and P4.25). Clean up.
2 Save Song – compare with project4/4.7.

Figures P4.24 and **P4.25**
Cello, Score and Matrix view

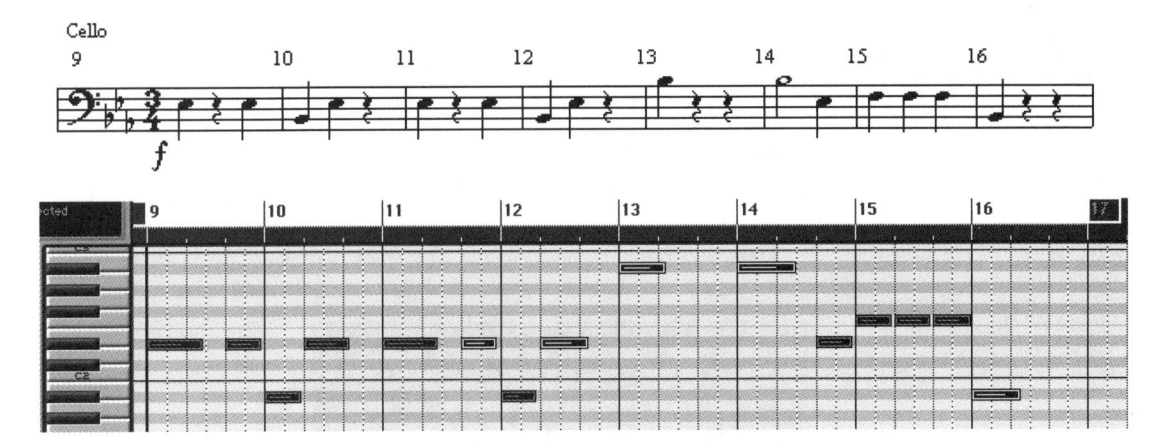

Take 8

Track 6: Strings | Double Bass
Sequence Parameters box: Qua 1/8 – note, Dynamics 75%.
Instrument Parameter box: Cha 6, Prg 48, Transpose –12
Transport Bar: (L) 9.1.1 (R) 17.1.1

Have a look at the double bass part on the score. You have probably noticed that it looks identical to the cello part above it. Well it is, but with one exception. The double bass sounds an octave lower than it is written. We now have a choice. We either record the bass part in the usual way or copy the cello sequence to track 7 and transpose it down one octave.

Although it takes a little longer, I prefer the first option. Why? Because the velocities and note lengths will be different and this adds to the overall realism of the sequence. Two sequences with identical data, playing together, often sound naff!

Follow these steps:

1 Record the double bass between the Locators (Figures P4.26 and P4.27). Ensure that transposition is set to –12 in the Instrument Parameter box. Clean up any overlaps.
2 Save Song – compare with project4/4.8.

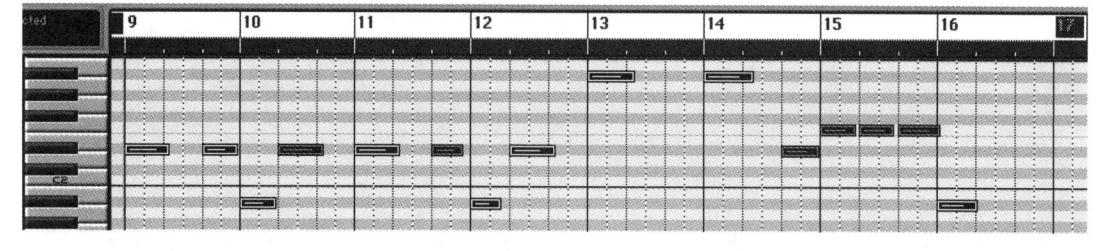

Figures P4.26 and **P4.27**
Double bass, Score and Matrix view

Automated mix

1 Open the Track Mixer [Windows >Open Track Mixer]. A mixer appears containing six channel strips that correspond to our six tracks in the Arrange window (Figure P4.28). The track names are listed at the top of each strip. The faders at the bottom are for controlling volume.

Figure P4.28
Track mixer.

2 Play the piece through and adjust the volume levels until you achieve an acceptable balance. Now this is a clarinet solo, so obviously that instrument needs to be louder than the others. On the score, the first eight measures of the strings are marked piano (quiet). I set my faders (Figure P4.29) to the following levels:

Clarinet: 115
Violin 1: 95
Violin 2: 95
Viola: 95
Cello: 95
Bass: 85

Figure P4.29
Volume and pan settings.

You may well need to set your faders to different levels for a nice balance, depending on how you played and the particular characteristics of your GM sound module. Whatever you decide, keep the clarinet prominent.

In a real string orchestra first and second violins are positioned to the left of the conductor and the viola and cellos to the right. The double basses are behind the violas and cellos. To achieve something similar in our stereo picture:

3 Adjust the pan control – the first row of knobs above the faders in Figure P4.29 – to the following:

Clarinet: 0 in the centre. It's his/her big moment!
Violin 1: minus 42
Violin 2: minus 28
Viola: 27
Cello: 41
Double Bass: 36

Tip

When mixing, keep the solo instrument – in this case the clarinet – in the centre of the stereo picture and, if necessary, raise its volume for prominence.

4 Return to the Arrange window. You will notice that the pan settings in the Instrument Parameter box have changed to reflect the mixer settings. One difference though! The numbers used here are MIDI Controller numbers 0 – 127 with 64 representing the centre position.
5 Refer to the score. In bar 8 (at 8.1.3. to be precise) the strings change to forte (loud). Set up a cycle starting a bar or two before the forte mark (f) and ending a bar or so afterwards.
6 Return to the Track Mixer, press the Cycle button and practise raising the fader levels for the strings to about 105 each time the music reaches bar 8.
7 When you're ready press the Record button and, channel by channel, record the fader movements. The data will be recorded into their respective tracks. When you're finished press Stop!

> **Tip**
>
> To ensure that the faders return to their original positions when re-playing a Song, ensure that 'Chase Control 0 – 15' and 'Send full MIDI Reset before Chasing' are checked in the Song Settings [Options >Settings >Chase Events].

8 Press Stop again to return the Song position to zero and play the sequence back. Gaze in wonder as the faders move all by themselves when the music reaches bar 8! I love it. Could watch them all day. Sad, really, isn't it?

7 You can view the fader movement reflected in the Event List window as Controller #7 data (Figure P4.30).

POSITION				STATUS	CHA	NUM	VAL	LENGTH/INFO	
7	2	4	240	Note	1	D#3	50	_ _ 1	232
7	3	2	232	Note	1	F3	55	_ _ 1	232
8	1	1	1	Note	1	D3	70	_ 1 0	5
8	1	1	150	Control	2	7	96	Volume	
8	1	2	110	Control	2	7	97	Volume	
8	1	3	42	Control	2	7	98	Volume	
8	1	3	230	Control	2	7	99	Volume	
8	1	4	186	Control	2	7	100	Volume	
8	2	1	236	Control	2	7	101	Volume	
8	2	2	70	Control	2	7	103	Volume	
8	2	3	105	Control	2	7	104	Volume	
8	2	3	221	Control	2	7	105	Volume	
8	3	4	233	Note	1	A#3	80	_ _ 3	232
9	2	1	10	Note	1	D#4	66	_ 1 1	232
9	3	3	8	Note	1	G4	85	_ _ 1	222

Figure P4.30
Controller #7 data.

8 Because this is 'straight' music we quantized everything, for accuracy. Sounds a bit stiff though, don't you think? In the Arrange window select all the objects [Edit >Select All] and open the Transform window [Windows >Open Transform].

9 Choose the Humanize preset. The randomize values all show plus or minus 10 ticks by default. Scroll 'Vel' and 'Length' values to zero and leave 'Position' at 10.

10 Press the 'Select and Operate ' button to perform the black magic and play back the piece.

That's better. Just a little looser. After all, straight players are human! Of course this randomization will have caused the odd overlapped note here and there but they're too small to notice. If you're feeling 'picky' clean them up from within the Matrix Edit window [Functions >Note Events >Note Overlap Correction].

11 Save Song – compare with project4/automix.

Finding and developing ideas 3

So far we have talked about and sequenced other peoples music – well mine actually, apart from the classical stuff – and I'm sure you are itching to put some of the topics covered into practice by composing music of your own. Before you can start doing this you will need ideas. No doubt some of you will have dozens of ideas already. Many people though, find it difficult to be inventive and will either stare blankly at the screen or doodle for hours with nothing to show for it at the end. 'I can't think of anything', they say.

The old saying, 'Composing is one percent inspiration and ninety-nine percent hard work,' is spot on. Beethoven for example – a creative genius if ever there was one – would tortuously re-work a fragment of melody over and over until he considered it perfect. From that one tiny idea a symphony would develop. One percent eureka, ninety-nine percent hard graft. So it is for the rest of us in most cases.

Finding new ideas

So how do we get ideas for compositions in the first place? Can we use Logic? Will Logic give us ideas? Well it might. It's not my favourite way to start but it undoubtedly works for some. If you are constructing loop based Techno or Dance music then using sample CDs with pre-recorded material is the obvious way to go. However, this will not work very well if you've been given a specific brief for a commercial project and you are being paid for it. Other people's licks are not guaranteed to fit the bill. Even if the style of music requires loops and grooves it may well be quicker to invent and record your own. The result is going to be far more original for a start.

At the computer?

A tentative yes. Keep control. A computer running Logic is a very powerful tool – and a tool is all that it is. It will not, as some mistakenly believe, compose or arrange your music for you. Does a carpenter tell his tools to build him a beautiful piece of furniture, sit back, open a six pack and watch? He'd have a long wait.

There are special random generator programs available which will turn small ideas into complete compositions of a sort. These are great for experimental music, but I'm sure even the authors of such software would be the first to admit that they are not intended for producing commercial music.

You could import MIDI files into Logic, chop up the material and re-use it for your own compositions. Not really a good idea though. You could end up in court for breach of copyright!

What about importing classical music MIDI files, chopping those up and re-working them? After all the composers are mostly long dead and the tunes are out of copyright. Well you can I suppose – I can think of one well known composer who does just that or something similar – but it will not help much if you've been asked to supply a heavy metal background to a motor racing video clip!

No, I'm sorry. Ideas are what we need and where is the best place to get them?

Away from the computer?

Leonard Bernstein got them lying on the sofa and staring at the ceiling. When his wife entered the room and asked him what he was doing, he would reply, 'I'm working!'

One thing's for sure. Ideas come more readily if you tell your subconscious that you want them. You may think this is barmy but it works. Give your subconscious instructions. Be specific and set a deadline. Start small. Don't ask for a symphony. You will not get it! Something like:

'I want the beginnings of a tune for a children's song by tomorrow morning'. The more you develop this habit of asking for ideas the more they begin to come. It's habit forming and self generating. Ideas generate more ideas.

I get ideas first thing in the morning as soon as I wake up. They are usually melodic – I don't dream chord sequences – and fortunately my bedroom is right next door to my studio, so I can leap (crawl, more like) out of bed, boot up Logic and record them before breakfast. After the all important pot of tea, I can evaluate these gems, delete them (often the case) or file them away in an ideas folder for later development.

Ideas tend to come in a flash and often fade away just as quickly. It's important to act quickly and retain them somehow. If you have a great memory, then fine. If not and you are familiar with music notation then it's a simple matter of keeping a manuscript note pad handy. A portable cassette or mini disk recorder and vocal chords are an alternative.

Don't doodle!

'What a load of cobblers!' I hear you say. 'I get my ideas at the keyboard. I fire up Logic, press Record and improvise until the ideas start to flow. Surely that's the best way to get ideas.'

Well good on you. That's great. I envy you. Trouble is, I can't do that, and nor can many others.

For those of you who are good keyboard payers I have only one word of warning. Beware of doodling. Improvising is not composition. Well it is, in a group environment when we tear off a solo on our chosen instrument over a pre-determined chord sequence. For this we generally need a good technique. There lies the problem.

A common scenario. A keyboard player with a fantastic technique sits down at his synthesizer to compose and record in Logic. What happens? Before he knows it his fingers have taken over. They are following patterns that have been learned and subconsciously stored over the years. Out they all come and into Logic they all go. A half hour later he plays it all back. Has he got a composition at the end of it? I doubt it. Music composed or arranged for a specific purpose generally needs discipline and a degree of planning. A balanced composition, particularly a lengthy one, is rarely conceived as an improvisation. That half hour may have been better spent lying on his back like Leonard Bernstein.

Developing your ideas

Dave's got a great idea for a tune. It came like a bolt of lightning while he was waiting for the bus. He hums all the way home – in case he forgets it – and quickly records the melody into Logic as an eight bar lead synth part. 'It's brilliant', he thinks. 'Absoloutely brilliant!' He cycles it round a few times and hits upon a killer bass line. 'Fantastic!', he yells.' He improvises some drums over that and records a funky chord sequence using a favourite guitar patch. 'This is it. This is gonna make me a fortune', he cries. 'Strings! It needs strings,' he bellows, and he sets about adding a string pad. Already his musical canvas is pretty full. He can't think of anything else to add at the moment so he saves the file and goes off to make a cuppa.

A while later Dave returns to his masterpiece. He plays the eight bars. 'Hmm, it's only eight measures long. It definitely needs more, but I can't think of anything else. I know, I'll do a rough mix instead. Something will come to me later.'

Dave sets about the mix and experiments with the levels in Logic's Track Mixer. He used the ES P Instrument for the lead synth and tries out dozens of different plug-in effects to fatten it up (does it really need them?). A couple of hours later he sits back to have a listen. 'Mmm, it doesn't sound quite as good now. It's not quite what I had in mind when I was on the bus. Perhaps that bass line needs to be a bit different. ' And so he changes the bass line, which in turn requires a modification to the chord sequence. 'That's better, but hold on.. the melody needs altering to fit that new chord.' Dave alters the melody. Oh dear! Wasn't that the brilliant bit, conceived at the bus stop. 'I'm not sure about that kick drum, it doesn't sound fat enough. Where's that article I read in *Sound on Sound* about compression, it's here somewhere. Oh well, maybe some EQ instead'.

He's lost the plot now, although I'm not so sure he had one in the first place. It was all so promising as well. What did he do wrong? Well he didn't know where he was going for a start.

Know where you are heading

Those sudden flashes of inspiration, so often likened to thunderbolts, the eureka if you like, are wonderful. Trouble is, once recorded they often turn into short, rather stubborn, fragments of material that refuse to move on. Why? Probably because we have not decided what we want to do in the first place.

The mind works all the time in the background. It will throw up all kinds of great, but totally unrelated ideas. If we decide what we want to write first, and then instruct our subconscious mind to get on with it, we stand a much better chance.

If someone has been commissioned to compose or arrange a piece of music for a specific purpose it is much easier to get going. The plan has been provided, and if you expect to be paid, then you had better stick pretty close to it. If however you want to write for the sheer pleasure of it, maybe for practice, then it's a good idea to invent a brief of your own. Give yourself a purpose for writing. Here's a rough guide on how to set about it.

1 Decide exactly what it is you want to write and why. If you are not sure, invent something like 'a local sports shop needs a short radio jingle'. Have a specific business in mind. You never know, if it turns out well they may decide to invest in a radio advertisement on the strength of your idea.
2 Decide what style the music should take and what instruments or sounds you intend to use. Obviously things may change, but it helps to have a clear mental picture from the outset as to how things will sound.
3 Decide on a basic form. If you can't envisage one mentally, invent one on paper. Keep it simple. ABA maybe. At least that way you have a structure to hang things on.

Now you know where you are heading. You have defined a set of problems to solve with your own skill and musical craftsmanship. Even if the result doesn't quite make it, you can get started and modify it later. As I said earlier, the mind is working constantly, all the time, in the background. If Dave had followed this route after that initial eureka he would maybe have recorded the broad outline of his project, and having done so had a further brilliant idea to help fill in the details, perhaps whilst waiting for the bus the next day. That's another thing the mind tends to do. Through up ideas at certain times and places.

Keep moving – work creates work

It is most important to keep moving. It can be a very daunting experience to stare at a blank Arrange window in Logic and not be able to start. Once you have set your criteria, record anything that it suggests. If you can only think up a tiny fragment of a tune, don't worry. Record it. That's enough. Remember how Beethoven built huge musical masterpieces from just such fragments. Don't dwell on it, but move on. Does that first phrase suggest something else? Does it beg an answer? Can it be repeated? Upside down or back to front. Keep moving. The more you write, even if it is not very good, the easier it will become. Work creates work and ideas produce yet more ideas. You can refine and improve them later.

Repetition and variation

OK so how do we keep things flowing if we can't think of anything? One method of course is simple repetition. It's an essential ingredient of most music. So many beginners are scared stiff to repeat an idea, afraid that it will be boring to do so. On the contrary, an opening phrase will often set a air of expectancy. When this phrase is repeated, the listener's subconscious picks up on it and a basic psychological and emotional sense of musical fulfillment is achieved. Of course it would be utterly boring if the same phrase were repeated endlessly. This is why we also need variation. Repetition and variation, hand in hand. Together they make a very powerful composition tool for almost any style of music.

Keep it simple – details later

As well as moving on it is important to keep it simple. Save the detail until later. If it's melodic material the details such as choice of harmony and rhythm will suggest themselves at a later stage. This is exactly what Dave did not do. He started right. He recorded eight measures of terrific melody, but then stopped and concentrated on the detail instead of moving forward. Paralysis by analysis! In the end he actually ruined the tune he started out with.

Review your work – less is more

Once your idea has been developed and recorded in Logic, take time to review it objectively. It's usually best left until later or even the next day. You will see a clearer, fresher picture. Those first ideas, great at the time, may require more work. First ideas are not always the best ideas and you may see ways of improving them. Maybe an introduction will suggest itself out of the general thematic material. Intros are paradoxically best left until the end. When composed first they often end up having nothing to do with what follows. Either that or they remain just great intros that go no further.

One more thing. When reviewing your work look for ways of cutting down on unnecessary details. They can usually be found, and a bit of ruthless pruning often yields a leaner but more effective composition. If you can't find any, all well and good, but do ask yourself a few questions like: Am I keeping that clever break because it really works? Or am I keeping it because I can't bear to let it go? Be objective. If a particular ingredient is not serving a definite purpose, get rid of it!

Oh! and for goodness sake don't do what Dave did and start mixing after only eight bars. It happens, I can assure you.

Project 5 – a computer game track

We will now follow the creative composition process through using a set brief and applying principles and techniques discussed in previous chapters. The music composed here does not use melodic development to carry it forward, but an additive technique whereby small fragments and cells of material are repeated and transposed to form blocks of material. These blocks are repeated in a loop like fashion and new layers of material are introduced in subsequent cycles to maintain interest. The overall effect is a static one, but that is precisely what we want – atmospheric background music.

Musical objectives

- To build a complete composition with Logic from small fragments and motifs using simple techniques of repetition and harmonic variation.
- Paint an atmospheric musical landscape suitable for background music to match the demands of the brief.
- Achieve clarity and balance through choice of instruments (timbre) stereo placement and mixing.

Logic skills

In the Matrix Edit window
- Alter note lengths.
- Change velocity values.
- Apply Legato.

In the Sequence Parameters box
- Use the Transpose feature.
- Apply Dynamics – compression.

In the Arrange window
- Repeat Objects.
- Create Aliases.
- Normalize sequence parameters.
- Use the Transpose feature in the Sequence Parameters box

Adaptive Track Mixer
- Use MIDI controllers Volume, Pan, Reverb and Chorus.
- Insert and utilize ES E virtual softsynth.

- Set up and utilize bus sends.
- Insert and utilize SilverVerb plug-in

Preparation

1 From the CD, copy the folder named project5 to your computer.
2 On your computer, create a folder named mywork5 or something similar in which to save your work.
3 From the project5 folder, open template – templt5.
4 In your new mywork5 folder, save the template as myproj5 or something similar.

The assignment

OK, here's the scenario. A computer game company has commissioned you to compose the music for a scene in their latest historical title set in Elizabethan times. The piece must run for a minimum of three minutes.

It's night-time and we see a lone sailor searching a misty quay side for a hidden treasure map. Moored sailing ships bob gently on the tide. Apart from the sailor, the scene is mostly static. We need something repetitive to underpin the structure. Let's start by recording a short ostinato. A simple line on the lower strings of an acoustic guitar will do nicely.

To gain an overall picture, at this point you may prefer to listen to the finished thing rather than let things unfold. To do so, load project5/5.mix.

Take 1

Track 1: Nylonstr. | Guitar 1
Sequence Parameters box: Qua 1/8 – note
Instrument Parameter box: Cha 1, Prg 24
Transport Bar: (L) 1.1.1 (R) 5.1.1

Guitar parts are usually written an octave higher than they sound, even on a Concert score. In this case, as we are playing a keyboard, it has been left at concert pitch. Play exactly as written.

1 Record the guitar ostinato (Figures P5.1 and P5.2). Although it's only a one bar repeated figure, it is better to play it four times in succession. This is better than recording it once and duplicating it because the velocities will be more varied and the result more realistic. I have used a tempo of 105 bpm. You may prefer a lower speed for recording. Depending on your playing style, the result may sound a little stilted if there is too much of a gap between notes. As we know, plucked guitar strings have a resonant quality and are slow to decay. If this is the case, Select the sequence and open the Matrix Edit window [Window > Open Matrix Edit]. If it looks anything like Figure P5.3 – the notes do not quite meet each other – select all the notes and apply Legato [Functions >

> **Info**
>
> The template has a time signature of 4/4 and the tempo is 105 bpm. Now this may be a bit fast for you. If so scroll the tempo to suit you. When listening back, scroll back to 105bpm.

> **Info**
>
> Ostinato – a posh word for riff!

> **Tip**
>
> When loading example files containing MIDI settings its quite likely that you will initially hear the wrong sounds (very likely those from a previous project or song). Use [Options > Song Settings > Used Instrument MIDI Settings] to correct them. A faster way – quickly cursor up or down the tracks using the arrow keys on your computer keyboard.

Figures P5.1 and **P5.2**
Guitar ostinato, Score and Matrix view

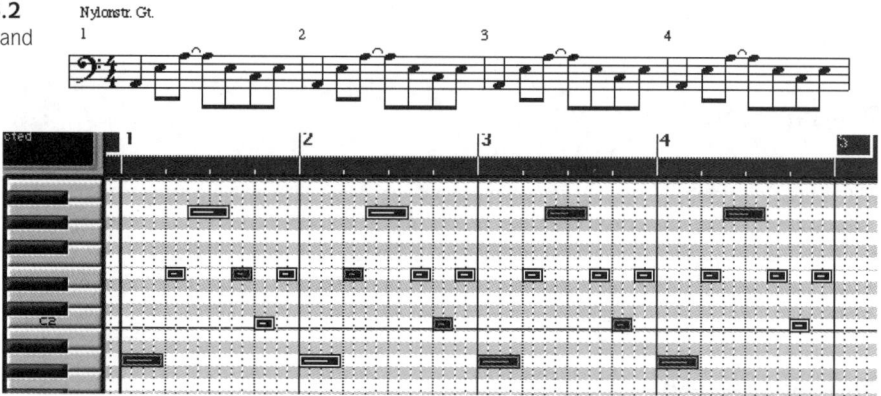

Figure P5.3
Note the gaps between notes.

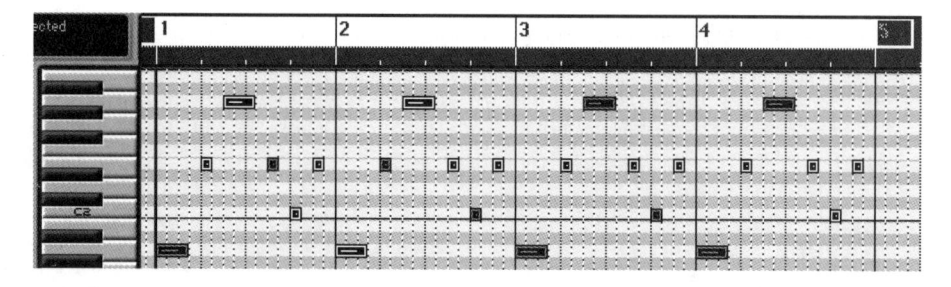

MIDI>Note Events > Note Force Legato (selected/any)] to lengthen them. The notes are now placed end to end and should appear like those in Figure P5.2.

2 Save Song – compare with project5/5.1

OK we've made a start. What next? It's night time and it's misty. How about some minor chords over that riff? Simple triads (three note chords) will do. 'But a guitar has six strings' I hear you say. True, but this is not a real guitar and six notes will prove too dense for the simple effect needed to create our moody atmosphere. However, if we use open spacing the triads will produce the depth we need.

Take 2

Track 1: Nylonstr. | Guitar 2
Sequence Parameters box: Qua 1/8 – note
Instrument Parameter box: Cha 2, Prg 24
Transport Bar: (L) 1.1.1 (R) 5.1.1

1 Record the chord sequence in Figures P5.4 and P5.5.

Listen to the result. If any notes sound too short, check them by viewing in the Matrix Edit window. Unlike Guitar 1, the notes need not line up end to end. If any are obviously too short, then lengthen them by grabbing the bottom right-hand corner – a finger appears – and dragging to the required length (Figure P5.5a and P5.5b). Alternatively, use the index finger tool from the Tool box (Figure P5.6).

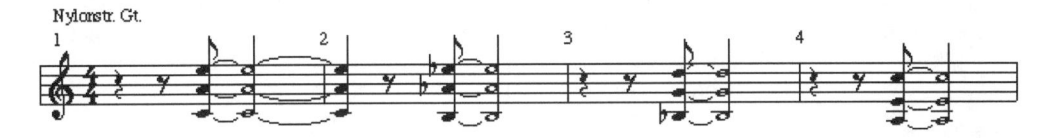

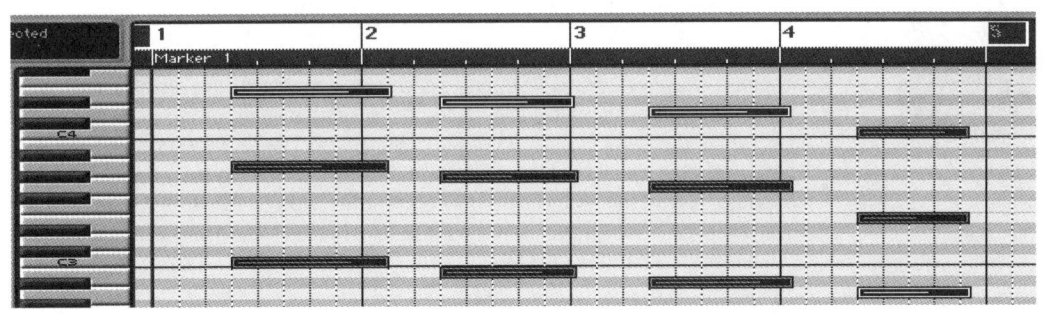

Figures P5.4 and **P5.5**
Chord sequence, Score and Matrix view

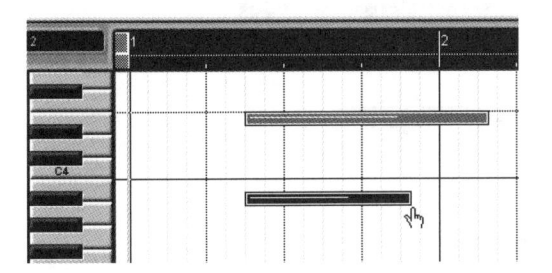

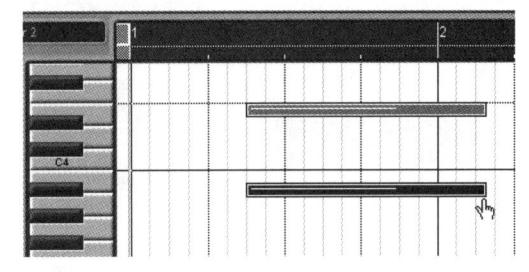

2 Select both recorded sequences, and use the Repeat objects command [Functions > Repeat objects...] to replicate them. In the resulting dialogue box, you will be asked:

- Number of Copies – type 1 here.
- Adjustment – select Auto here.
- as – select Copies here.

We now have eight measures of music on tracks 1 and 2 (Guitar 1 and 2).

3 With the Glue Tool, join the two sequences on track 1 together.
4 Repeat the procedure with the two sequences on track 2.
5 Save Song – compare with project5/5.2a

OK so far, so good, but we can't repeat the same eight bars indefinitely without some form of variation. On the other hand, we must not overdo it. It's a predominately static scene remember. Let's try repeating the same eight bar sequence but drop the pitch a perfect fourth whilst doing so. That way we keep the minor chords and retain the moody atmosphere.

1 Select the sequence on track 1 (bars 1 – 9) and duplicate it [Functions >

Figures P5.5a and **P5.5b**
Lengthening a note with the Index finger tool (**Figure P5.6** below).

Info

How much you can lengthen notes in the Matrix Editor depends on the display resolution. Change this in the small window found on the left – below the Tool box. This is linked directly to the display resolution on the Transport bar (Figure P5.7) In our case a value of 16 is fine.

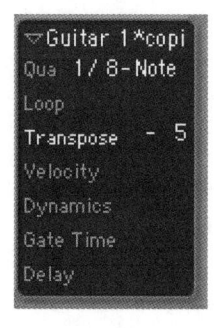

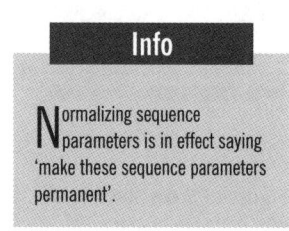

Objects > Repeat objects (x1)] between bars 9 and 17.
2 Select the new, copied sequence (9 – 17), and using the Sequence Parameters box, enter a Transpose value of –5 (Figure P5.8). There are other ways of doing this, but our chosen method is convenient for now. If we don't like the result, it's easily changed.
3 Repeat the above procedure with the sequence on track 2.

Set the Locators to cycle between (L) 1.1.1 (R) 17.1.1 and play the piece back a couple of times. 'Sounds good to me maestro' (as a well known session bass player was fond of saying to the musical director when he wanted to get home early without doing another take!) We're happy with that (well I am anyway) so let's make a commitment! If you were to view the transposed sequences in the editors at this point they would still show their original pitch, even though we now hear them a perfect fourth below. We'll now make these changes permanent.

1 Select the two sequences (bars 9 – 17) on tracks 1 and 2.
2 Use Functions > Sequence Parameter > Normalize Sequence Parameters (Figure P5.9) to make the transposition for real. Play things back to check. A look in the Editors will reveal the data changes.

Figure P5.8
Transpose value – Sequence Parameter box.

Figure P5.9
Normalizing sequence parameters.

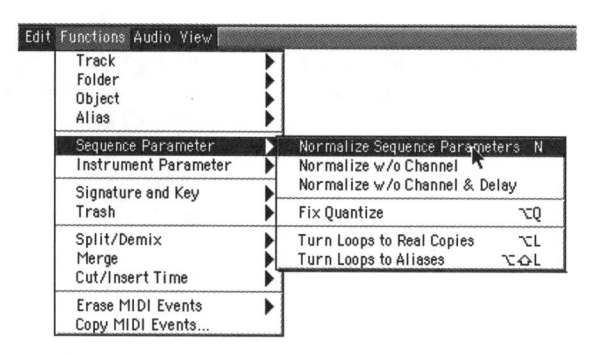

Info

Normalizing sequence parameters is in effect saying 'make these sequence parameters permanent'.

3 Save Song – compare with project5/5.2b
We now have 16 bars that can be repeated ad.finitum as long as we dream up interesting variations to overlay.
4 Using the Glue tool, join the two sequences together on track 1.
5 Repeat the procedure on track 2.
6 Copy and paste the sequences on both tracks (bars 1 – 17) to bar 17.
7 Save Song – compare with project5/5.2c

We now have 32 bars of guitars. A different texture perhaps? Strings come to mind, and movement. A rhythmic figure maybe.

Take 3

Track 3: (Ch 3) Strings
Sequence Parameters box: Qua 1/8 – note
Instrument Parameter box: Cha 3, Prg 48
Transport Bar: (L) 17.1.1 (R) 21.1.1

Follow these steps:

1 Record the string part (Figure P5.10 and P5.11). Note the accent on the first eighth note in each measure. Play this with slightly more emphasis than the other notes. Visualize the string section bowing this figure and transfer that to your own playing. Imagine yourself actually playing in that string section. It may sound crazy, but that's how it's done! Logic will receive these accented notes at slightly higher velocity values.

Figures P5.10 and **P5.11**
Strings, Score and Matrix view

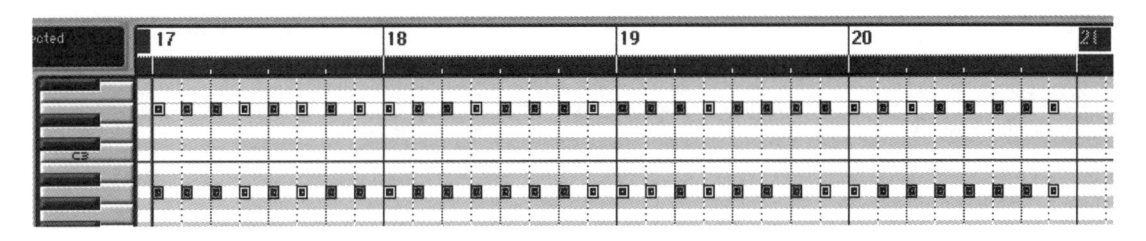

2 Check these velocity values in the Matrix Edit window. Click on a note and the Info Line appears. If you under played the accented notes increase their velocities by clicking on them with the Velocity tool (Figure P5.12 right) and scrolling the value in the Info Line.

Figure P5.12
Velocity tool.

We now have another short ostinato figure ready for repetition and variation.

3 Save Song – compare with – project5/5.3a
4 Copy and paste the string sequence (bars 17 – 21) to bar 21 and glue the two resulting objects together.
5 Copy and paste this new sequence (bars 17 – 25) to bar 25. Once again we have two string sequences.
6 Select the second sequence (bars 25 – 33) and as we did with the guitars, transpose it down a perfect fourth (–5) in the Sequence Parameters box, and use Functions > Sequence Parameter > Normalize Sequence Parameters to make it permanent.
7 Select all the sequences on all the Tracks between bars 17 and 33. Copy and paste them to bar 33. We now have 48 bars of music.
8 Save Song – Compare with project5/5.3b

Let's review things so far. We have set a nice background scene through the use of repetitive ostinato figures and limited harmonic variation. Nothing here to distract the game player whilst he noodles around the murky dockyard looking for treasure maps. Even so, to repeat it again would run the risk of sending him to the land of nod. We need some melody, but nothing too intrusive. A fragment lasting around four measures would be ideal. Choice of instrument? What about clarinet. Nice and dark when played in the lower register.

Take 4

Track 4: (Ch 4) Clarinet
Sequence Parameters box: Qua 1/16 – note
Instrument Parameter box: Cha 3, Prg 71
Transport Bar: (L) 33.1.1 (R) 37.1.1

Follow these steps:

1 Record the clarinet part (Figure P5.13 and P5.14).
Note we have changed the Quantize value in the Status bar to 16. This is to accommodate the sixteenth notes at the beginning of the melody. Clarinets are members of the woodwind family and a vibrating wooden reed produces the sound. Clarinet players articulate with their tongue, by striking this reed. Observe the written articulation – legato slurs and staccato notes – when playing the part into Logic.

Figures P5.13 and **P5.14**
Clarinet, Score and Matrix view

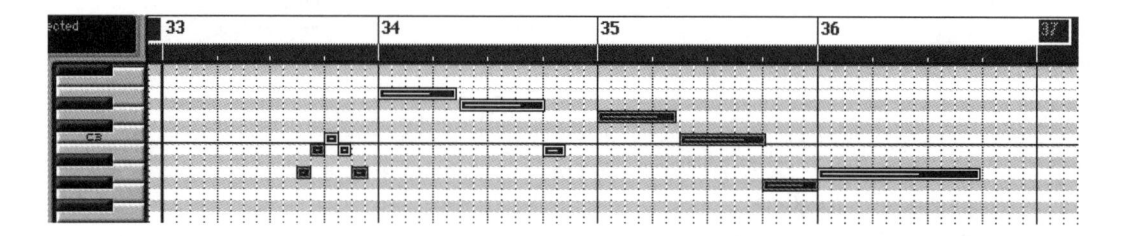

2 Copy and paste the newly recorded clarinet sequence (bars 33 – 37) to bar 37 and glue both sequences together.
3 Copy and paste the resulting sequence (bars 33 – 41) to bar 41. Once again, we have two sequences.
4 Transpose the second sequence (bars 41 – 48) down a perfect fourth (-5) using the Sequence Parameters box and Normalize it [Functions > Sequence Parameter > Normalize Sequence Parameters].

Incidentally, we have now taken the clarinet below its normal range. No matter. In the real world a bass clarinet would play this part. As the GM sound set does not contain a bass clarinet, transposing the normal clarinet this low is acceptable.

OK this seems to be working. Let's copy another 16 bars. This time we'll do it a slightly different way.

5 Set the Locators between bars 33 and 49.
6 Select the sequences [Edit > Select Inside Locators] and Copy

[Edit>Copy]. Make sure the Song Position Line is set to 49. 1. 1 and Paste [Edit> Paste] the copied sequences to their new location.
7 Save Song – compare with project5/5.4

Something new? I love pizzicato strings used to add that atmospheric touch. We will now add a simple arpeggio figure.

Take 5

Track 5: (Ch 5) Pizzicato Str
Sequence Parameters box: Qua 1/8 – note
Instrument Parameter box: Cha 5, Prg 45
Transport Bar: (L) 49.1.1 (R) 53.1.1

Follow these steps:

1 Record the pizzicato strings (Figure P5.15 and P5.16)
Figure P5.15 Pizzicato strings.

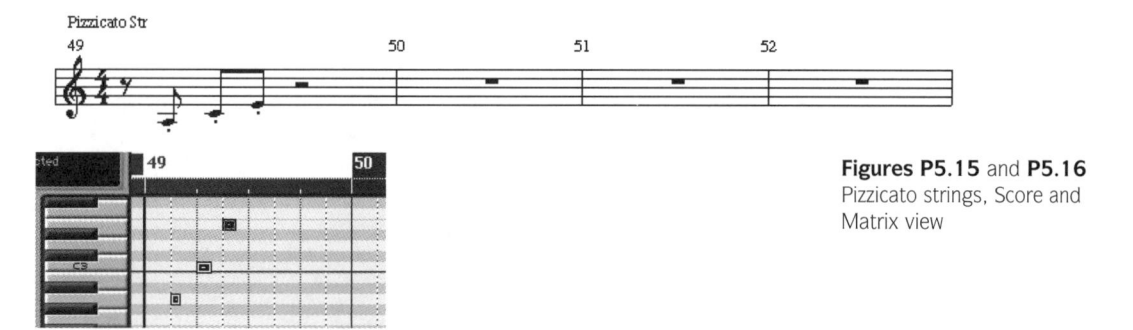

Figures P5.15 and **P5.16**
Pizzicato strings, Score and Matrix view

This figure is played at the beginning of the bar, just before the clarinet entry, and therefore avoids any confusion, that may have resulted, had we placed it elsewhere in the four bar cycle.

2 Copy and paste the pizzicato sequence (bars 49 – 53) to bar 53. Glue the two sequences together.
3 Copy and paste the resulting sequence to bar 57. Once again, we have two sequences.
4 Transpose the second sequence (bars 57 – 65) down a perfect fourth (-5) using the Sequence Parameters box and Normalize it [Functions > Sequence Parameter > Normalize Sequence Parameters].

Our musical canvas is filling up nicely but the stereo picture needs sorting out. We need not make any final decisions just yet, so let's use the Instrument Parameter box to try out a few preliminary settings.

5 Set the Locators between 49 and 65. Enable cycle and play.
6 Using the Instrument Parameter box, separate the two virtual guitarists

by panning the first to a value of 40 and the second to 88. Leave the strings in the centre (64). Place the clarinettist at 48 and the pizzicato strings at 80. We now have quite a nice spread. Have a peek in the Track Mixer [Windows > Open Track Mixer] and you'll notice the changes reflected in the Pan settings (Figure P5.17).

Figure P5.17
Pan settings

7 Set the Locators – (L) 49.1.1 (R) 65.1.1, Select all sequences [Edit>Select>Inside Locators], and copy and paste to bar 65.
8 Save Song – compare with project5/5.5.

It's all going swimmingly so far and there's room on our canvas for more. Something nautical? A fragment from a well known sea shanty perhaps? The Drunken Sailor obviously! Played on the accordion? Of course!

Take 6

Track 6: (Ch 6) Accordion Fr.
Sequence Parameters box: Qua 1/16 – note
Instrument Parameter box: Cha 6, Prg 21
Transport Bar: (L) 57.1.1 (R) 61.1.1

Follow these steps:

1 Record the accordion part (Figures P5.18 and P5.19). This fragment works best over the lower transposed section, hence the Locator positions of 57 – 61.
2 What do we do with the drunken sailor? Dump him on the far left! – Instrument Parameter box – Pan value 10.
3 Copy and paste the accordion sequence (bars 57 – 61) to bar 61. Glue the two sequences together.
4 Copy and paste the new accordion sequence to bar 73.
5 Save Song – compare with project5/5.6.

[Accordion score and matrix view, bars 57–60]

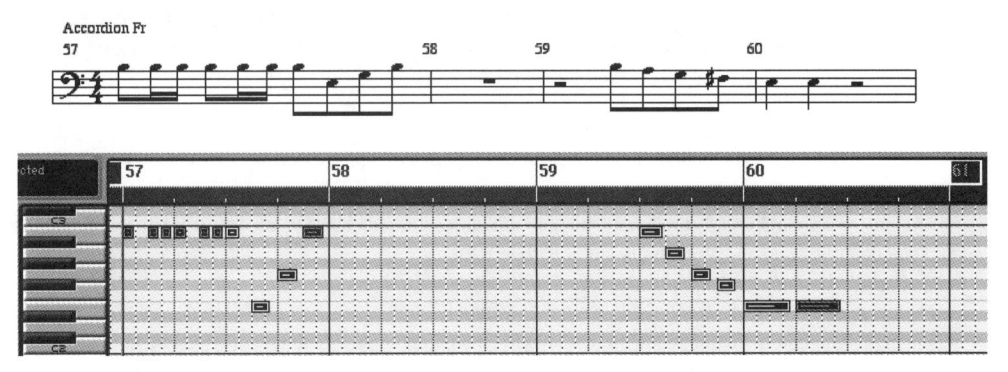

I think we've got room for a little more nautical nonsense. How about a Hornpipe?

Figures P5.18 and **P5.19**
Accordion, Score and Matrix view

Take 7

> *Track 7:* (Ch 7) Piccolo
> *Sequence Parameters box:* Qua 1/16 – note
> *Instrument Parameter box:* Cha 7, Prg 72
> *Transport Bar:* (L) 64.1.1 (R) 66.1.1

Follow these steps:

1 Record the piccolo part (Figures P5.20 and P5.21). Play it one octave higher than written. This fragment is placed at the end of the clarinet line and just before the pizzicato strings. No confusion.

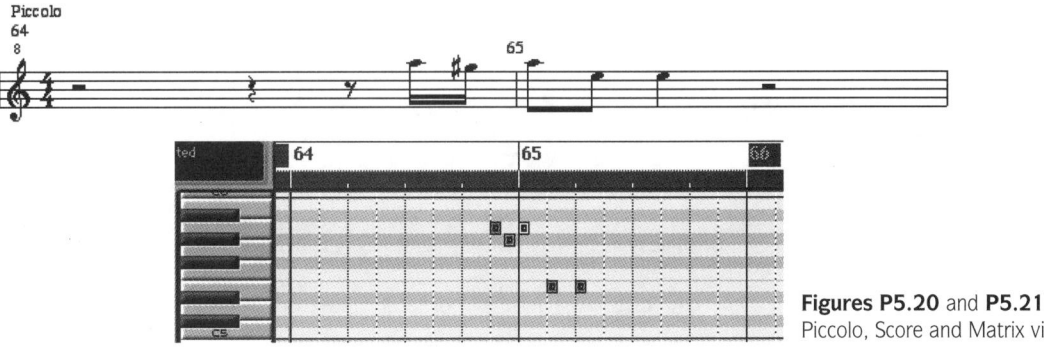

[Piccolo score and matrix view, bars 64–65]

Figures P5.20 and **P5.21**
Piccolo, Score and Matrix view

2 Copy the piccolo sequence (bars 64 – 66) and paste to bars 68, 72 and 76. We now have four piccolo sequences.
3 Select the last two sequences (bars 72 – 74 and 76 – 78) and using the Sequence Parameters box, transpose them up a fifth by adding a value of seven (7 semitones) in the Transpose section. Yes, I know everything else went down a fourth, but I fancied a change! Make this permanent with

Functions > Sequence Parameter > Normalize Sequence Parameters.
4 Where shall we place the piccolo player? Over on the right, away from the drunken sailor – Pan value 117!
5 Save Song – compare with project5/5.7.

At this point I think a couple of effects would work a treat at instilling yet more atmosphere to this backdrop. GM effects are not noted for their realism but used carefully, in the background, can work quite well. Let's try the Seashore effect. Back to the top!

The Seashore effect – Program 122 on the GM sound set varies considerably from one sound module to another. Some are quite convincing and others are plain awful. Let's hope yours is not like mine, which includes a flock of seagulls!

Take 8

Track 8: (Ch 8) Seashore
Sequence Parameters box: Qua 1/8 – note
Instrument Parameter box: Cha 8, Prg 122
Transport Bar: (L) 1.1.1 (R) 9.1.1

Follow these steps:

Figures P5.22 and **P5.23**
Seashore, Score and Matrix view

1 Record the seashore effect (Figure P5.22 and P5.23). It doesn't matter which note you use. They all play the same sample. I have used middle C. We'll leave it in the centre (64).

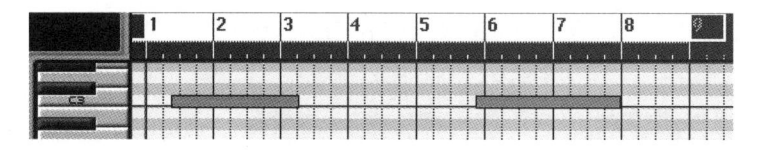

2 Save Song – compare with project5/5.8.

Something else? A ship's bell perhaps. Ghost-like in the mist.

Take 9

Track 9: (Ch 9) Tubular-bell
Sequence Parameters box: Qua 1/8 – note
Instrument Parameter box: Cha 9, Prg 14
Transport Bar: (L) 1.1.1 (R) 9.1.1

Follow these steps:

1 Record the tubular bell (Figures P5.24 and P5.25). It works a treat. Pan it to value 94 for now.

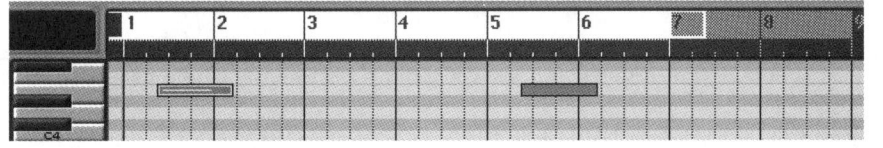

Figures P5.24 and **P5.25**
Tubular bell, Score and Matrix view

2 Now we calculate how many times to repeat the seashore and tubular bell. 72 bars, divided by 8 = 9 times. Use Functions > Object > Repeat Objects... In the resulting dialogue box, you will be asked:

- Number of Copies – type 9 here.
- Adjustment – select Auto here.
- as – select Aliases here.

3 Save Song – compare with project5/5.9.

What now? We have 80 bars of music, a full sound canvas with no room left for any moving parts without the risk of confusing the listener. I still think it needs something else ... a pad of some kind ... high strings in fifths will create a nice backdrop and sit well with the descending guitar chords. Now it just so happens that Logic's own virtual softsynth, the ES E (Figure P5.27) is capable of some great pad sounds.

> **Info**
>
> An alias looks like an object (Figure P5.26), but doesn't contain data. It's a reflection of the original. Any further changes to the original are reflected in the alias. It's recognizable by italic text.

Figure P5.27
ES E virtual softsynth

> **Info**
>
> The ES E (es ensemble) is an eight-voice polyphonic softsynth and very useful for a variety of 'pad' and ensemble sounds.

Take 10

Track 10: (Ch 10) Audio Instrument 1 | ES E Pre-set [Factory 1 > bright_PWM_Strings]
Sequence Parameters box: Qua 1/4 – note
Instrument Parameter box: Cha 1
Transport Bar: (L) 1.1.1 (R) 9.1.1

I have chosen the ES E pre-set called bright_PWM_strings. You may prefer another, or you may want to experiment and edit the chosen pre-set. To do so:

1 Select track 10 – Audio Instrument 1 – and open the Track Mixer [Windows > Open Track Mixer]. On the mixer, the Audio Instrument 1 object will be framed in red (Figure P5.28).
2 Double click on the blue, illuminated ES E button to reveal the ES E instrument (Figure P5.29a) – click and hold to choose another – (Figure P5.29b).

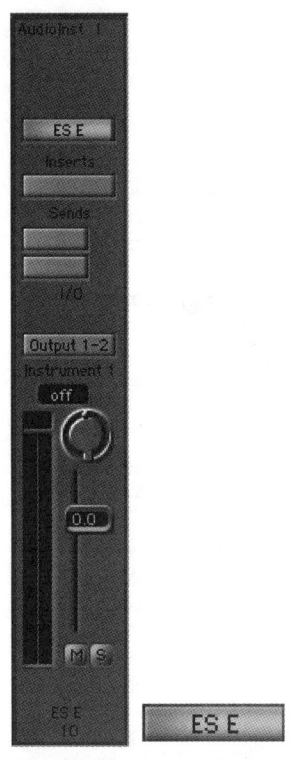

Figures P5.28 and **P5.29a**
Mixer track 10 – ES E, and ES E button.

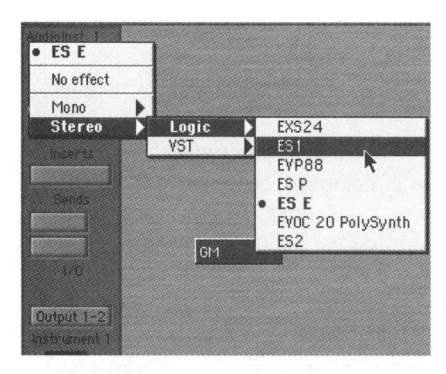

Figure P5.29b (right)
Choosing instruments.

3 Choose a pre-set from the drop-down menu (Figure P5.30).

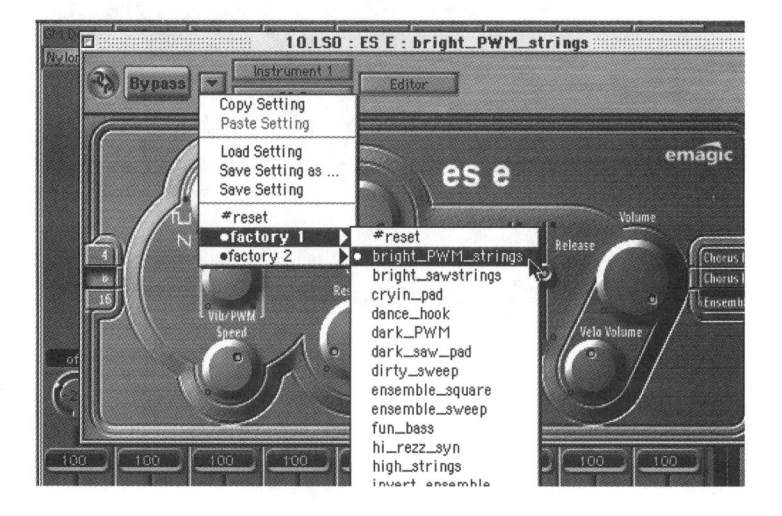

Figure P5.30
Choosing pre-sets.

Now follow these steps:

1. Record the string pad (Figures 5.31 and P5.32) – play these gently. If you find it difficult to do so, use the Dynamics section in the Sequence Parameters box to reduce the velocities. Try 50% or 75% (Figure P5.33).

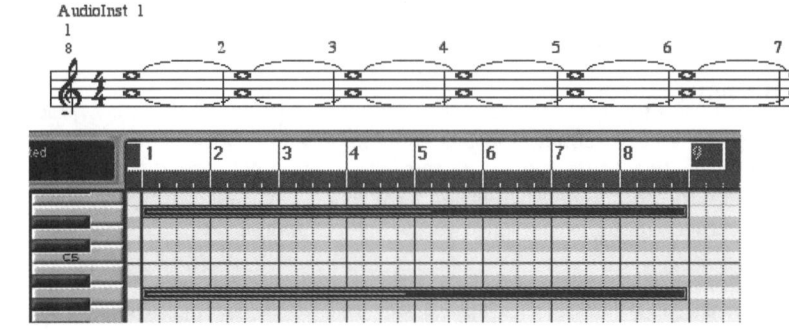

Figures P5.31 and **P5.32**
String pad, Score and Matrix view

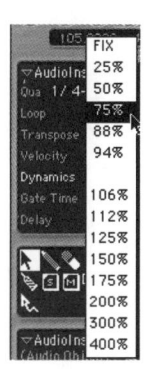

2. Copy and paste the sequence (bars 1 – 9) to bar 9 [Functions > Object > Repeat Objects... x1]
3. Transpose the new sequence (bars 9 – 17) down a perfect fourth (-5) using the Sequence Parameters box and Normalize it [Functions > Sequence Parameter > Normalize Sequence Parameters]. Glue the two Parts together.
4. Copy the new sequence (bars 1 – 17) to bar 17 until the end of the piece [Functions > Object > Repeat Objects... x4]
5. Glue all the sequences on track 10 together.
6. To make the string line continuous:

(a) Select the track and open the Matrix Edit window [Windows > Open Matrix Edit].
(b) Select all the notes [Edit > Select All].
(c) Apply Legato [Functions > Note Events > Note Force Legato (selected/any)].

Figure P5.33
Compressing velocities.

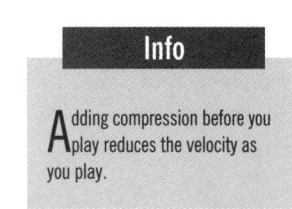

7. Save Song – compare with project5/5.10.

OK we have 80 bars, just over three minutes long. Time to end it. If used with a game it probably wouldn't need one. But what the hell! I like endings. We're going to add a very simple one note ending on the Guitar 1 track.

Info

Adding compression before you play reduces the velocity as you play.

Take 11

Track 2: (Ch 2) Nylonstr. | Guitar 2
Sequence Parameters box: Qua 1/4 – note
Instrument Parameter box: Cha 2, Prg 24
Transport Bar: (L) 81.1.1 (R) 83.1.1

Follow these steps:

1 Record the guitar (Figures P5.34 and P5.35).
2 Save Song – compare with project5/5.11.

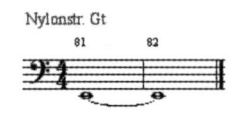

Figures P5.34 and P5.35
Guitar, Score and Matrix view

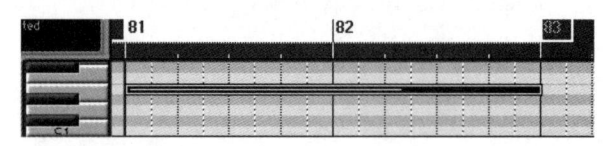

The Mix

Mixing this piece is straightforward enough. A label – KISS (Keep It Simple, Stupid) – is stuck to my monitor because it's easy to get carried away, especially with the comprehensive mixing facilities now available with Logic, but I have learned through experience to use effects and signal processing sparingly.

Everybody does it differently, but I like to get the stereo picture and volume levels clear before I decide to add effects. Up to now we have left Volume at a value of 100 in the Instrument Parameter box. Before changing them I listened back and decided to alter the stereo picture slightly.

Pan settings

- Guitar 1 actually functions as a kind of bass line. It's usual to place the bass in the centre (64) so that's what I did.
- Guitar 2 was upsetting the balance a little. I left where it was (88) but applied 75% compression.
- The Clarinet was competing for space with the Accordion, so I moved it to the right (80).
- The pizzicato strings have changed sides (48). They enter after the clarinet, which is on the right, and I wanted a contrast.

Volume levels

I used the Track Mixer to play around with the volume levels until I found a suitable balance. The main thing to remember here is to keep the ES E pad fairly low to begin with. Think of it as a back-drop, a kind of musical canvas on which the other instruments are painted, one at a time. As each one appears it should sound clear and detailed against the back-drop, but never too dominant. I ended up with the settings in Figure P5.36. Yours of course will be different.

Reverb settings

That settled, I listened again. The obvious candidate for reverb was the 'Seashore' sound. It needed more ambience. I set this at 95 for a distant effect. For the remaining GM sounds I used a value of 55. Any more would have robbed them of detail and muddied the mix. These settings work fine for my GM sound module but may be unsuitable for yours. Make your own judgements and adjustments.

Now for the ES E. The chosen pre-set already utilizes an Ensemble effect

Figure P5.36
Track mixer settings.

to thicken the sound but reverb was needed to provide a sense of mystery. So I:

Figure P5.37
Bus object.

1 Made sure a bus object was present in the Environment and Track Mixer (Figure P5.37).
2 In the Track Mixer, selected the ES E Object and clicked on one of the buttons named Sends.
3 From the drop-down menu, chose Bus 1 and Post – post fader (Figure P5.38).
4 Set the Send Knob to -0.10 – about 1 o'clock (Figure P5.39).

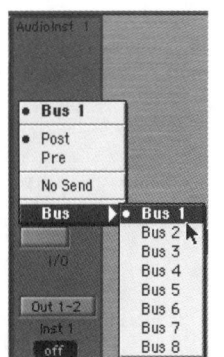

Figures P5.38 and **P5.39**
Sends menu and Send knob

5 Selected the Bus 1 object and clicked on one of the buttons named Inserts.
6 From the drop-down menu, chose Stereo > Reverb > SilverVerb.
7 Double clicked on the blue SilverVerb button to reveal the SiverVerb send effect itself (Figure P5.40).

Figure P5.40 SilverVerb, choosing a pre-set.

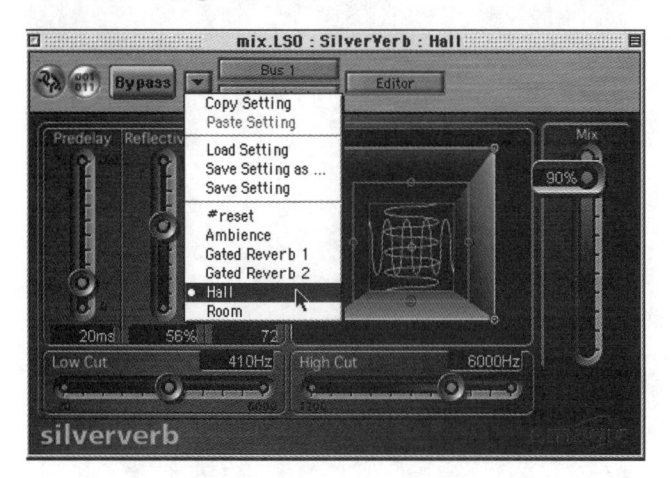

8 Chose the Hall pre-set and adjusted the Mix to 90%, I wanted it nice and wet.

None of the above took as long as it takes to read! It's quite easy when you get the hang of it.

Chorus

I decided the guitar would benefit from some judicious use of a chorus effect. All right, I know they didn't have digital effects processors back in Sir Francis Drake's day, but who cares! It serves our purpose of beefing things up a little. I set a value of 35 which worked fine on my GM sound module. It'll no doubt be different for yours.

The result? I'm happy. There's always another way to do it but part of doing this kind of thing for a living is deciding when to stop. Time's money. Commitments have to be made. No doubt you would do it another way. Open project5/5.mix. Go ahead! Experiment! That's how you learn but don't even think about altering it and claiming copyright – I have a brilliant lawyer!

4 A look at musical form

Practically all music has form – a structure or framework, often planned before the composition process even begins. I'm referring here to composed music as opposed to improvised music (although improvisation is often based on form anyway). The casual listener does not always notice the form, nor should they because in most cases it's a hidden element. They enjoy the music on a superficial level, and quite rightly so. After all, when we gaze at a work of art we are not necessarily examining its hidden form. We appreciate the whole picture.

Sometimes the musical form is very simple and glaringly obvious, the 12 bar blues being a perfect example. Other times it's very complicated and stretched across a long time span. A classical symphony, for instance, may contain four complete movements and last up to 45 minutes or more.

One thing's for sure. Although the listener may not be consciously aware of musical form they certainly know when it's missing! Formless music – and plenty has been composed and forgotten – lacks the sense of completeness which is perceived by the listener and held in their memories. Of course good music has been written without conventional musical form but it has no place in this book which is primarily concerned with producing commercial music.

Form can be anything you want it to be. It's about organization. However, over time, certain musical forms have appeared and remained embedded in popular culture. They've stood the test of time and provided a basic structure for composers to use repeatedly. Let's take a quick look at some established musical forms in three very different genres.

Simple three part forms

A simple three part form is referred to as ABA. The third section is a recapitulation of the first, sometimes harmonically and melodically modified. The middle section is a contrast to avoid monotony.

- Load form/haydn and view the Arrange window (Figure 4.1).

This extract is from a Haydn Piano Sonata (Figure 4.2). Track 1 contains the right hand parts and track 2 the left. You will notice that the Marker contains a reference to the form. Section A is 16 bars long. It is in fact an eight bar segment played twice.

An analogy: think of A as the homepage on a themed Internet site. B is a contrasting section and consists of nine measures. The rhythmic structure and phrasing are similar to the A section but the harmony sets it apart. The

> **Info**
>
> To examine the Logic files for this chapter, copy the folders named 'form' and 'exile' from the CD to your computer.

A look at musical form 101

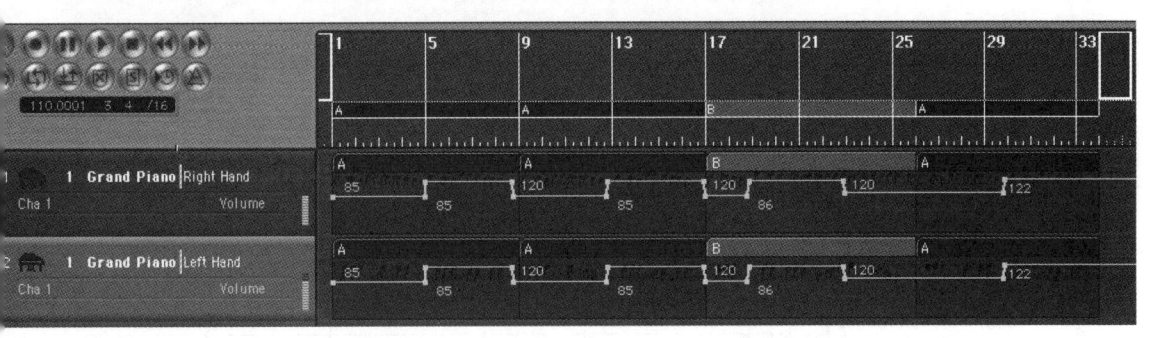

Figure 4.1 (above)
haydn.lso

Figure 4.2 (left)
haydn.lso

scenery is familiar but we've definitely left the homepage. The piece finishes with a note for note repetition of A. Back home! It would be more accurately described as an AABA structure.

Here's another example – form/minuet – this time from Bach's French Suite (Figure 4.3).

Again we have the A section followed by a contrasting B section. However, in this example the recapitulation has been varied. The reason?

Well A ends on the dominant and sounds incomplete. Bach needed an ending. He begins the recapitulation the same (for two bars) but then leads us home to the tonic in the last bar. The Marker Track shows this structure as A1, B and A2.

Figure 4.3
minuet.lso

Jazz standards

Jazz musicians often use the classic standard song repertoire from the first half of the twentieth century for their improvisations. 'I Got Rhythm' by Gershwin is a typical example. Although in a completely different style from the minuet above it's form is basically the same: AABA. Here's a tune in a similar style called 'Raising Standards'.

- Load form/raisings (Figure 4.4).

The Marker shows the form. Section A1 and A2 are both eight bars long. The difference between them lies in bars 15 and 16, in the A2 section, where the melody and harmony have been modified. Section B is a contrasting section, generally referred to by jazz musicians as the 'bridge'. The tune finishes with eight bars of A3. Again, things have been changed slightly to bring about the ending.

Figure 4.4
raisings.lso

Pop songs

Pop songs are varied in their structure. However one form seems to be more predominant than most. A verse followed by a chorus is repeated two or three times and contrasted with a bridge. This gives way once again to the verse and chorus. Sometimes the bridge is used again. This corresponds to an ABABCAB structure. Here's an example.

- Load exile/exile and view the Arrange window (Figure 4.5, page 104).

This tune, although an instrumental, follows the format of many a rock song in it's construction. Medieval in character it could have been played by an electric folk band from the seventies such as Fairport Convention.

It kicks off with a verse (A) lasting 14 bars followed by an eight bar chorus (B). The verse and chorus are then repeated. This takes us up to bar 42. To repeat things again would be bordering on the tedious so a 10 bar bridge is introduced for relief (C). Now that could have led straight back to either the verse or chorus (as it does in millions of songs) but in this case the bridge has been extended by adding another eight bar section (D). This helps build a sense of expectancy. The verse returns and is followed by a chorus and ending. What we have then is a ABABCDAB structure.

It's a good idea to have a basic form in mind before starting a composition. Although you will probably modify it as you write the piece, jotting down a simple structure first will serve as a guide.

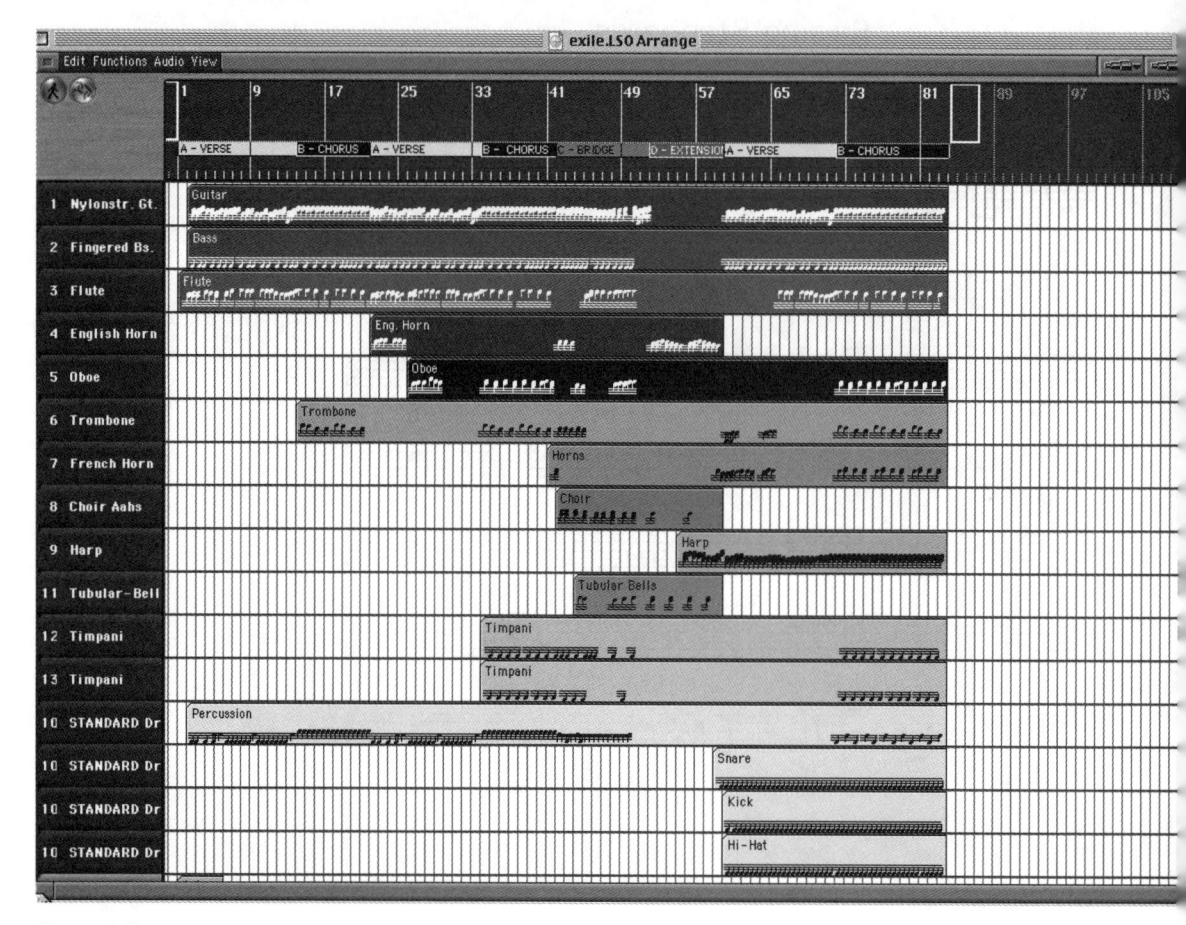

Figure 4.5

The building blocks of composition 5

In Chapter 1, MIDI sequencing, I explained how technically challenged keyboard players like myself can record a difficult piece of music by breaking it down into manageable chunks. We dismantle the composition, piece by piece and rebuild it again as sequencing objects on a track in the Arrange window within Logic. You could liken this process to a building being dismantled and reassembled, brick by brick, in a new location. There is much to be learned by doing this, and Logic is an ideal place to do it because we can see the constituent parts, or building blocks, of a composition clearly displayed in the Arrange window.

> **Info**
>
> To examine the Logic files for this chapter, copy the folders named 'exile' and 'blocks' from the CD to your computer.

The phrase

You probably discovered earlier, when sequencing three completely different styles of music, that musical common sense prompted you to play and record the music as complete phrases. We can assume then, that a phrase is the smallest structural unit used for composition. It has a sense of completeness. It can be sung or played in a single breath and has a definite beginning and ending.

- Load exile/exile and view the flute (track 3) in the Score window.

The first phrase is coloured red. It's a complete unit. Think of it as a musical sentence. Better still, think of it as a musical question. It's followed by another phrase, the answer, marked blue. After this there are two more question and answer phrases. Look through and play the score to identify other such phrases. I've marked a few to get you going.

What do these phrases consist of? What is the main ingredient? Well melody for a start. For me, this is usually the most important part of the creative process. The melody comes first and the rest follows later.

Melody

OK, not all music relies on melody but the overwhelming majority does. How many times have you heard a snatch of melody and it's instant recall time? You know exactly where it came from. Even if you can't remember where its origins lie, the damn thing nags you silly until you eventually find out. That's the power of melody. That recall – depending on how old you are! – will often bring to mind a particular memory. It may well bring submerged emotions to the surface. Powerful stuff!

What constitutes a melody? At its most basic, a string of notes which rise and fall. But that's not enough.

- Load blocks/oddnotes (Figure 5.1).

Figure 5.1
oddnotes.lso.

Listen to this group of notes. Not very memorable, is it?

- Now load blocks/igetit (Figure 5.2).

Figure 5.2
igetit.lso

It's the same order of notes, but what a transformation. It's instantly recognizable as Eine Kleine Nacht Musik by Mozart, an absolute master of melody. What brought about the transformation? The rhythm. Without a rhythmic shape the melody does not exist.

What else? A distinctive shape, brought about by the pitch of the notes as a melody unfolds. A string of adjacent notes soon becomes monotonous without a leap – large or small, up or down – of some kind.

Take another look at the first few phrases of Exile (exile/exile). Now this is a gentle melody, nothing very dramatic, which gradually climbs a scale. To make it a little more interesting there is a leap of a fourth between the first two notes (A and D). Each time the melody climbs a step there is a return to the A before leaping back up again and continuing the ascent.

High climax points within the melodic shape are also important for emotional intensity. In this case the highest note arrives at the beginning of each chorus (high E – marked green).

Low notes can have the opposite effect and are often used to calm things down. The English horn does just that between bars 53 and 61 (track 4).

A good melody can be likened to well written prose. A readable page of text contains clearly defined phrases and frequent use of punctuation. Bear this in mind when writing melodies. Time taken crafting a memorable melody is time well spent.

Harmony

A vast subject which needs a complete book of its own. In fact there are several excellent books available. If you're into composing and arranging – you must be if you bought this book – I'm assuming that you already have a basic knowledge of the subject. However, I can supply a few guidelines.

Beginning composers working with Logic or similar sequencers often make the mistake of attempting to write a chord sequence and melody together. It doesn't usually work! Not many people can control all these elements at once, not least a beginner. The usual result of this way of writing is either a few measures of block chords following every single melody note with the bass playing only root notes or a few measures of repetitive chords and a boring melody line. Everything grinds to a halt pretty soon after. It's a very common mistake and simply the result of trying to think of two things (sometimes three if rhythm is included) at once.

It's far easier to get the melody down first. It's what people are going to remember after all. Craft the melody, make it interesting, and add chords afterwards. You will discover that a melody often suggests the harmony anyway.

It depends on the style of music of course, but when you add the harmony avoid having the bass constantly following the chords in root position. One way to get a more interesting harmonic structure is through careful construction of the bass line. Make it distinctive. Give it a life of it's own and where possible, and appropriate, have it move in the opposite direction to the melody. This will nearly always give a good result. This movement inevitably provides interesting inversions and passing notes.

- Load exile/dullbass and play it through.

The guitar is playing this chord sequence:

Dm / A7 / | Dm / / / | Dm / A7 / | Dm / / / |

F / Gm / | Am / / / | C / E7 / | Am / / / ||

The chords are OK, simple yes, but it's a rather plaintive melody and doesn't need complicated chords. Not quite right though, is it? How can we make it more harmonically interesting?

- Switch to exile/exile (the previous song) and play the opening measures.

By having the bass move, for the most part, in the opposite direction to the melody we have created the following:

Dm / A7 / | Dm7 / / Bbmaj7 | Dm / A7 / | Dm / / Gm9 |
    C#   C   A

F / Gm7 / | Fmaj7 / / / | C / E7 / | Am / Am / ||
   F   B   C

That's better. The bass is now playing a kind of counter melody – appropriate here because the drums have yet to enter – and created several inversions, new chords and interesting passing notes along the way.

Modulation is another way to make the harmonic structure interesting. It's often best to write what the melody suggests and the modulation should be smooth and natural sounding. The listener will not consciously perceive these key changes – but their subconscious will.

Exile is a simple enough song but helped along the way with several key changes. You can see them indicated in the Marker:

The verse is in D minor, the chorus in G minor and the bridge uses D flat major and A major. The bridge extension returns to D minor. These modulations are the direct result of the melody. Not the other way around.

> **Info**
>
> Modulation is the changing from one key to another within a composition.

Rhythm

Another vast subject. We have seen how a rhythmic design can change an ordinary string of notes into a memorable tune. Its most important role though is in the accompaniment. It can probably be best studied in piano music, where it is usually evident in the left hand part.

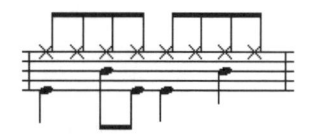

Most instrumental music used in the commercial world, makes extensive use of rhythm in the accompaniment, usually drums and percussion and is often derived from the character of the melody. For example, I wrote the melody for Exile before adding rhythm and harmony. The melody suggested both.

Take another look at the melody in the beginning phrase and you will notice that the first nine notes are eighth notes (quavers). Pretty straightforward stuff that, to my ears, suggested a classic rock drum rhythm (Figures 5.3, 5.4 and 5.5) used on countless recordings over the last four or five decades. Simple but effective. Of course we all hear things differently and had that melody been written by someone else (you?) the rhythmic scheme may well have taken a different turn.

Of course rhythmic accompaniment need not be restricted solely to drums. It is very easy to create rhythm in Logic without the use of percussion sounds. Rhythm can be generated with absolute accuracy using synthesized sounds to play arpeggios and other percussive patterns. These take on a more pulsating effect than the humanly played equivalent. For example: in Exile the drums don't appear until the third verse. However an eighth note pulse has been implied by the guitar arpeggios (track 1), which also happen to supply the harmony. This is reinforced by a sixteenth note arpeggio pattern played by the harp (track 9) on the last verse and chorus.

Techno and dance music are playing an increasing role in music for the media. Melody is a secondary consideration in this style of music and the composition process would probably start from the bottom up, with rhythmic patterns and loops being created first.

Figure 5.3
Rock rhythm.

Figures 5.4 and **5.5**
Rock rhythm, Hyper view, and matrix view

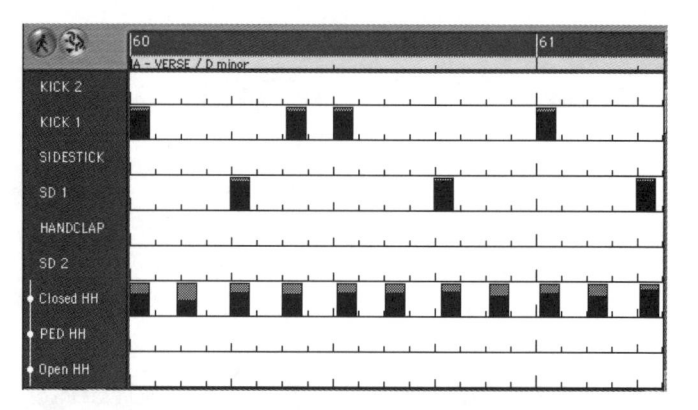

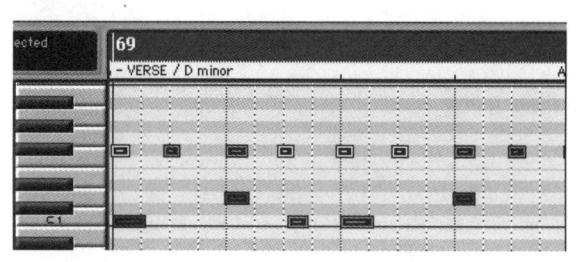

Melody making   6

In the previous chapter we used small melodic fragments to build a kind of musical collage suitable for background use. The fragments remained undeveloped. We'll now have a look at how small fragments of melody can be expanded into larger structures. In other words we will construct a melody.

'Construct a melody! ' I can hear you saying, 'surely melodies aren't constructed but revealed, in moments of divine inspiration, to extremely gifted musical people like, Mozart, Irving Berlin, Lennon and McCartney and the like. Not ordinary people like us.

Not so. The first ideas are often inspirational but the hard work of building and constructing soon takes over. As usual it's one percent brain wave, 99 percent hard slog. So you're in with a chance.

So how's it done? Well, there are no hard and fast rules. However, there are some guidelines and general principles that have worked well over the last few hundred years or so. Why do we remember certain melodies, and not others? In most cases we remember the well crafted ones that are carefully developed from a few distinctive ideas. These ideas, are then repeated and varied to form a complete melody. The two key ingredients are repetition and variation. Without repetition the listener has nothing to hold on to and soon becomes bewildered. Without variation boredom sets in.

> **Info**
>
> To examine the Logic Audio files for this chapter, copy the folders named 'cells' and 'exile' from the CD to your computer.

Cell construction

Don't be frightened of repetition. Without it nobody will be likely to remember anything you compose. A good way of getting started on developing and constructing melodies is to write a short motif or phrase, repeat it several times and introduce variations in pitch. Here is a melody constructed this way (Figures 6.1 and 6.2)

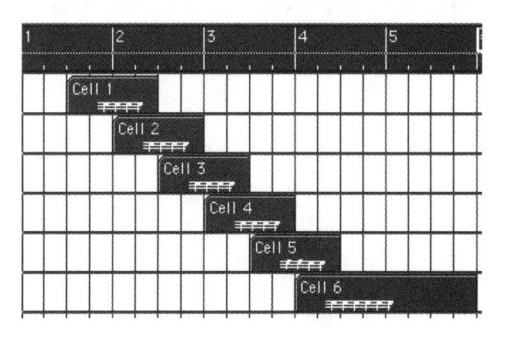

Figure 6.1
Motif cells.

Figure 6.2
Motif cells, staff

After creating a short motif, I duplicated it five times and varied the pitches of the notes each time, to form a continuous flowing melody. I used several tracks, for clarity, but of course, it could all be done on a single track!

- Load cells/cells and examine the sequences one by one.
- Cell 1: The so-called inspirational beginning. Although it ends on the tonic (we are in the key of F) it has an air of expectancy about it which suggests continuation.
- Cell 2: By raising the pitch of all but the first note I was able to create a new phrase. The air of expectancy continues. We are climbing.
- Cell 3: Another copy is added. The pitches are raised and the climbing continues.
- Cell 4: ... and continues
- Cell 5: We begin a descent.
- Cell 6: This time the motif is extended to complete a musical sentence.

Info

If you are stuck for an idea, try constructing a small rhythmic framework and experiment with various pitch combinations.

Musical questions and answers

Another way of developing melody is to create musical statements that suggest an answer. The melody for Exile was constructed this way.

- Take a look at the beginning of the flute part in Exile (exile/exile).

The opening phrase (marked red) poses a kind of musical question that begs an answer. We'll call it Q1. The answer follows in the next phrase (marked blue). We'll call it A1. Although different to Q1 – note how it rises higher in response – the last five notes are a recall of the last five notes of Q1. Already we have repetition with a slight variation (Figure 6.3).

The next phrase (again in red), call it Q2 follows the same rhythmic pattern as Q1 but the notes are completely different. That air of expectancy has been fulfilled and a new question asked. A2 the next phrase (in blue) again answers the question and is a varied repetition of A1.

All this often comes naturally, without thinking. We have merely analysed it. However, if you're stuck for ideas this is a sure fire method of keeping things moving. There are so many ways to achieve this onward flow that a whole book is needed on the subject. You can though, learn a great deal by taking time to listen and analyse other melodies in this way. Reading music, although helpful, is not always necessary.

Figure 6.3
Exile

7 Audio recording

The next project in the book incorporates the use of a pre-recorded audio track containing an improvised saxophone solo behind the main tune. This can be replaced with another instrument or a vocal track. At this point then, it seems appropriate to have a quick look at the basic audio recording procedure and microphone techniques needed to do this. If you don't happen to play an acoustic instrument and can't stand to hear the sound of your own voice use a synthesized sound instead!

Recording vocals

To record vocals, a directional mic mounted on a stand is the usual method and the singer will most likely be standing up. If you have a wobbly wooden floor, isolate the stand from the floor to prevent low frequency rumble travelling up the mic stand and on to your recordings. If you can afford it, a condenser mic is best – AKG C-414, AKG C-3000 or the Audio Technica are good – but a dynamic mic such as the trusty Shure SM57 or SM58 will still produce good results.

Although most vocal mics have built-in wind shields it is still a good idea to use a pop screen. There are several types on the market these days. The DIY alternative, a pair of tights stretched over a bent wire coat hanger does the same job. Apart from preventing sudden pops, if you are recording a vocalist other than yourself, it will also prevent them getting too close to the microphone.

A distance of between 15 and 60 cm between the mouth and microphone is usual, depending on the strength and character of the vocalist, with the mic tilted slightly, either up or down, away from a direct line with the mouth. A greater distance is fine but bear in mind the fact that more gain may be needed and if the vocalist has a quiet voice problems with noise could arise. Keep the mic away from reflective surfaces, walls being an obvious example.

Recording electric guitars

A dynamic mic such as the Shure SM58 is the usual choice for the job. To begin with place it between 15 and 30 cms from the centre of one of the speakers in the amp cabinet. Experiment by moving it off centre from there to alter the tone. Try using two mics, one further away or at the side, or even behind the speaker cabinet. Use a similar method for bass guitar, but place it further away to avoid a boxy sound.

Recording acoustic guitars

A directional mic is best, preferably a condenser type, however reasonably good results can still be achieved with a dynamic mic. Position it about 45 cm from the sound hole. Avoid the temptation to place it any closer unless you want a boomy sound!

Recording brass and woodwind

The SM58 will do fine, but a better choice is a condenser mic. Where you place the mic depends very much on where most of the sound comes from – saxes and brass from the bell, flute from the mouthpiece etc. However, particularly with woodwind, the sound emanates from other parts of the instrument and it is better therefore to keep the mic at a reasonable distance from the player, 45 cm or so is usually OK.

Recording strings

Treat individual stringed instruments such as violin in the same way as the acoustic guitar. If you are fortunate enough to have the space to rcord a small string ensemble, use two mics suspended above the players mounted at right angles to each other for a good stereo image.

From microphone to audio track – the signal route

OK, you are all set to record that blistering solo but how do you actually get the audio signal into Logic? If you are new to recording and find it confusing, here's a summary of the main things to do.

- Connect the audio signal from your external mixer to the audio card input.
- Choose an Audio Path [Audio > Set Audio Recording Path...]. This is where you will store your recorded files. It makes sense to keep them in the same folder as your song file.
- In the Arrange window, select an Audio Object and rename it with a relevant name. This makes it easy to find in the Track Mixer, when you're mixing.
- In the Environment, select the Audio Object and choose an Input.
- Decide on either a stereo or mono Audio Object.
- In either the Arrange or Environment windows, arm the Audio Object by clicking on REC.
- Adjust the input level using your external mixer or your sound card's software mixer.
- Record the audio using the Transport bar, as you do with MIDI Tracks.
- View the recorded audio files in the Audio window [Audio > Audio Window...]

You will be using the Arrange, Audio and Environment (Audio Layer) windows and it's a good idea to have these open together, as a screenset, for an overall view of the proceedings. Figure 7.1 displays these windows as used in Project 6.

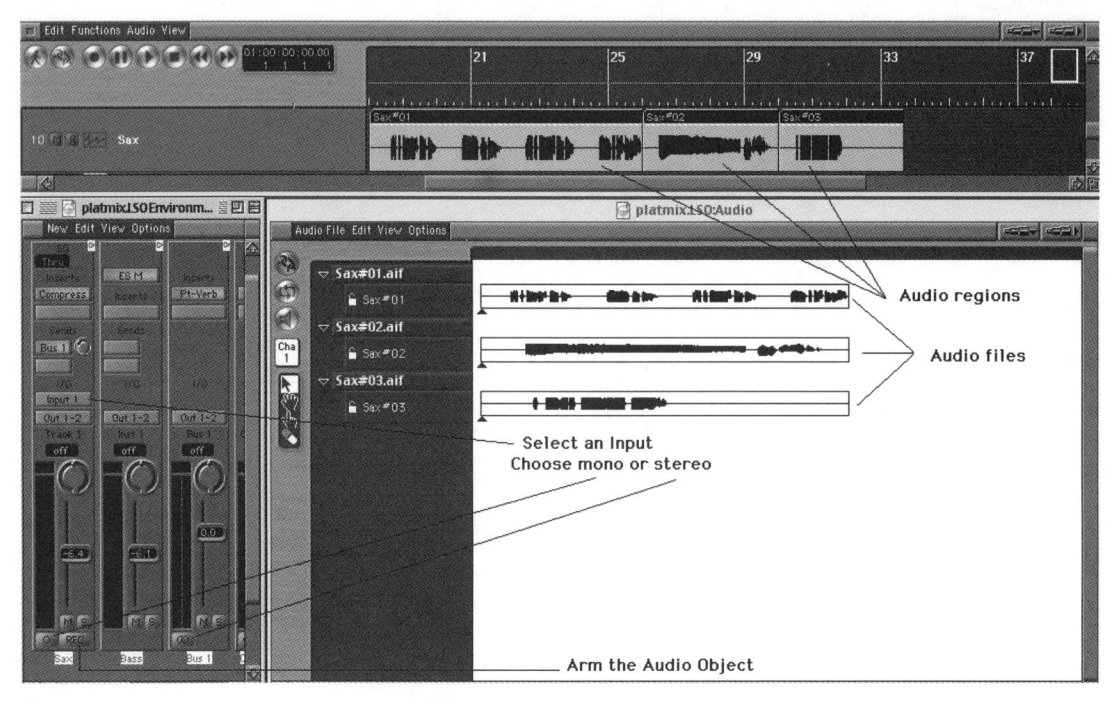

Figure 7.1
Audio screenset.

At the top we see part of the Arrange window displaying the renamed Audio Object, 'Sax', and three separate Audio Regions. These relate directly to the audio files displayed in the Audio window below. On the left we see the Audio Objects contained in the Environment window (Audio Layer).

Project 6 – a football theme

Musical objectives

- Construct a melody from a small melodic 'cell' by applying repetition and pitch variation.
- Compose a rhythmic bass part to compliment the newly invented melody and consider the harmonic possibilities this implies.
- Use three part sectional harmony to build a "brass section".
- Use tenor sax or other instrument to provide an improvised solo behind the main melody.

Logic skills

In the Transform window
- Lengthen a selected group of notes.

In the Arrange window
- Arm and record enable an Audio Object.
- Record an audio track.

In the Adaptive Track Mixer
- Verify input signal, check and adjust audio signal input levels.
- Apply dynamic processors - Compressor and Silver Compressor - to the recorded audio signal.
- Apply send effects - PlatinumVerb and SilverVerb - to the recorded audio signal.

In the Transport window
- Set up a drop-in/drop-out recording region.
- Utilize the Audio Instrument ES E.

Preparation

1 From the CD, copy the folder named 'project6' to your computer.
2 On your computer create a folder called 'mywork6' or something similar in which to save your work.
3 From the project6 folder, open the template - templt6.
4 In your new 'mywork6' folder, save the template as myproj6 or something similar.

> **Info**
>
> The template has a time signature of 4/4 and the tempo is 140 bpm. Now this may be a bit fast for you. If so scroll the tempo to suit you. When listening back, scroll back to 140 bpm.

> **Info**
>
> When loading example files containing MIDI settings its quite likely that you will initially hear the wrong sounds (very likely those from a previous project or song). Use [Options > Song Settings > Used Instrument MIDI Settings] to correct them. A faster way – quickly cursor up or down the tracks using the arrow keys on your computer keyboard.

The assignment

You have been commissioned to compose a 1 minute theme for a football program. It must be upbeat in tempo, attention grabbing, and uplifting in character.

To gain an overall picture, at this point you may prefer to listen to the finished thing rather than let things unfold. To do so, load one of the three mixes contained in the Proect 6 folder.

Take 1

Track 1: (Ch 1) Brass 1 | Tpt 1
Sequence Parameters box: Qua 8C Swing
Instrument Parameter box: Cha 1, Prg 61
Transport Bar: (L) 1.1.1 (R) 3.1.1

A blank Arrange page presents a daunting prospect. But wait – an initial fragment of melody has presented itself and stubbornly sticks in the mind, refusing to go away (Figure P6.1 and P6.2). Let's record it and take it from there. I've chosen a Brass Synth sound to get that 'uplifting' quality. To achieve a loose march feel, I've chosen 8C Swing from the Quantize menu. The result of the chosen groove can be seen in the List Edit window. Note how all the off-beat eighth notes are delayed by 81 ticks (Figure P6.3).

Figures P6.1 and P6.2
A fragment of melody, Score and Matrix view

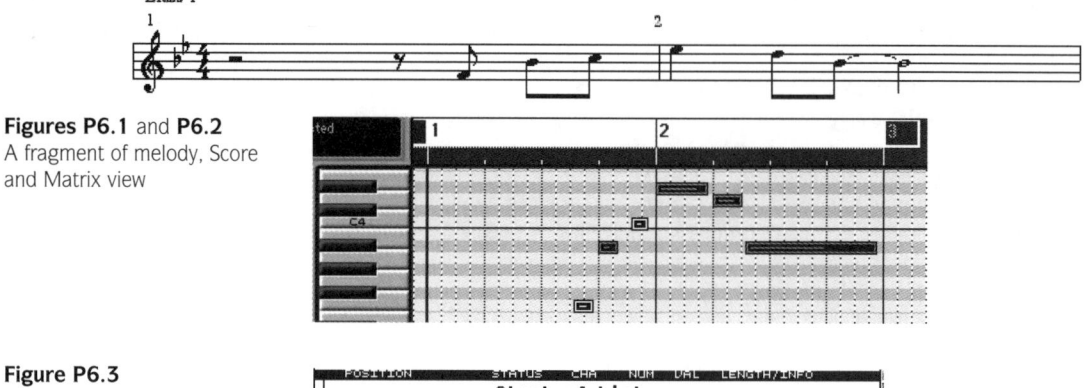

Figure P6.3
Delayed eighth notes

- Save song – compare with project6/6.1a.

The plan here is to construct a theme by repeating this fragment and applying variation to it in the various editors.

First let's repeat the sequence seven times. [Functions > Object > Repeat Objects... x7]. We now have a 16 bar section comprised of eight two bar sequences to work on. I shall refer to these sequences or objects as Cells 1 – 8. (Figure P6.4).

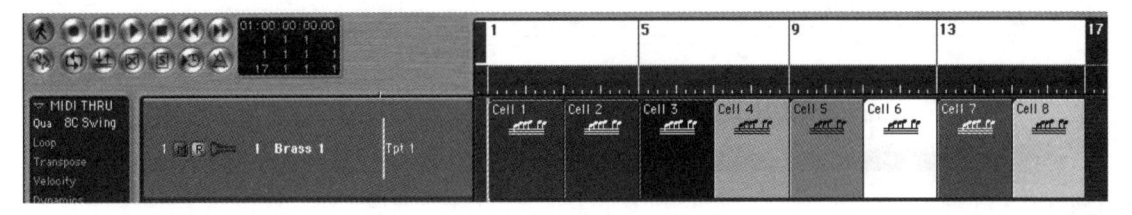

Figure P6.4
Cells 1 – 8

Here's what we do (Figures P6.5 and P6.6):

1 Cell 1: bars (1 – 3) Although it ends on the tonic (we are in the key of Bb) it definitely suggests continuation so ...
2 Cell 2: (bars 3 – 5) By keeping the rhythmic framework of Cell 1 intact and altering the pitch of the notes we generate more melody. Alter the pitch of the notes as shown by using either the Score or Matrix Editors.

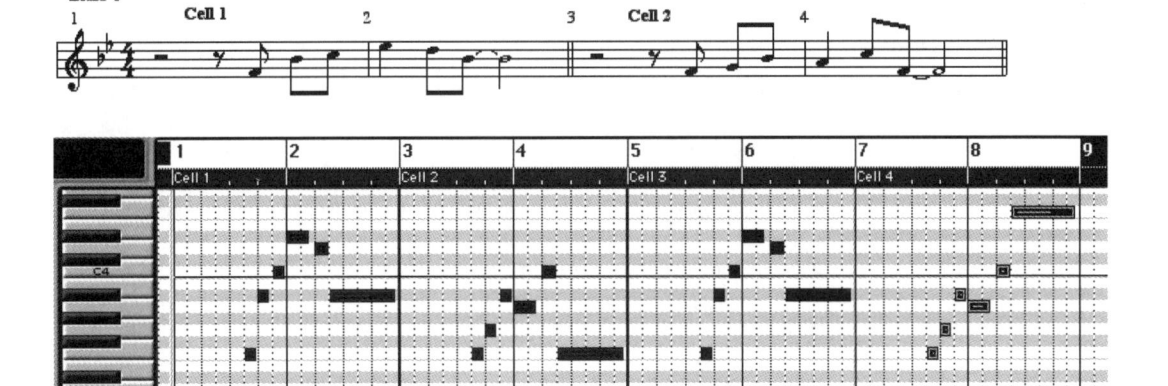

3 Cell 3: (bars 5 – 7) The initial phrase can be repeated again without risk of boredom so leave it untouched.
4 Cell 4: (bars 7 – 9) We use the same note pattern as Cell 2 but raise the last note by an octave. This really does suggest continuation. Upwards! The brief stated uplifting, remember?
5 Save song – compare with project/6.1b.

Figures P6.5 and P6.6
Cells 1 – 4, Score and Matrix view

After saving the song we continue with Cells 5 – 8 (Figures P6.7 and P6.8).

1 Cell 5: (bars 9 – 11) We change the notes to continue the ascent to C and have the melody fall from there.
2 Cell 6: (bars 11 – 13) Our listeners are unconsciously expecting yet another fall in pitch and a repetition of the familiar rhythmic pattern, but this time we surprise them by applying the brakes. We delete the first

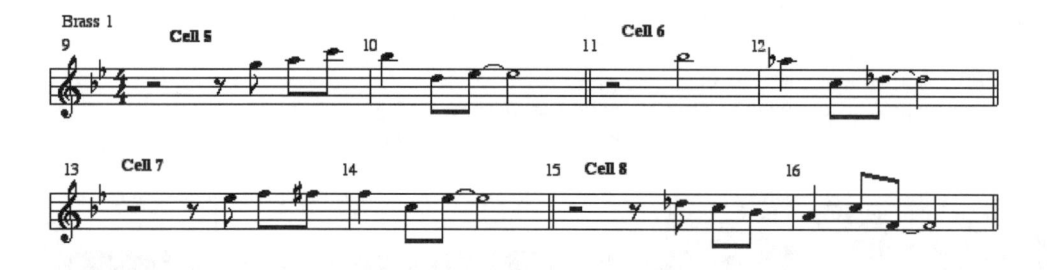

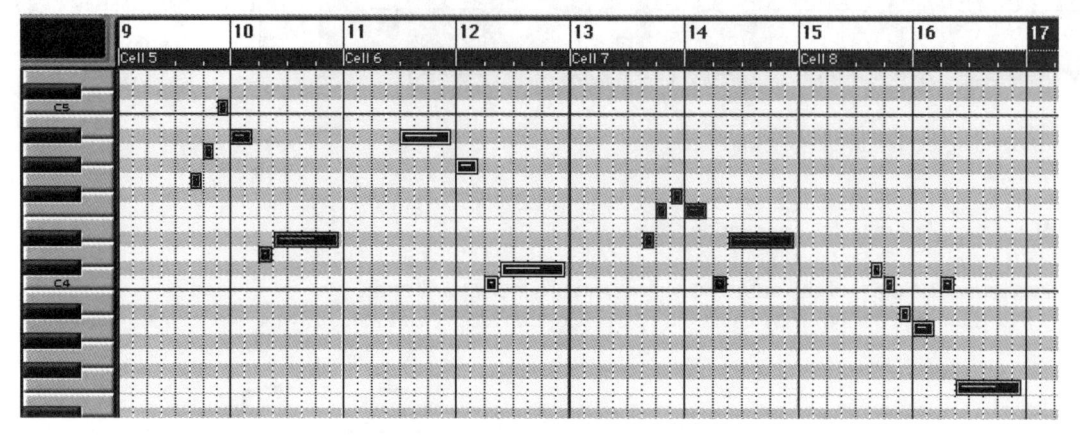

Figures P6.7 and **P6.8**
Cells 5 – 8, Score and Matrix view

three notes – in the Score or Matrix Editors – and replace them with a half note (minim) half a beat earlier than expected, and continue the descent.

3 Cell 7: (bars 13 – 15) We hover around a bit ...
4 Cell 8: (bars 15 – 17) ... before landing back on the tonic, where we began.
5 Save song – compare with project/6.1c.

Play it through. I think the last note in each cell should be a bit longer by a couple of beats. Now there are several ways to do this. We could alter each note manually with the pencil tool, but that's tedious. A quicker way would be to select all the notes in the Matrix Edit window and use the pencil tool to lengthen them all together, in one fell swoop. However, I'm feeling masochistic and have decided to do it the hard way. Yes it's time to get to grips with that most terrifying of Logic's features the Transform window (Figure P6.9).

Before we start, let's have a look around. In the Arrange window, select the track and open the Transform window [Windows > Open Transform]. Pretty scary eh! Now, don't quit Logic and throw the book out of the window, it really isn't too bad. You know what they say? It's easy when you know how.

There are two main sections in the Transform window:

- Select by Conditions – where we select events to change.
- Operations on selected Events – where the selected events are changed.

Directly above them are three buttons to implement the changes. Select and Operate is the most commonly used. To the left of these are two boxes. The topmost is for selecting and creating Parameter Sets. The lower is a checkbox which allows you to hide all the unused pull-down menus in the conditions and operations boxes.

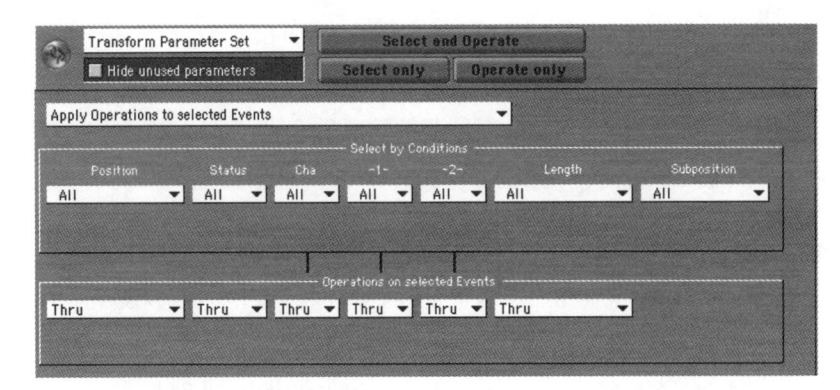

Figure P6.9
Transform window

The eighth notes we need to lengthen (one in each object or cell) are all exactly the same length because we duplicated them. In my example this length is 0.2.1.76 but will almost certainly be slightly different in yours. I'm going to lengthen them by two whole beats. The lowest note is F3 and the highest is F4.

The chances are, when you opened the Transform window it was displaying a pre-defined Parameter Set. Logic comes with over a dozen of these but none of them will do what we need. So, we'll have to create our own set.

Follow these steps:

1 In the Parameter Set box, choose **Create User Set!** from the drop-down menu. The text will change to Transform Parameter Set. All the menu boxes are now displayed in the Conditions and Operations sections below.

Figures P6.10, 6.11 and 6.12
Conditions status, pitch and length boxes

Working from left to right in the Conditions section and using the drop-down menus:

2 In the Status box select: = and Note. (Figure P6.10).
3 In the Pitch box choose: Inside and enter F3 and F4. (Figure P6.11).
4 In the Length box choose: = and enter a value (Figure P6.12).

Note that the Position, Cha, Vel and Subposition boxes remain unaltered. Now, in the Operations section:

5 In the Length box choose: Add and enter 2.0.0 (Figure P6.13).
Note that the Position, Status, Cha, Pich and Vel remain unaltered.
6 Press the Select and Operate button (Figure P6.14).
You have now successfully changed eight events at once in a matter of moments. Well that's the theory anyway.

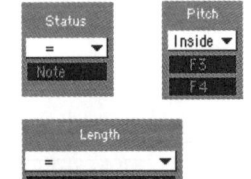

Figure P6.13
Operations length box

What we actually told Transform to do was:

- Conditions – find all notes between F3 and F4 that are 0.2.1.76 in length and:

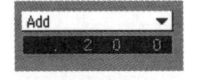

Figure 6.14
Select and Operate button

> **Info**
>
> The Transform window has the power to perform complex edits and transformations of MIDI data.

- Processing Section – lengthen those notes by two whole beats.

To complete the procedure:

1 Type a name (Lengthen Notes) in the Parameter Set box.
2 Check the Hide Unused Parameters box and all the unaltered menus disappear.
3 In the Arrange window, lengthen the last sequence – Cell 8 (bars 15 – 17) by one bar to accommodate the longer note we have just created and glue all the sequences together.
4 Save song – compare with project/6.1d.

Now this was a very simple operation compared to the complex tasks that Transform can handle and was used as an example to demonstrate the power of this feature. Using it will become easier in time, I promise! Believe me, it really does save a great deal of time. Check out the pre-sets.

What next? It obviously needs a pretty lively rhythm but all I can hear at the moment (mentally) is a four-to-the-bar bass drum.

Take 2

> *Track 8:* (Ch 10) Standard Drum | Kick Drum
> *Sequence Parameters box:* Qua 1/8 – note
> *Instrument Parameter box:* Cha 10, Prg 0
> *Transport Bar:* (L) 2.1.1 (R) 6.1.1

Follow these steps:

1 Record the four bars of kick drum (C1) (Figure P6.15, P6.16 and P6.17) and copy the resulting sequence three times to complete sixteen bars [Functions > Object > Repeat Objects... x3] Choose Aliases from the dialogue box.
2 Save song – compare with project/6.2.

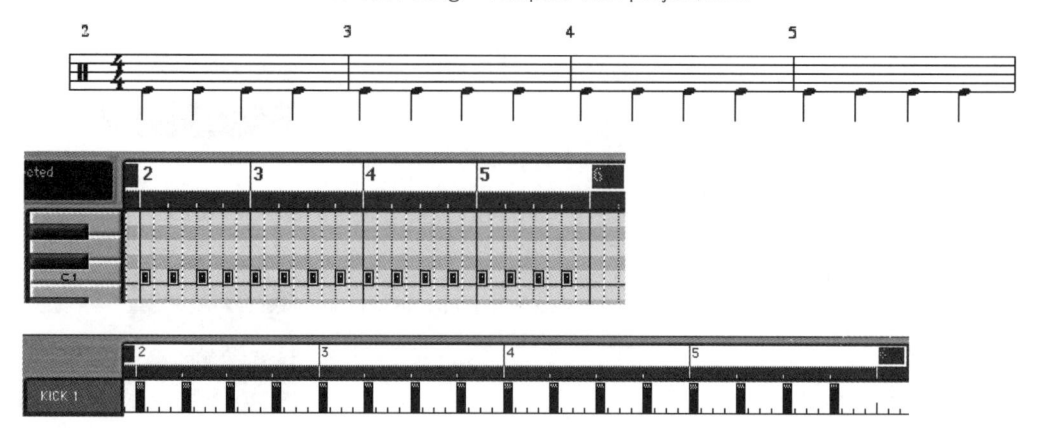

Figures P6.15, P6.16 and P6.17
Kick drum, Score, Matrix and Hyperview

A bass line is needed. Because of the drum machine style kick drum, a bass synth sound suggests itself. Time to launch Logics ES M.

Take 3

Track 6: (Ch 1) AudioInst 1 | ES M
Sequence Parameters box: 8B Swing
Instrument Parameter box: Cha Inst 1, MIDI Cha 1
Transport Bar: (L) 2.1.1 (R) 18.1.1

Follow these steps:

1 Open the Track Mixer [Windows > Open Track Mixer], select the Audio Instrument 1 object (Bass), and from the drop-down menu, insert the ES M (Figure P6.18). A blue button named ES M appears.
2 Click on the blue button to reveal the ESM itself and select the acid preset [factory 2 > acid] (Figure P6.19).

3 Record the bass (Figures P6.20 and P6.21). Breaking it down into four bar cycles is favourite! Probably the easiest way. Note bars 6 – 10 are a repeat of bars 2 – 6, so copying that will save time. Note too, the Quantize setting is 8B Swing, slightly different to the brass track.. The choice of notes for the first eight bars (2 – 10) are pretty straightforward stuff. Tonic to Dominant etc. Things get more interesting in bars 10 – 16 where chromatic movement is beginning to suggest more adventurous harmony.
4 Save Song – compare with project/6.3.

Info

The ES M (es mono) is a specially designed bass synthesizer in permanent portamento mode (one note glides to another). It can, of course, be used for lead synth work if assigned to higher voices.

Figure P6.18
Inserting ES M.

Figure P6.19
Choosing a pre-set.

Tip

Writing the bass line and melody will often suggest interesting harmony that may never have occurred had the chords been worked on first.

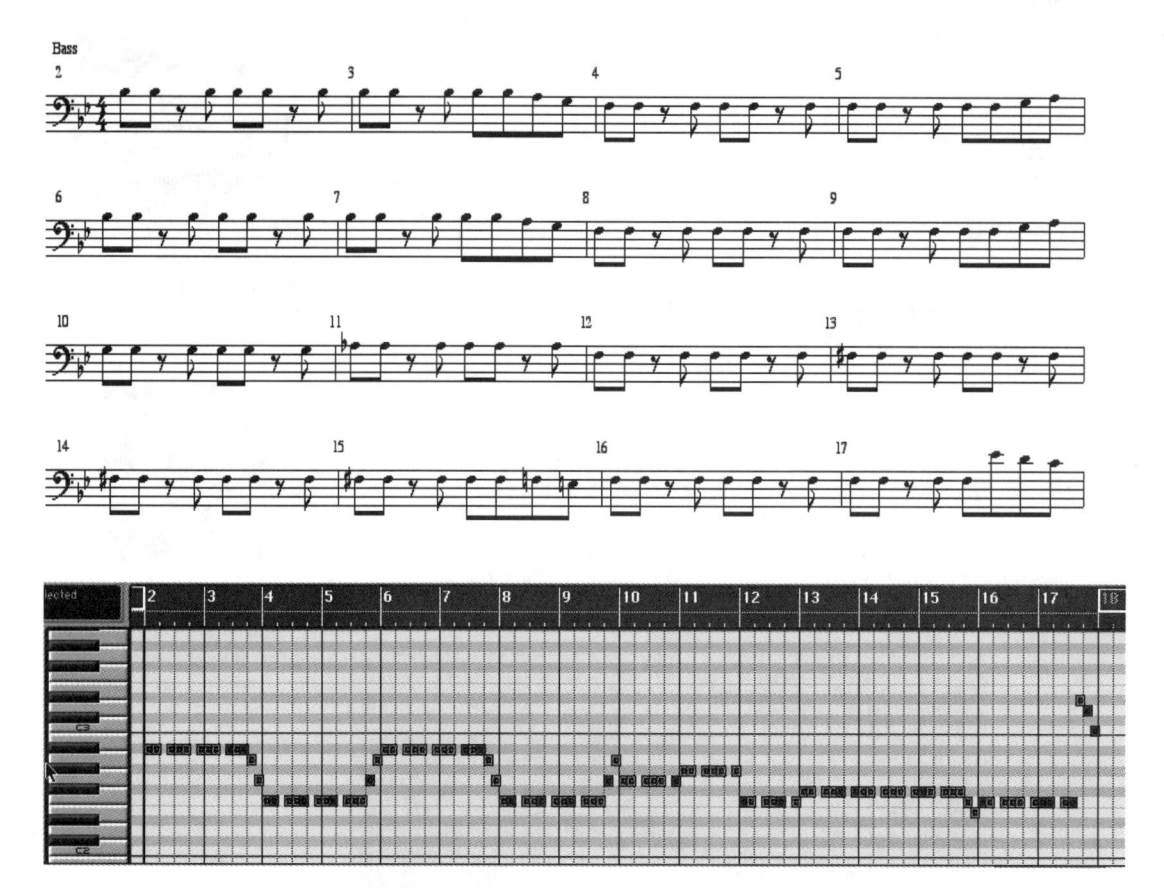

Figures P6.20 and **P6.21**
Bass, Score and Matrix view

Take 4

Track 2: (Ch 2) Brass 1 | Tpt 2
Sequence Parameters box: Qua 8C Swing
Instrument Parameter box: Cha 2, Prg 61
Transport Bar: (L) 2.1.1 (R) 18.1.1

Follow these steps:

1 Record Tpt 2 (Figure P6.22 and P6.23). Break it down if necessary. It's a harmony part and we will examine it closer after the next track is recorded.
2 Save Song – compare with project/6.4.

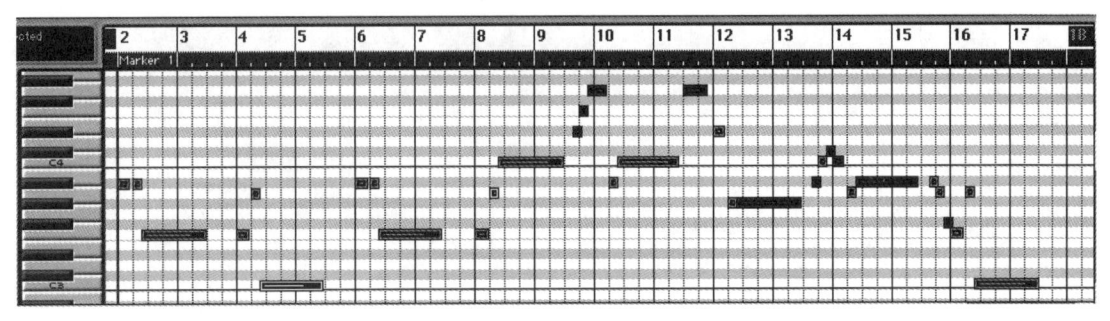

Take 5

Figures P6.22 and **P6.23**
Trumpet 2, Score and Matrix view

Track 3: (Ch 3) Brass 1 | Tpt 3
Sequence Parameters box: Qua 8C Swing
Instrument Parameter box: Cha 3, Prg 61
Transport Bar: (L) 2.1.1 (R) 18.1.1

Follow these steps:

1 Record Trumpet 3 (Figure P6.24 and P6.25). Break it down if necessary.
2 Save Song – compare with project/6.5.

By selecting all the brass sequences we can examine the harmony in the Score window. Three-part, close voicing is used to provide a full brassy sound and for the first half of the tune, the anacrusis (a posh word for 'pick-up' – the note(s) preceding the main part of a musical phrase) is left to just Brass 1.

The kick drum is providing the 'umph' required but a simple snare drum part will give it a lift.

> **Tip**
>
> As rule of thumb, in three part sectional harmony, it's a good idea to have the outside parts form a duet and move together in parallel sixths where possible.

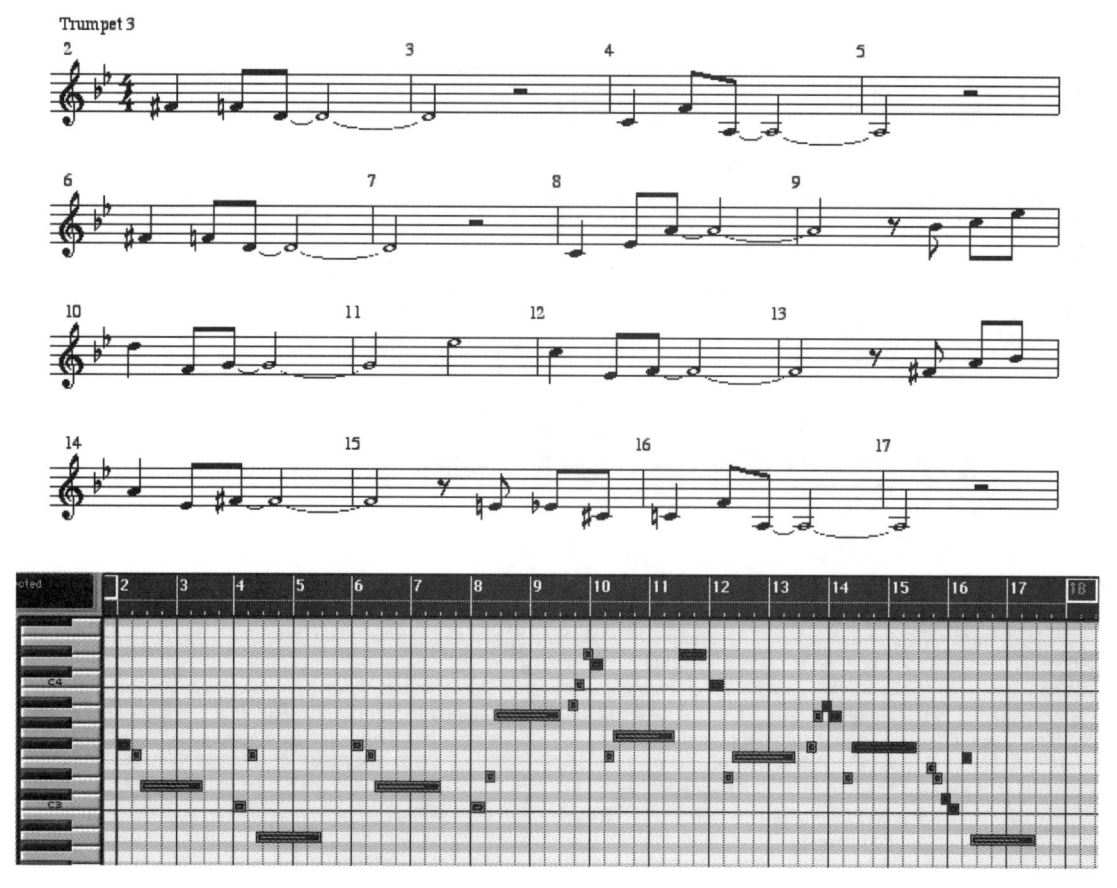

Figures P6.24 and **P6.25**
Trumpet 3, Score and Matrix view

Take 6

Track 8: (Ch 10) Standard Drums | Snare
Sequence Parameters box: Qua 8B Swing
Instrument Parameter box: Cha 10, Prg 0
Transport Bar: (L) 2.1.1 (R) 6.1.1

Follow these steps:

1 Record the Snare (Figure P6.26 and P6.27). Note, we have returned to quantizing at 8B Swing.

2 Copy the resulting sequence three more times to complete 16 bars.
3 Save song – compare with project/6.6a.

The entire 16 bars will stand a repeat, but first:

1 With the Song Line on 2.1.1, use the Scissors tool, make a cut between bars 1 and 2 on the Trumpet 1 track, to isolate the 'pick-up'.
2 Drag a copy of the new sequence (bar 1) and drop it on top of bar 17 to create another pick-up.

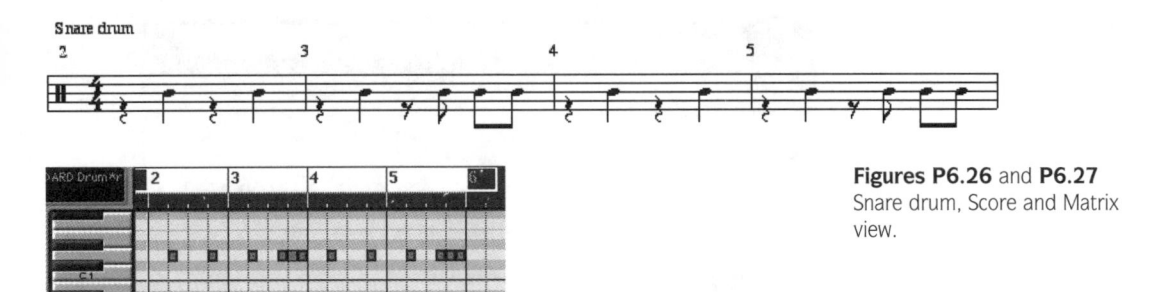

Figures P6.26 and **P6.27**
Snare drum, Score and Matrix view.

3 With the Glue Tool, join all the sequences on each track together between bars 2 – 18. Do not include the 'pick-up' at bar 1.
4 Now set the Locators at (L) 2.1.1 (R) 18.1.1, select everything between [Edit > Select Inside Locators] and repeat once [Functions > Object > Repeat Objects... x1]. Choose Copies from the dialogue box.
5 Save Song – compare with project/6.6b.

The piece is now one minute long. Time for an ending. It has to be short and snappy to fit the brief.

Take 7

1 Set the Locators to (L) 34. 1. 1 (R) 37. 1. 1
2 Record the Brass, Bass and Kick Drum parts in Figure P6.28. The brass needs to be straight here so use 1/8 – Note quantization.
3 Save Song – compare with project/6.7.

Figure P6.28
Brass, bass and kick drum parts

Figures P6.29, P6.30 and **P6.31**
Matrix views of Trumpet 1, Trumpet 2 and Trumpet 3.

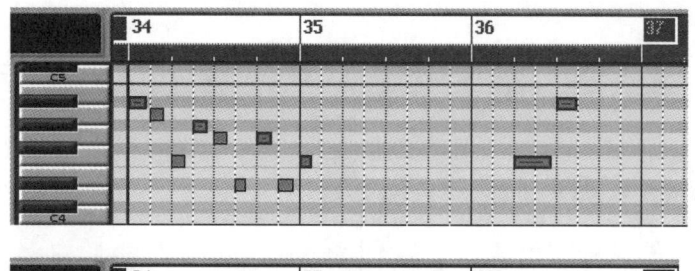

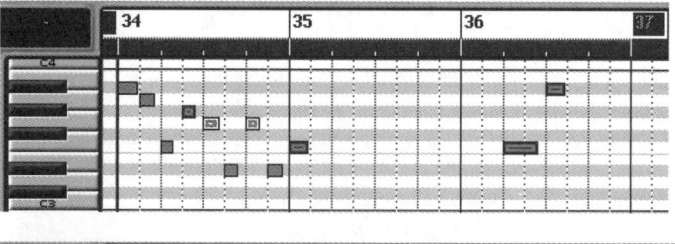

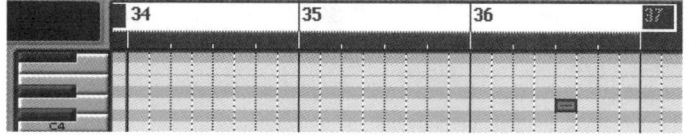

The repeated section from bar 18 onwards sounds fine but there's room for something else. What will provide a lift? The whole piece is dominated by brass and a touch more will not do any harm. Something very high might do the trick – Maynard Ferguson style.

Take 8

Track 4: (Ch 4) Brass 1 | Solo Tpt
Sequence Parameters box: Qua 8C Swing
Instrument Parameter box: Cha 4, Prg 61
Transport Bar: (L) 18.1.1 (R) 37.1.1

Follow these steps:

1 Record the solo trumpet part. (Figure P6.34 and P6.35) Break it down into four bar chunks if need be. Note the transposition (12) in the Instrument Parameters box. The notes in Figure P6.34 are written one octave lower than they sound.
2 Save Song – compare with project/6.8.

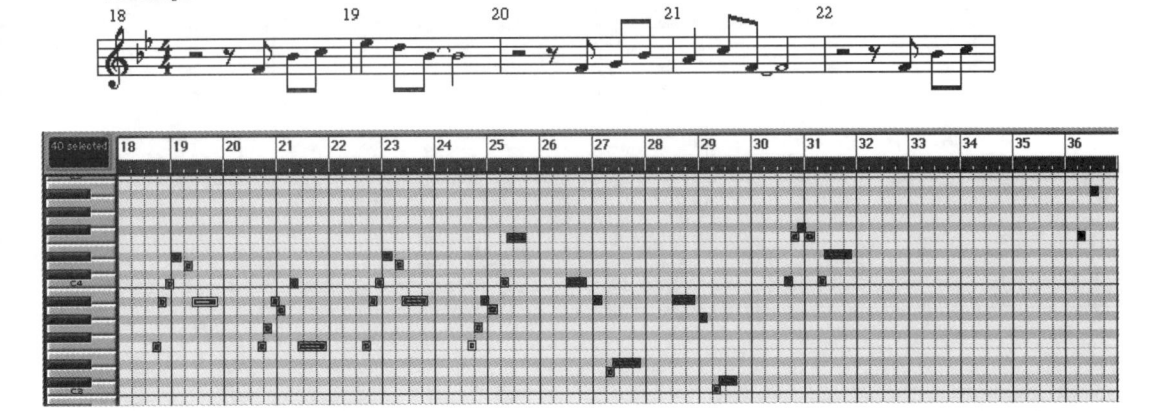

Up to now we have left the harmony to the brass. On reflection, I think the piece may now benefit from some rhythm guitar. Something sparse and choppy.

Figures P6.34 and **P6.35**
Solo trumpet, Score and Matrix view.

Take 9

Track 2: (Ch 5) Overdrive Gt.
Sequence Parameters box: Qua 8C Swing, Dynamics 75%
Instrument Parameter box: Cha 5, Prg 29
Transport Bar: (L) 2.1.1 (R) 18.1.1

Guitar parts are usually written an octave higher than they sound, even on a Concert score. In this case, as we are playing a keyboard and giving a general impression of what a guitar might do here, it has been left at concert pitch. Play exactly as written. Now I don't know about you, but I tend to play rather hard when bashing out chords, guitar style, on a keyboard. This is why I've used 75% compression. Unless you're a rather more gentle soul, you may have to do the same! I also broke it down into four bar sections. Follow these steps:

1 Record the first guitar part (Figures P6.36 and P6.37).
2 Save Song – compare with project/6.9.

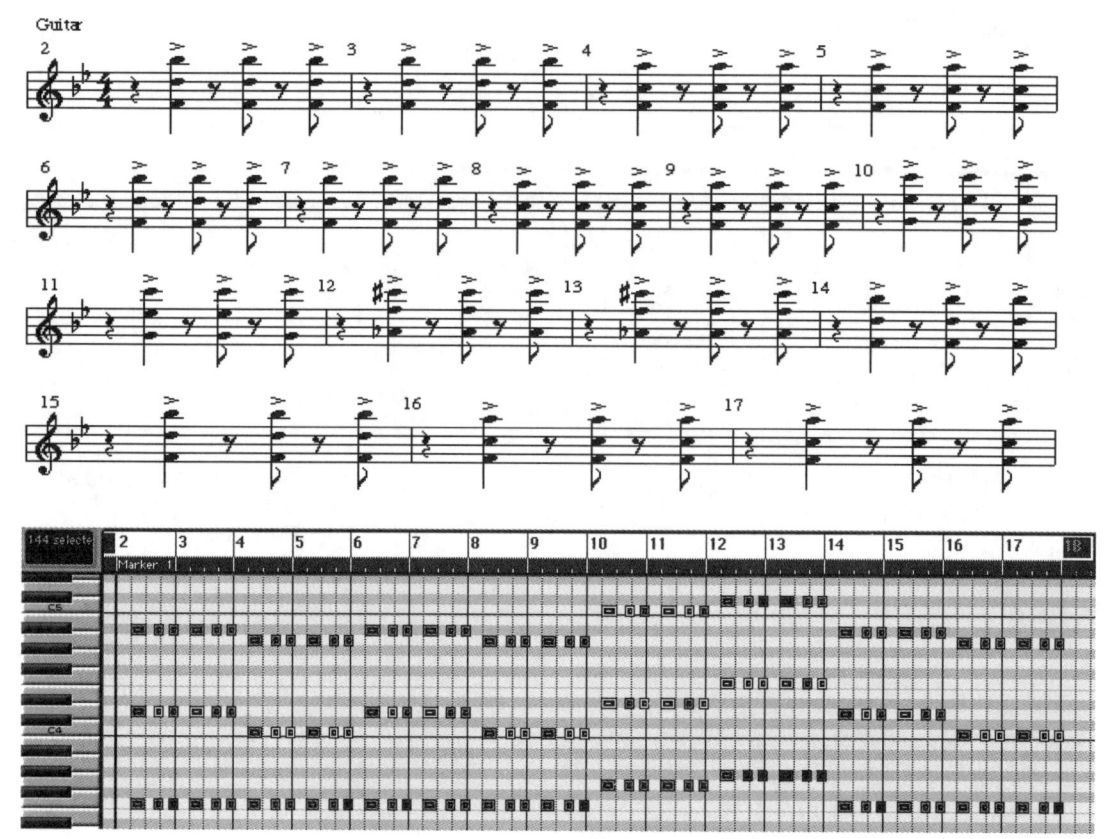

Figures P6.36 and **P6.37**
Guitar, Score and Matrix views.

3 Select the newly recorded guitar sequence(s) (bars 2 – 18) and repeat them between bars 18 and 34 using Functions > Object > Repeat Objects... (x1).

Now for the coupe de grace!

Take 10

Track 10: (Ch 10) Standard Drums | Referee
Sequence Parameters box: Qua 16C Swing
Instrument Parameter box: Cha 10, Prg 0
Transport Bar: (L) 35.1.1 (R) 37.1.10

Follow these steps:

1 Record the whistle (Figure P6.38), using note B3 on the keyboard.
2 Save song – compare with project/6.10.

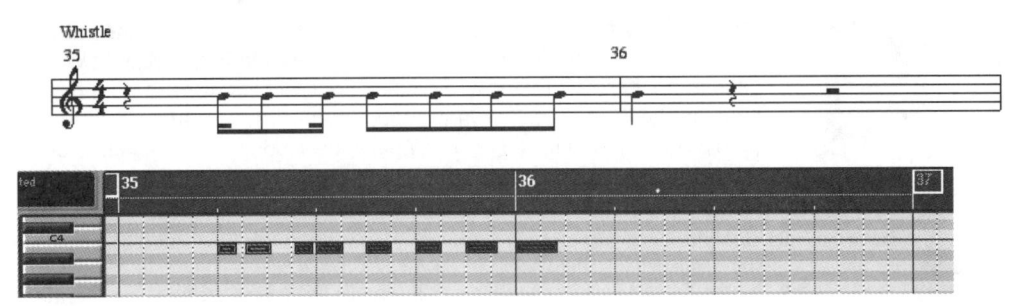

Figures P6.38 and P6.39
Whistle, Score and Matrix view.

Take 11 – We record an audio track

OK, apart from the mixing we're finished. Or are we? Now I'm a saxophone player and although I'm happy enough with the solo brass part, I can mentally hear a tenor sax answering those brass phrases. So I recorded an audio track.

Obviously, every reader can't follow me step by step as with the MIDI side of things so far (unless they happen to play tenor sax), but I can explain the process. This will serve as a guide to the general principles involved in recording vocal tracks and acoustic instruments.

Before proceeding further, I would advise readers – if they have not yet done so – to thoroughly read their manuals for a complete understanding of how Logic handles the audio recording process. On the surface, in the Arrange window, audio objects look the same as MIDI objects and are manipulated in a similar fashion. However, behind the scenes, in the editors, things are somewhat different.

OK, here's how it's done. Recording a saxophone is not so different to recording vocals. I'm using a good quality condenser mic, in preference to a dynamic type and routing the signal through an external mixing console to my sound card. To record the audio track I:

1 In the Environment, made sure an Audio Object existed.
2 In the Arrange window, selected the Audio Object and renamed it 'Sax'.
3 Armed the Audio Object by clicking on the button marked R, to the left of the Audio Object (Figure P6.40). The Audio Object was now prepared for recording.
4 Set a Record Path [Audio > Set Audio Record Path... or Key Command A]. A dialogue window appeared (Figure P6.41). I checked the box in the

> **Tip**
>
> To make them easy to find in the Track Mixer, rename Audio Objects with a meaningful name before actually recording.

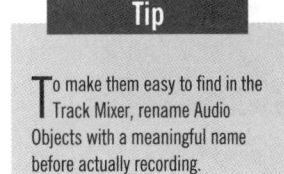

Figure P6.40
Arming an Audio Object

Figure P6.41
Setting a recording path

> **Tip**
>
> When setting a recording path, choose the Song Recording Path as opposed to Global Recording Path to save all your audio in the same folder as your Song files.

Figures P6.42a and **b**
Mono track and stereo track.

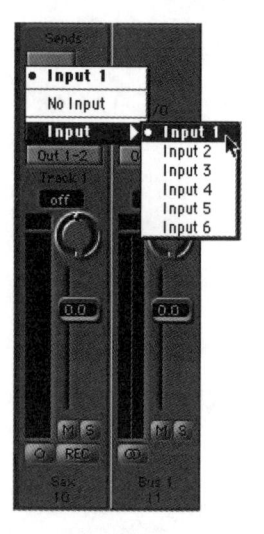

Figure P6.43
Choosing Inputs.

Info

The faders in the Track Mixer are not used to alter the input level, only the recorded signal.

Figure P6.44
Auto-drop button

Tip

To avoid distortion, make sure the input signals do not exceed 0.0dB.

top panel – Use Audio Object Name for Filename. The third panel from the top – Maximum Recording Time: 5 min. – should be checked by default. It's best left that way! Selecting Song Recording Path from the menu in the fourth panel from the top, I then clicked on the Set button (audio device), and in the resulting dialogue window, typed a name for the audio files and chose a path to store them. I chose the name Sax and navigated a path to the project6 folder.

5 The sax, as would most vocals, was recorded in mono. I verified this in the Track Mixer (Figures P6.42a and P6.42b).

6 In the Track Mixer, I chose Input 1 (Figure P6.43) – audio was entering on the left input of my stereo card as a mono signal.

At this point I began playing the saxophone. Partly to warm up! – and partly to check the input level. This was adjusted using the output fader on the external mixer until a satisfactory level was achieved in the Track Mixer.

By blowing as loud as I knew I would be when actually recording, the red clipping indicator (at the top of the fader) was lighting up. This was cured by reducing the fader level on the external mixer.

Everybody finds their own way of doing things. It's possible to cycle record several takes and either choose the best or edit them. I prefer to record a 'take' and listen back. If I like it – great. If I don't, I delete it and record another straight away. In Logic this 'take' – referred to as an Audio Region – is not actually deleted, but remains on the hard disk, in the Audio window, so I can change my mind and recall it later.

Audio regions are the equivalent of MIDI sequences. In the Arrange window, they look similar but there is a difference. Regions are only a reference to parts of audio files on the hard disk whereas sequences actually contain MIDI data.

Playing the saxophone and recording – pressing record buttons on and off at the same time etc. – is an unwieldy, and potentially dangerous task to say the least. Fortunately the whole process can be automated in Logic. (Not the sax playing of course!) Before recording the sax I:

1 Muted the solo trumpet on Track 4.
2 Set the Locators at (L) 18. 1. 1 (R) 26. 1. 1
3 Activated the Auto-drop button on the Transport bar (Figure P6.44).

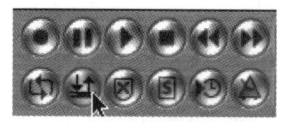

4 Scrolled back a few bars and pressed Play. When the Song Pointer reached bar 18, on came the red light and Logic entered record mode. I blasted away on the tenor sax for eight bars, and when bar 26 arrived, off went the red light, and back on the stand went the tenor sax. A brand new Audio Region looking very much like its MIDI counterpart had appeared on the audio track.

After listening back I decided that I could do better. I could slice it up and drop in and out at various points but in my experience it's better to get things down in one take. So, I deleted the Audio Region (remember this is non-destructive, it's still in the Audio Window) and repeated the recording process. This time I'm happy. I can live with that.

Again, I knew what I wanted between bars 26 and 30, and I knew it wasn't easy, which is why I didn't include it in the first take! A very high altissimo C (concert Bb) may well need a few attempts. It did! After a satisfactory take I moved on to the last four measures. Easy by comparison. One take was all that was necessary. I now had three Audio Regions. After playing back the whole piece, I decided to keep them all.

Now, I don't have unlimited hard disk space, (and neither, I expect, do you) so I opened the Audio window [Audio > Audio Window...] (Figure P6.45). Here I found four audio files, one of which is referenced to the Audio Region I deleted earlier from the Arrange window. I only wanted to keep the three good takes so I deleted it permanently [Select and backspace].

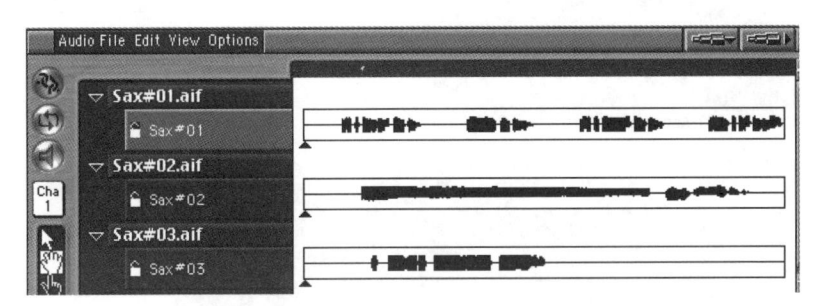

Figure P6.45
Audio window

The mix

I kept things simple on all of them and a summary is all that is necessary.

- Bass and drums are in the centre.
- Brass 1 is in the centre because it carries the tune.
- Brass 2 and 3 are supporting parts and are set at lower levels than brass 1. However they are panned left and right and provide the main stereo spread.
- Solo trumpet is in the centre but not too loud (muted if the sax is used).
- Guitar is placed left and kept low in the mix.

Info

There are three mixes on the CD, Platinum (Figure P6.46), Gold and Silver, each using slightly different plug-ins. However, should a plug-in not be found, just replace it with the equivalent included with your particular version.

Figure P6.46
6platmix.lso

Modest amounts of reverb are applied to the MIDI tracks.

6silvmix
On 6silvmix, Siver Compressor (Figure P6.47) has been inserted on the sax track and a vocal pre-set has been applied. The sax is then sent to SilverVerb (Figure P6.48) via Bus 1 and treated with the Hall pre-set as a starting point.

Figure P6.47
Silver Compressor

Figure P6.48
SilverVerb

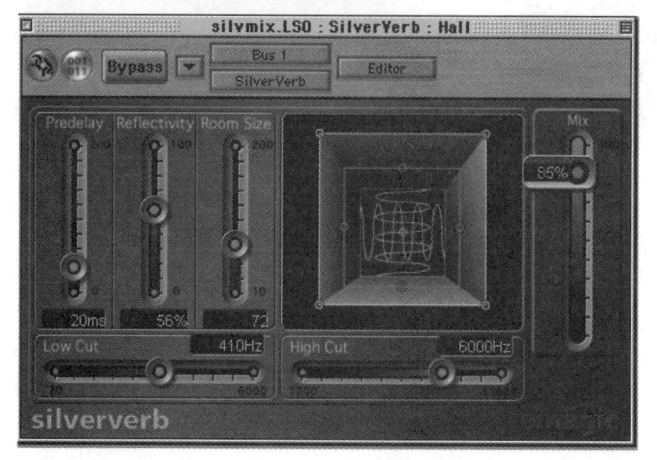

6goldmix
On 6goldmix, Compressor (Figure P6.49) has been inserted on the sax track and a vocal pre-set has been applied. The sax is then sent to GoldVerb (Figure P6.50) and treated with the Long Reverb pre-set as a starting point.

Figure P6.49
Compressor

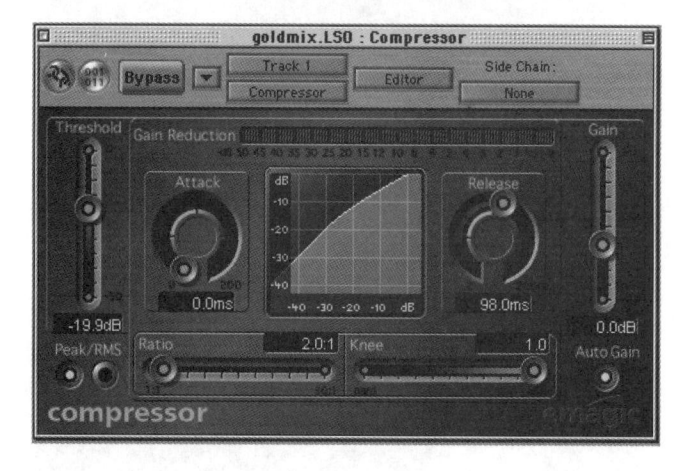

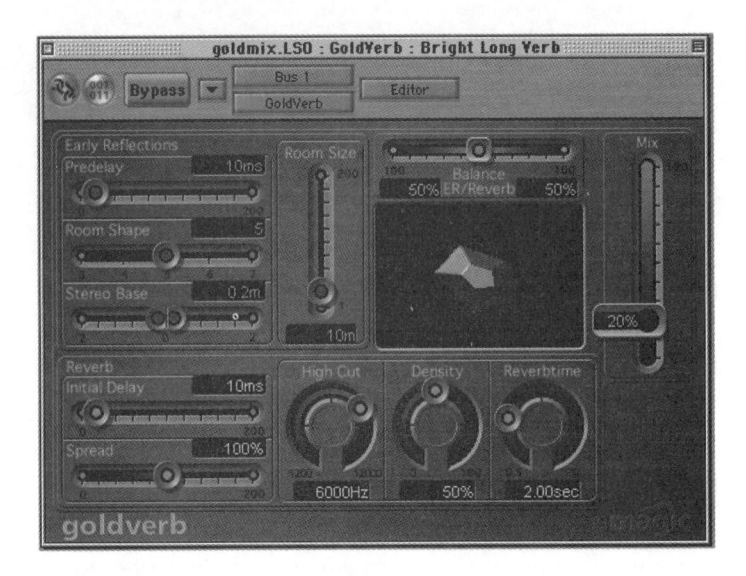

Figure P6.50
GoldVerb

6platmix

On 6platmix, Compressor (Figure P6.49) has been inserted on the sax track and a vocal pre-set applied. The sax is then sent to PlatinumVerb (Figure P6.51) where a Bright Long Reverb pre-set is applied as a starting point. The overall effect is similar to many up-front pop vocal treatments.

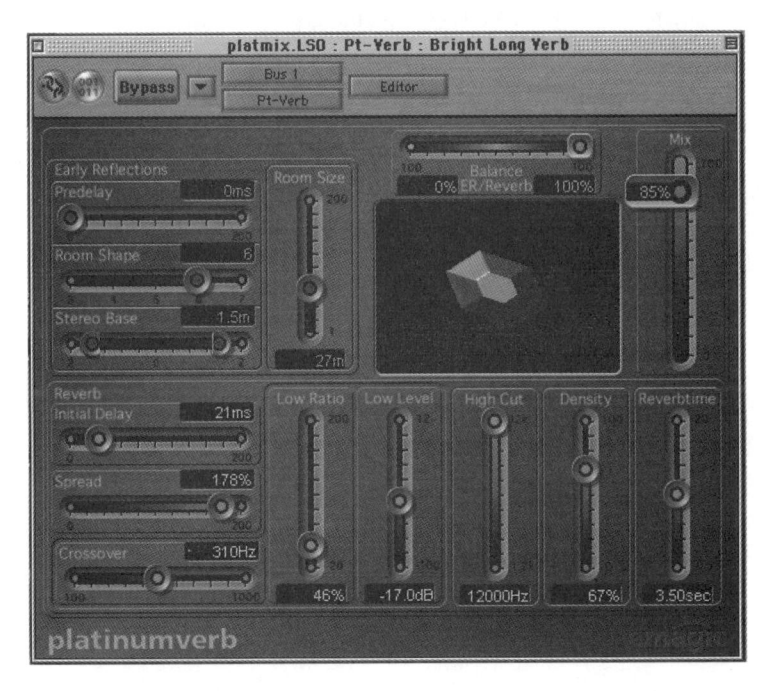

Figure P6.51
PlatinumVerb

View and listen to the results in project6/6silvmix, project6/6goldmix and project6/6platmix alternately muting Track 4 (MIDI – solo trumpet) and Track 10 (Audio – tenor sax) to compare versions. Now experiment with the compressors and send effects. That's how you learn. Happy twiddling!

8 Create illusions – a big band radio jingle

> **Info**
>
> To examine the Locic files for this chapter, copy the folder named 'big band' from the CD to your computer.

Jack has a small studio set-up and runs Emagic Logic software. Some local jingle work has been coming his way recently and a client calls to say that he needs some big band swing music, 1940s style. He really liked the Vangelis 1980s style synth music Jack supplied for the last job, but this is a bit different. A jazz big band is comprised of 17 instruments for a start and some pretty smart arranging techniques are needed. He decides to take on the challenge, confident that he can handle the sequencing. A friend, fresh from music college, agrees to score the 30 seconds of music required.

A day or so later his mate arrives clutching a 'hot' score for five saxes, four trumpets, four trombones and rhythm section but they soon realize that no matter how skillfully things are sequenced using sampled sounds, the end result will not be convincing enough.

It's always a little tricky to sequence acoustic instruments, even with the very best sampled instrument sounds available, but the problem seems to compound itself when a large ensemble is needed such as a symphony orchestra. Brass bands are particularly difficult, due mainly to the fact that all the instruments are using the same type of sample. As the layers are piled on, a kind of MIDI soup develops. The problem is not quite so bad with a jazz big band, but care must taken to avoid too thick a texture.

Back to Jack's problem. What's the solution? Well, he could book a large studio or a local hall and hire 17 musicians, but in Jack's case, that's the route to bankruptcy. He has another idea. Apart from being a dab hand at arranging his pal also plays a mean saxophone. Jack decides to create an illusion.

Audio and MIDI Tracks combined

Once a large collection of MIDI instruments are combined as an ensemble it soon becomes obvious, even to the untrained ear, that synthesized sounds are being used. In Jack's case hiring 17 musicians is out of the question so he decides to ask his friend to replace the virtual saxophone section with the real thing. Five saxes are used in the score, two altos, two tenors and one baritone. He doesn't own a baritone so they decide to leave that as it is.

- Open Logic Song File bigband/jitterbug (Figure 8.1).

Entitled 'Jitterbug Jump' this is a 29 second 'sting,' composed in a 1940s big band swing style and originally intended for use as library music. It's very similar to Jack's tune!

Figure 8.1

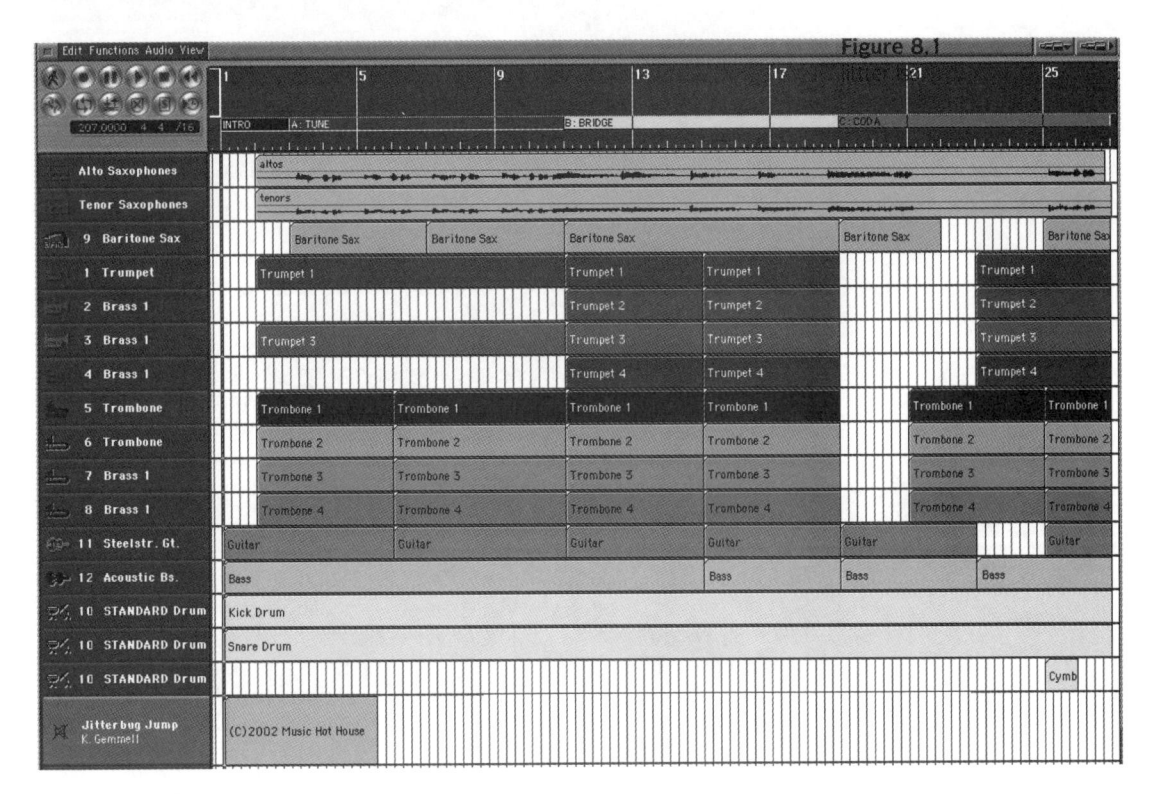

Jitterbug Jump

This version has in fact been heavily edited from around five minutes to 30 seconds to achieve a punchy fast moving sound track suitable for the role of background music to a radio jingle or similar use. This editing requires a great deal of savagery on the part of the composer. It's no good being precious about one's art in a commercial world. Things have to go. In this case it was four and a half minutes of music including a tenor saxophone jazz chorus. The Marker track indicates the construction.

Intro	This was reduced from four bars to two.
A	The main tune, carried by trumpets, backed by riffing saxes and wailing trombones and reduced from 16 bars to eight.
B	The bridge, eight bars long and carried by saxophones survives intact!
C	A huge cut to a coda and ending.

By moving quickly from one section to another within a 30 second framework the listener's attention is kept throughout. Of course it all gets shoved in the background behind somebody talking anyway, and that's another reason not get too intense about cutting things out.

From top to bottom we have two audio tracks, 11 MIDI tracks and three drum tracks.

The first track contains two alto saxophones and the second, two tenor saxophones. You may be wondering if I used two players on each track. I did not. Neither did I play two saxophones at once! 'Jitterbug Jump' was originally recorded on a 16 track analogue tape machine and each saxophone had its own track. To save unnecessary overload on my computer CPU (and yours) I doubled them up whilst transferring them across to Logic.

It's worth taking a closer look at 'Jitterbug Jump' because many of the topics and principles discussed in this book so far are used here.

The saxophone section

Just as a magician distracts our attention away from what he does not wish us to see, the same technique is used here. By keeping the saxophone section fairly prominent (but never dominant) our attention is focused on these 'real' instruments rather than the artificial ones. Even the fifth member of the section – the sampled baritone sax – is not really noticeable as such. There is a fair bit of unison doubling throughout and had this been a MIDI saxophone section, much pruning would have be needed to 'thin' the texture at those points. With real saxes it doesn't matter. The more the merrier.

The trumpet section

Only the lead trumpet has been assigned to the GM preset 'Trumpet' (Prg. 56) This sets it apart from trumpets 2, 3 and 4 which use the 'Brass Section' preset (Prg. 61) Where unison doubling occurs, care has been taken to avoid using the same GM voice. For example, in the opening bars, only trumpet 1 and 3 are playing. If trumpets 2 and 4 were added, MIDI soup would result. However, if this were a real brass trumpet section all four trumpets would be playing in unison here.

The trombone section

Trombones 1 and 2 have been assigned to the GM preset 'Trombone' (Prg. 57) and trombones 3 and 4 to the 'Brass Section' preset. (Prg. 61) As with the trumpets, although unison doubling does occur it only happens on separate presets to avoid unnecessary thickening of the texture.

Pitch bend was used between bars 2 and 11 to create the slurs. Viewed In the Score window, the notes are displayed at a constant pitch. Use either the Matrix, Event List or Hyper editors to view the pitch bend data.

The rhythm section

Piano has been omitted. In a real big band it would very likely be used. However the acoustic guitar provides all the rhythm and harmony needed here along with acoustic bass. Guitar chord voicing is mostly open and restricted, in the main, to four notes.

The drums have been split over three tracks. In this kind of music a real drummer may well play his snare drum on all four beats in a bar and accent the second and fourth. However we achieve much the same effect here by omitting the first and third beats.

The mix

The instruments are panned roughly as a big-band would be seated. The only exception being bass and drums which are placed in the centre for balance. Modest amounts of reverb have been added to MIDI instruments and the saxophones are treated with a small dose of Logic's AVerb. Any more would have created too much of a distancing effect.

75% compression was added to all the MIDI Tracks as they were played and smoothes out any jerkiness due to my keyboard playing shortcomings!

Project 7 – a TV sitcom theme

Musical objectives

- To construct a melody using only the notes of a blues scale.
- Fill in the harmonic and rhythmic background with the sounds of a blues band.

Logic skills

- Re-record MIDI tracks as audio tracks ready for further processing and mixing.
- Use Logic's built in plug-in, Limiter, to reduce audio signal peaks.
- Use Track Automation and Hyper Draw to control volume and effects.

Preparation

1 From the CD, copy the folder named 'project7' to your computer.
2 On your computer, create a folder called 'mywork7' or something similar in which to save your work.
3 From the project7 folder, open the template – templt7.
4 In your new 'mywork7' folder, save the template as myproj7 or something similar.

The assignment

You've been commissioned to write a theme tune for a television sitcom. The main characters are two young, likeable 'no-hopers'. You know the kind of thing. They can't get the girls, they can't keep their jobs, and at the end of every episode, despite temporary success, are back where they started. The music required is to be fairly upbeat (it is a comedy) but at the same time, bluesy. Length: just under one minute. The producer is keen on tenor sax and if possible, would like it featured.

This is a bit of a tough one. How do we keep it lively and at the same time bluesy? An upbeat 12 bar blues maybe. The problem with '12 bars' is that it is hard to find a distinctive melody to fit the rather played out chord sequence. In my experience it is always a good idea to work on the melody first and harmony second. So how do we compose an instrumental blues melody line? Well the blues scale is a good starting point.

When stuck for ideas whilst writing melodies it sometimes helps to limit oneself to just a few notes. A pentatonic scale for example will provide a set

> **Info**
>
> A pentatonic scale consists of just five notes and is found in a huge amount of folk music around the world as far ranging as China, Africa and Scotland. Auld Lang Syne, for example, uses only the notes of the pentatonic scale.

> **Tip**
>
> It's possible to invent simple tunes very quickly using the pentatonic scale on the piano. How? – by using only the black notes starting with F#.

> **Info**
>
> A blues scale has only one more note than the pentatonic scale, but what a difference it makes! It's used frequently by jazz and rock soloists alike. In the key of C it will consist of: C D Eb E G A. but is usually played beginning on A, like this: A C D Eb E G A and referred to as the A blues scale.

of notes suitable for something rustic and folky. In our case the blues scale, which contains one more note than a pentatonic scale, is just the job.

A pentatonic tune in the key of C will consist of the following notes: C D E G A

OK, which key? Well tenor sax was mentioned in the brief. The key of Bb/Gm is a good key for tenor and actually puts the player in the nice easy key of C/Am. So the blues scale for this key is G Bb C C# D F G. 'That's all very well,' I can hear you say, 'the blues scale is fine for improvisation but surely it is too limiting for composing a theme tune.' Well, it's surprising just how much can be done with those six notes particularly if more than one blues scale is used. For this tune we are also going to use the C blues scale, C Eb F F# G Bb C and the D blues scale, D F G G# A C D. Let's construct a tune.

> **Info**
>
> Why does the key of Bb put the tenor saxophone player in the key of C? Because it is a transposing instrument. A tenor saxophone is pitched in Bb. When a pianist plays the note Bb, at concert pitch, the tenor sax player blows a tone higher – the note C. Likewise if the pianist was to play Eb then the tenor sax player would again play a tone higher – the note F. Of course they are really both playing the same note. The tenor sax player is just thinking, and as far as he is concerned, playing in a different key.

So, music for the tenor saxophone is notated a tone higher than it actually sounds. Now this is sometimes convienient for the player and reduces the number of flats he would have to play if his instrument was pitched in C. The key of Ab, concert pitch, (four flats) puts him in Bb (two flats) for instance. However, it is not so good for him in sharp keys. For example, the key of C, concert pitch, will put him in the key of D containing two sharps. The key of E (four sharps) puts him in F# (six sharps).

Other common transposing instruments are:

- In Bb: trumpet, clarinet, soprano sax
- In Eb: alto sax, baritone sax
- In F: cor anglais, French horn

Some instruments, such as the piccolo and guitar, sound one octave higher than they are notated on the staff. Others such as the double bass and bass guitar sound one octave lower than written.

To gain an overall picture, at this point you may prefer to listen to the finished thing rather than just let things unfold. To do so, load project7/7platmix (7goldmix or 7silvmix depending on your version).

> **Tip**
>
> When loading example files containing MIDI settings its quite likely that you will initially hear the wrong sounds (very likely those from a previous project or song). Use [Options > Song Settings > Used Instrument MIDI Settings] to correct them. A faster way – quickly cursor up or down the tracks using the arrow keys on your computer keyboard.

Take 1

Track 1: (Ch 1) Grand Piano
Sequence Parameters box: Qua 8 & 12
Instrument Parameter box: Cha 1, Prg 0

> **Info**
>
> The template has a time signature of 4/4 and the tempo is 105 bpm. Now this may be a bit fast for you. If so scroll the tempo to suit you. When listening back, scroll back to 105 bpm.

Because a blues shuffle feel is required here the Quantization has been set to 8T. The melody will eventually be played on tenor sax but we will construct it first using a piano pre-set.

To help you decide how to break it down here's a brief analysis of the melody (Figure P7.1).

Figure P7.1
The melody.

- Bar 1 poses a musical question, bar 2 answers it. Bars 1 to 3 then, are a phrase and uses all six notes of the G blues scale.
- The phrase is repeated between bars 3 and 5 but – for variation and continuation – the last note has been changed from Bb to G.
- Bars 5 to 7 is a repetition of the first phrase but this time uses the C blues scale. It's repeated between bars 7 and 9 with pitch variation on the last two beats.
- Bars 9 to 11 is an exact repetition of the first phrase using the G blues scale.
- Bar 11 uses the D blues scale. Bar 12 is a repetition but uses the C blues scale.
- Bar 13 is an exact repetition of bar 1. Bar 14 is a new ending phrase using part of the G blues scale.

Follow these steps:

Figures P7.2, P7.3 and **P7.4**
Matrix views of the melody, first section, second section, and third section.

1 Record the melody in Figure P7.1 How you do it is up to you. If you are an accomplished keyboard player it can be done in one pass. It's more likely that you will opt to record it in sections (Figures P7.2, P7.3, and P7.4).
2 Save Song – compare with project 7/7.1.

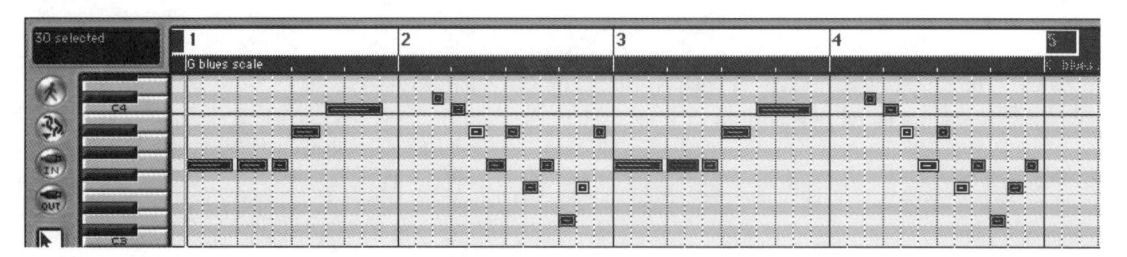

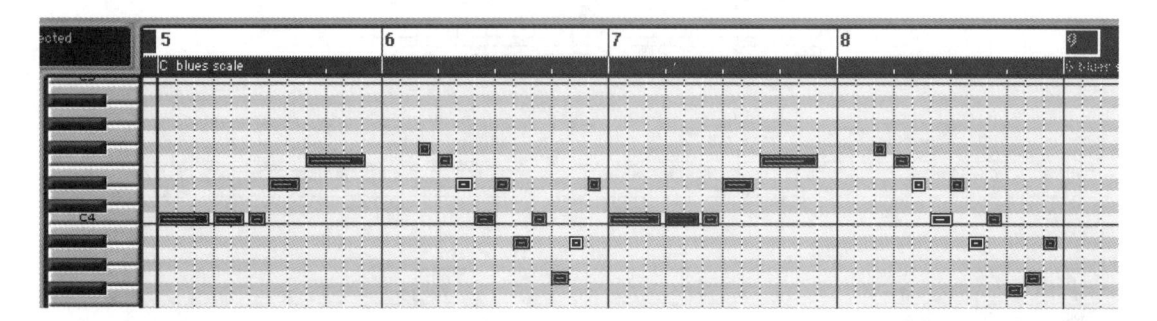

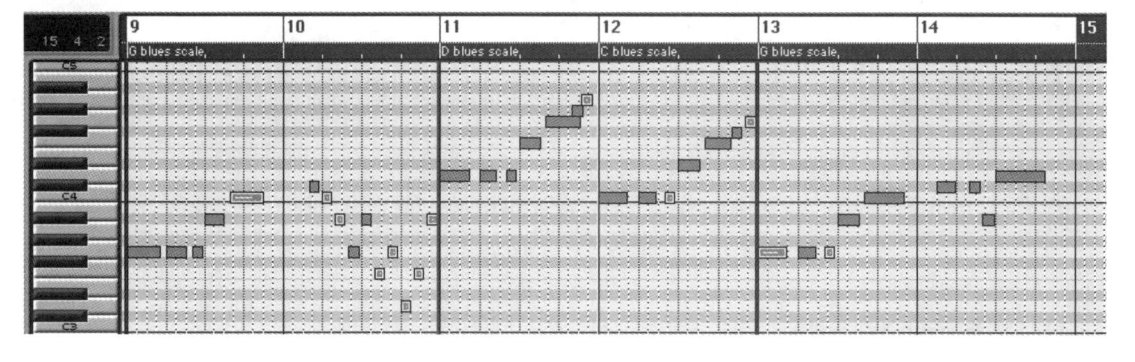

That's a chunk of the tune finished. The backing suggests itself.

Project 7 – a TV sitcom theme   141

Take 2

Track 1: (Ch 1) Fingered Bs.
Sequence Parameters box: Qua 8 & 12
Instrument Parameter box: Cha 2, Prg 33, Trannspose –12

For the bass a nice simple eighth note shuffle on the root note of each blues scale is really all that's needed. You can of course improvise on this, as would a real player. Keeping it simple though, for now at least, will help establish a clear harmonic structure.

Follow these steps:

1 Record the bass (Figure P7.5). (Note the transposition, –12). Even though the notes are written straight, play them with a triplet feel. Record it in sections maybe (Figures P7.6 and P7.7). Again how you break it down is up to you. It is not too difficult to play in one pass, except maybe for the last bar, which can be done separately. Have a go!
2 Save Song – compare with project7/7.2.

Figure P7.5
Bass part.

Figures P7.6 and **P7.7**
Matrix views of the Bass, first and second section.

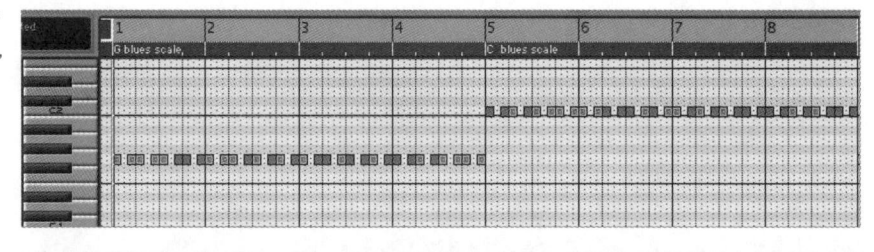

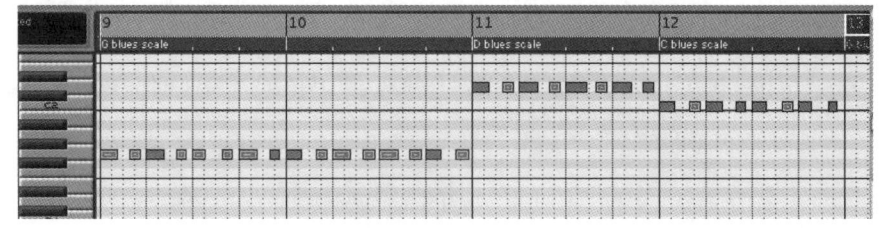

Take 3

> *Tracks 5, 6 and 7:* (Ch 10) Standard Drum | Kick Drum | Snare Drum | Crash Cymbal
> *Sequence Parameters box:* Qua 8 & 12
> *Instrument Parameter box:* Cha 10, Prg 0
> *Transport Bar:* (L) 1. 1. 1 (R) 14. 1 1

Again simplicity is the key to a solid track here so, in a shuffle style:

1 On track 5, record the kick drum (C1) (Figures P7.8 and P7.9).
2 On track 6, record the snare drum (D1) (Figures P7.10 and P7.11).

Figures P7.8 and **P7.9**
Kick drum, Score and Matrix view

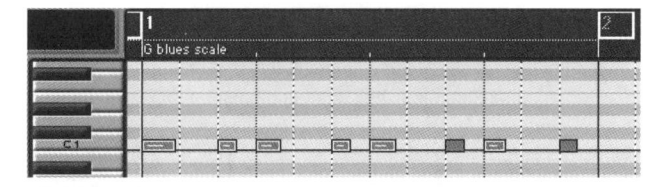

3 Record the snare drum fill (L) 14. 1. 1 (R) 15. 1. 1 (Figures P7.12 and P7.13).
4 On track 7, record the crash cymbal (C#2) on the first beat of bars 1, 5 and 9.
5 Save Song – compare with project7/7.3.

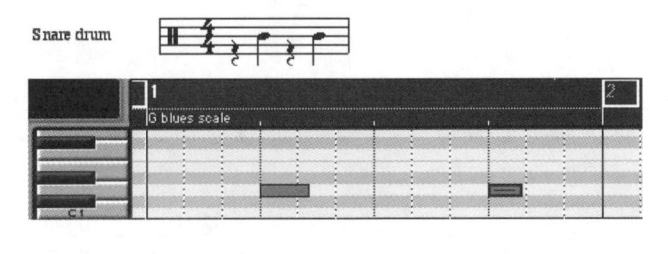

Figures P7.10 and **P7.11**
Snare drum, Score and Matrix view

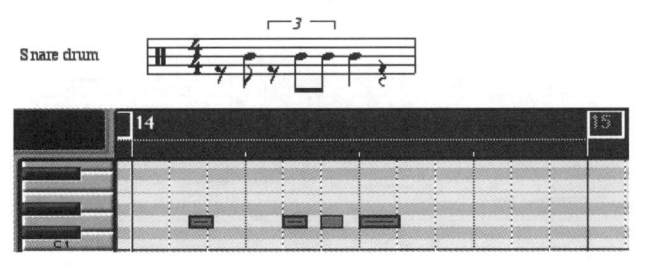

Figures P7.12 and **P7.13**
Snare drum fill, Score and Matrix view

It's coming along isn't it? Play it through and try to imagine the two characters, maybe in a dole queue or being rebuffed by two pretty girls. What next? Well we have the basics of a blues band. Why not add guitar and organ to complete the line up?

Take 4

Track 3: (Ch 3) Distortion Gt
Sequence Parameters box: Qua 8 & 12 Dynamics 50%
Instrument Parameter box: Cha 3, Prg 30

Guitar parts are usually written an octave higher than they sound, even on a Concert score. In this case, as we are playing a keyboard, it has been left at concert pitch. Play exactly as written.

1. Record the guitar (Figure P7.14). You may well have to break it down into sections (Figures P7.15, P7.16 and P7.17). Again it's a simple shuffle. A real guitar player would undoubtedly do more. However this creates the mood perfectly well.
2. Save Song – compare with project 7/7.4.

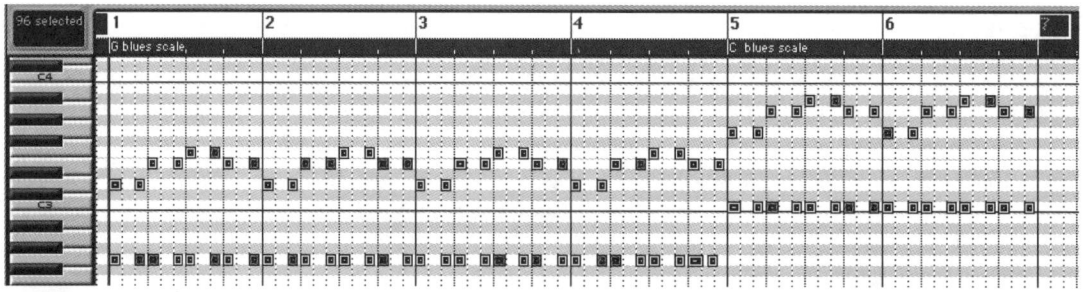

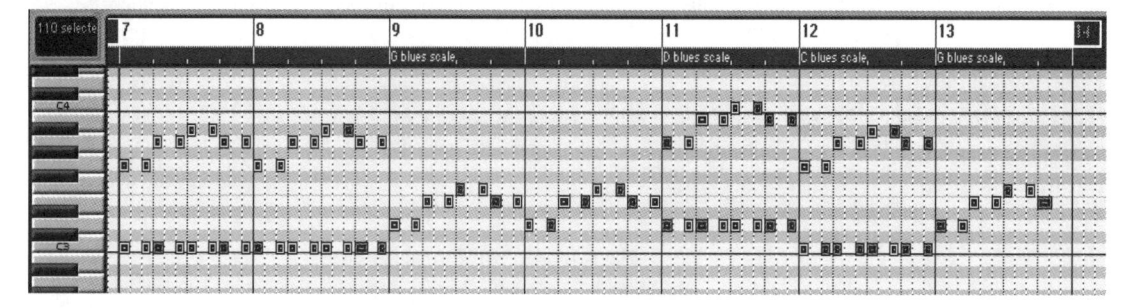

Figures P7.14 – P7.17
Guitar, Score view.
Guitar, first section, Matrix view.
Second section.
Guitar, last bar, Matrix view.

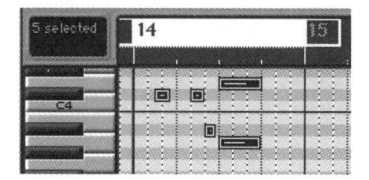

Take 5

Track 4: (Ch 4) RockOrgan
Sequence Parameters box: Qua 8 & 12 Dynamics 50%
Instrument Parameter box: Cha 4, Prg 18, Transpose +12

To repeat the shuffle pattern again would be too much of a good thing. So what to play? Something a little more spaced out is called for that does not interfere with the melody. How about this:

1 Record the organ (Figure P7.18). It sounds good one octave higher than written so use the transpose feature in the Instrument Parameters box (+12). Again, do it in sections if your keyboard skills are not too hot! (Figures P7.19, P7.20 and P7.21).
2 Save Song – compare with project7/7.5.

Figures P7.18 – P7.20
Organ, Score view.
Organ, first section, Matrix view.
Second section, Matrix view.

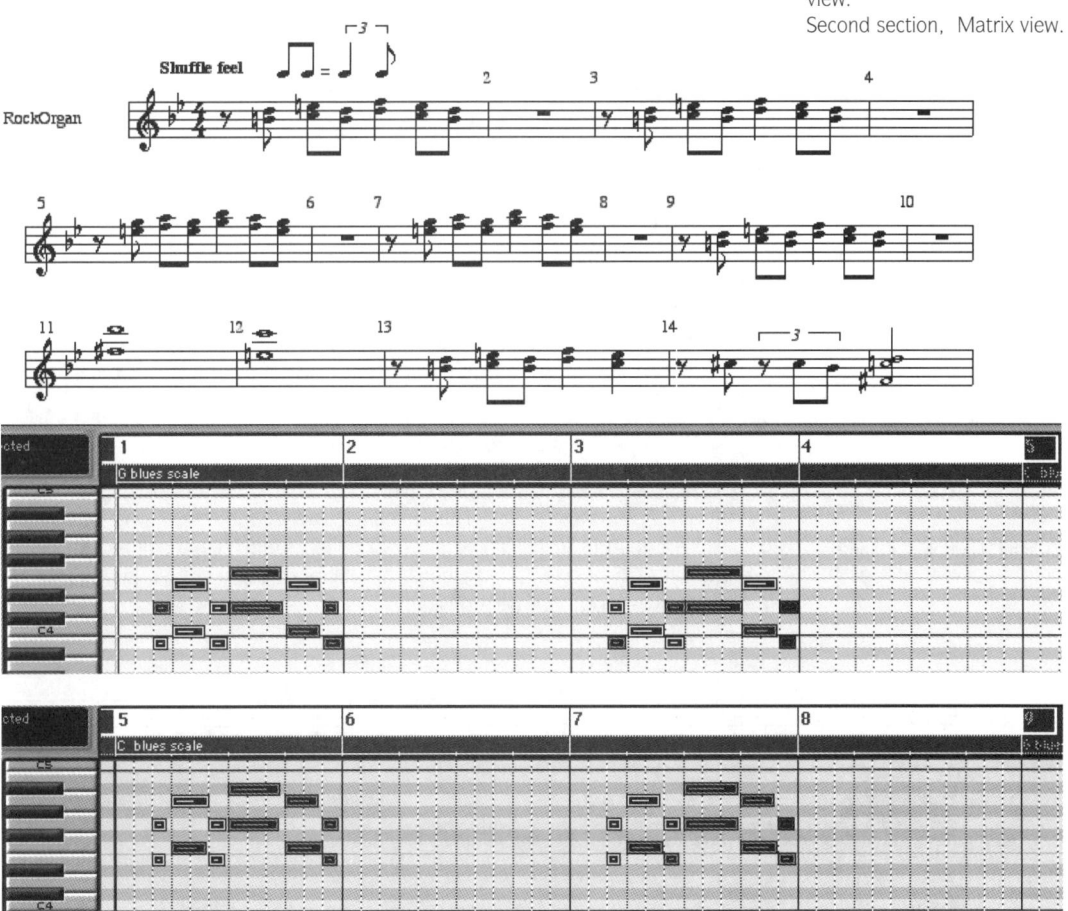

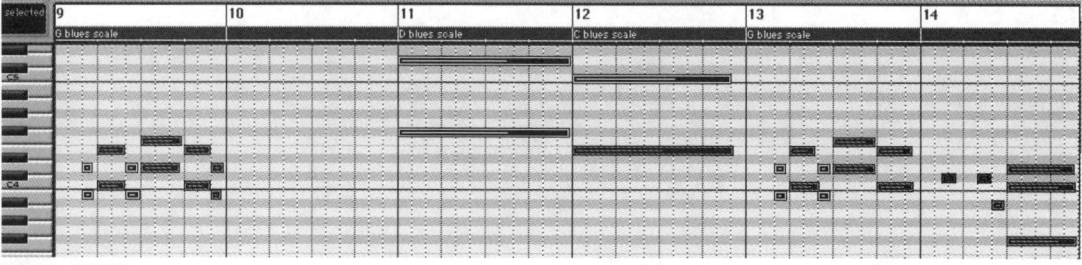

Figure P7.21
Organ, last section, Matrix view..

Nothing more is needed except for the tenor sax, to replace the piano. Nothing more in the way of instruments that is. We only have about 30 seconds of music and the brief requires around one minute's worth. How do we extend it? Well, we could repeat it again. It might work but boredom will almost certainly creep in. No, something new is needed.

Think back to the brief. It's a comedy, but there's something a little sad about those characters. A slight change of mood could be established. But how do we do that without losing the feel? Continue to use the blues scale of course, to provide unity. Back to the piano track and melody crafting.

Take 6

1 Return to the piano track (Ch 1) and set the Locators to (L) 15. 1. 1 (R) 17. 1. 1 and record Figure P7.22 and P7.23. This phrase uses the notes of the D blues scale and takes us up and away from what came before. We don't want to go higher so let's just repeat it in a descending pattern.
2 Repeat the sequence twice as far as measure 21. We now have three objects containing the same phrase.
3 Select the second object (17-21) and, using the Transpose feature in the Sequence Parameters box, transpose it down a tone (–2) to use a C blues scale.
4 Select the third object and transpose it down a fifth (–7) to use a G blues scale.
5 Set the Locators to (L) 21. 1. 1 (R) 23. 1. 1 and record more piano Figure P7.24 and P7.25). This takes us nicely back home to G, so:
6 Set the Locators to (L) 23. 1. 1 (R) 25. 1. 1 and record still more piano Figure P7.26 and P7.27) to finish off at about 55 seconds. Luv'ly job!
7 Save Song – compare with project7/7.6.

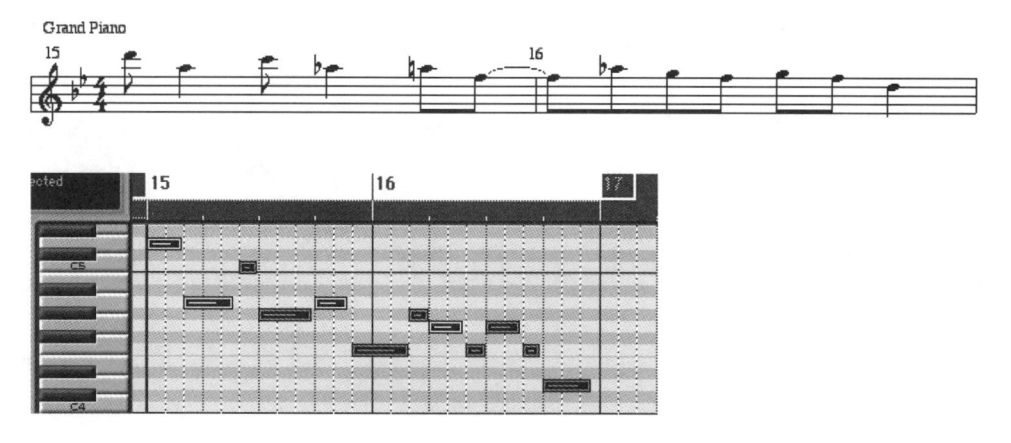

Figures P7.22 and **P7.23**
More piano, Score and Matrix view..

Project 7 – a TV sitcom theme   147

Figures P7.24 and **P7.25**
... and more piano, Score and Matrix view..

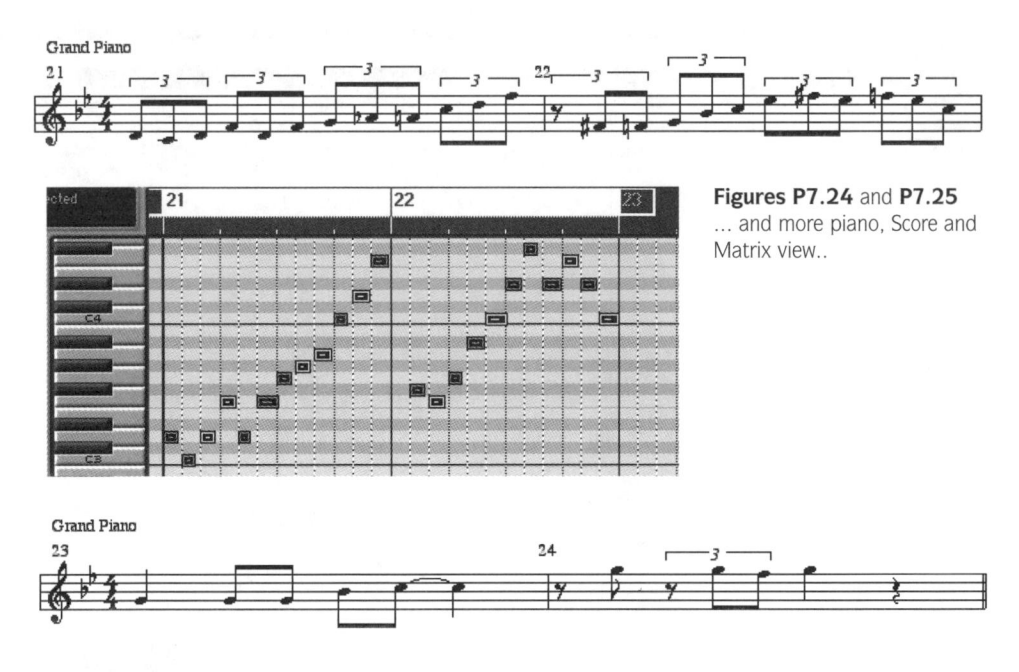

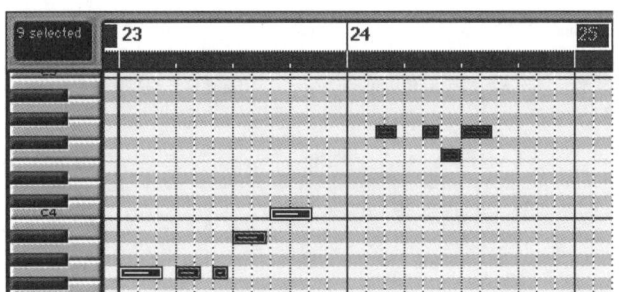

Figures P7.26 and **P7.27**
... and still more piano, Score and Matrix view..

Take 7

1. Return to the bass track (Ch 2) In order to change the mood:
2. Set the Locators to (L) 15. 1. 1 (R) 25. 1. 1 and record Figure P7.28. Do it in sections if you prefer (Figures P7.29 and P7.30).
3. Save Song – Compare with project7/7.7.

Figure P7.28
More bass, Score view.

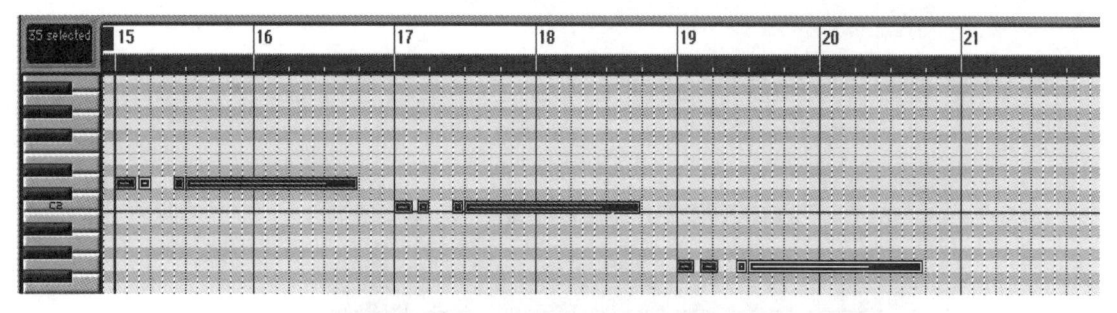

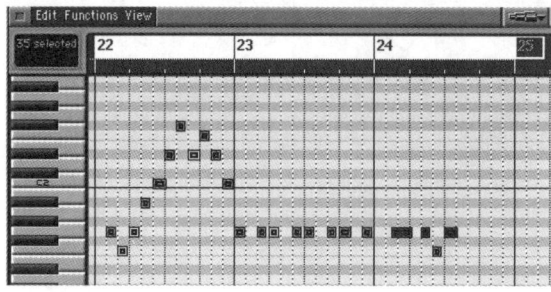

Figures P7.29 and **P7.30**
More bass, Matrix view of section one and section two.

Take 8

1 Return to the organ track (Ch 4)
2 Set the Locators to (L) 15. 1. 1 (R) 25. 1. 1 and record Figure P7.31. Do it in sections if you prefer (Figures P7.32 and P7.33).
3 Save Song – compare with project7/7.8.

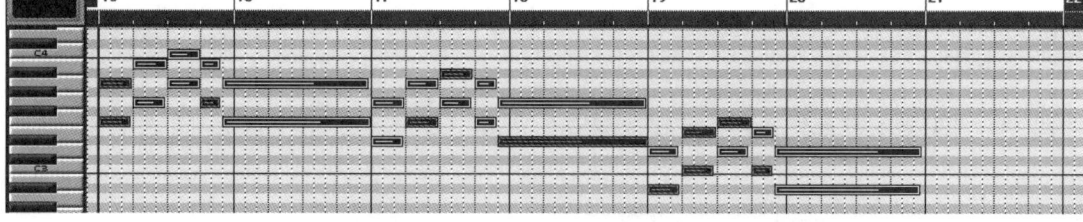

Figures P7.31 – P7.33
More organ, Score view, and Matrix view of section one and section two.

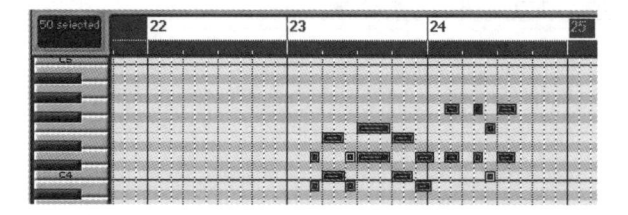

Take 9

1 Return to the guitar track (Ch 3).

How do we fit the distorted guitar into this more melancholic section? The most obvious answer is to leave it out. Not only would it spoil the mood, omitting it creates a nice sense of emptiness. However it will boost the unison line in bar 22, so:

2 Set the Locators to (L) 22. 1. 1 (R) 25. 1. 1 and record the ending. (Figures P7.34 and P7.35).
3 Save Song – compare with project7/7.9.

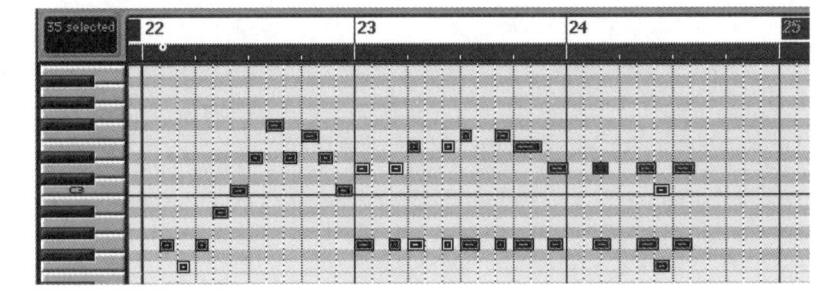

Figures P7.34 and **P7.35**
More guitar, Score and Matrix view.

Take 10

1 Return to the kick drum track (Ch 10). Set the Locators to (L) 23. 1. 1 (R) 25. 1. 1 and record the ending (Figures P7.36 and P7.37).
2 Return to the snare drum track (Ch 10). Set the Locators to (L) 22. 1. 1 (R) 25. 1. 1 and record the ending. (Figure P7.38 and P7.39).
3 Save Song – compare with project 7/10.

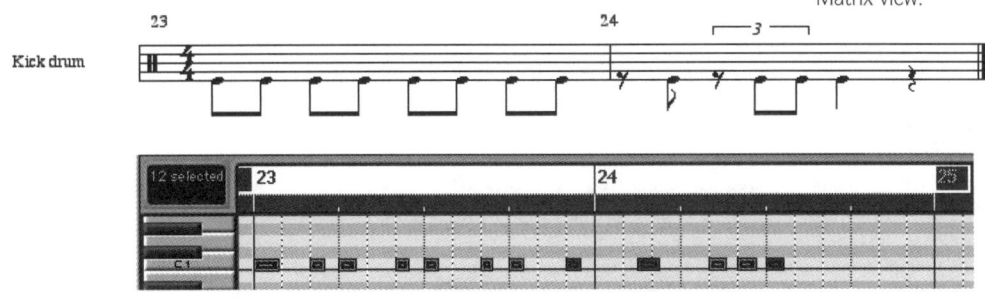

Figures P7.36 and **P7.37**
More kick drum, Score and Matrix view.

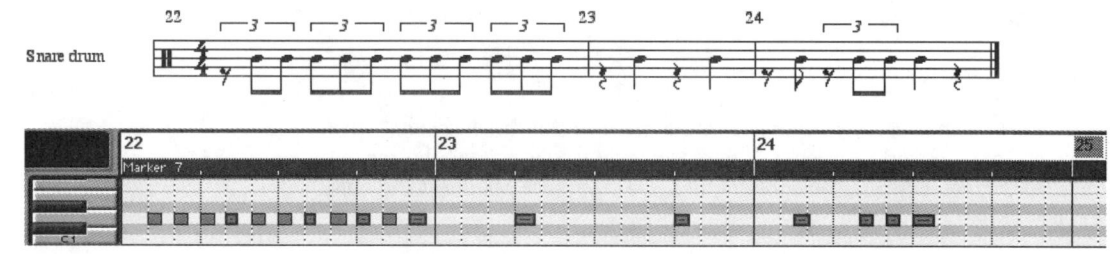

Figures P7.38 and **P7.39**
More snare drum, Score and Matrix view.

That's it. We're done. All that's needed is the tenor sax. This was recorded in one take using an external mixer and a Microtech Geffel condenser microphone. EQ was not used. For information on how to record vocals and acoustic instruments into Logic see Chapter 7 Audio Recording: The Basics. For a more detailed account see Project 6: We Record an Audio Track.

The Mix

Open project7/7platmix, 7goldmix or 7silvmix, depending on your version of Logic, to hear and view the tenor sax track which replaces the piano melody. A quick glance will reveal six additional audio tracks. For better mixing control, the MIDI tracks have been recorded as audio tracks. The main advantages of this? Well, once recorded as audio files they can be treated with inserts and send effects in the Track Mixer. How's it done? Route the audio output from your MIDI device to the input you use for recording audio into Logic. Exactly how this is achieved will depend on your particular hardware set-up. Likely sources will be either a sound module, synthesizer, sound card or external mixer. You may even have a sound card that includes an option to route the signal internally. Once the signal reaches Logic, just record the audio as you would any other audio source.

OK, let's examine 7platmix in the Track Mixer.

> **Info**
>
> There are three mixes on the CD, Platinum, Gold and Silver, each using slightly different plug-ins. However, should a plug-in not be found, just replace it with the equivalent included with your particular version.

> **Info**
>
> When mixing, MIDI tracks can be re-recorded as audio tracks. How? – route the MIDI output (audio) to the audio input used to record into Logic.

> **Tip**
>
> For flexibility, when re-recording MIDI tracks as audio, record each MIDI part as a separate audio file, including individual drum sounds. To do this, use the Mute and Solo functions.

- PlatinumVerb has been inserted on Bus 1.
- MIDI tracks – all five channels are muted now that we have re-recorded them as audio tracks.
- Tenor sax remains in the centre of the mix. There are sudden peaks in this recording and it's difficult to control them using just the volume faders, or indeed with a compressor. Logic's Limiter (Figure P7.40) plug-in is used as a channel insert and provides a solution. As an experiment, bypass the signal in the Limiter and raise the overall track volume. See what I mean!

After limiting, the signal is sent to Bus 1 and treated with PlatinumVerb's Bright Long Reverb pre-set, which if not overdone, enhances the solo tenor sax nicely.

- Drums are in the centre of the stereo picture and, in this case, the kick drum is left dry. A small amount of snare drum is sent to PlatinumVerb via Bus 1. Because of the long reverb being used, any more would sound very messy. To save processing power, only one reverb unit has been used. Feel free to add another if your computer's CPU can cope.
- Bass was recorded with a touch of reverb from the GM sound module. Nothing further is added and it's left dead centre.

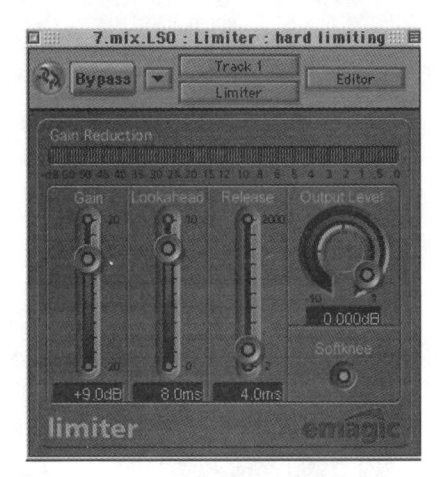

Figure P7.40
Limiter.

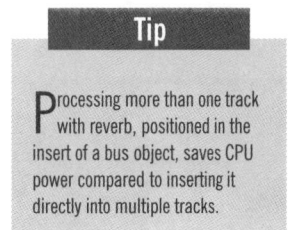

> **Tip**
>
> Processing more than one track with reverb, positioned in the insert of a bus object, saves CPU power compared to inserting it directly into multiple tracks.

- Guitar is panned left and a small amount treated with reverb.
- Organ is panned right and treated with a little reverb. Another device, Logic's Flanger (Figure P7.41), has been inserted here. Normally used as a bus effect, in this case it's ok as a channel insert because only one track is using it.

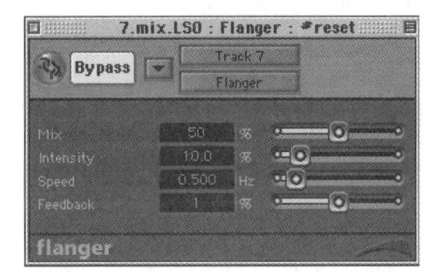

Figure P7.41
Flanger.

- Automation is used on the organ track. With the Track Mixer open, play the piece through. At bar 15, where things cool down a little, the Flanger kicks in (the channel insert button becomes illuminated – blue) and the volume fader rises a little. When the band returns in full, the volume returns to its previous level and the flanger is turned off. (I love all this! Could play with it for hours.)

Return to the Arrange window to view the automation data another way (Figure P7.42). Select the organ track (15/16) and you will see a coloured, horizontal line in the audio region marked 0.0db. Follow it along and you will notice it rise to +4.6 in bar 15. It returns to 0.0dB in bar 21. Select the track below (16) and you will see the Insert #1 Bypass automation data, represented as another coloured line. The flanger is bypassed until bar 15, where it is switched on. It's bypassed again at bar 23. 'That's all very well', you say, 'but how was it done?'

Figure 7.42
Organ track – automation data.

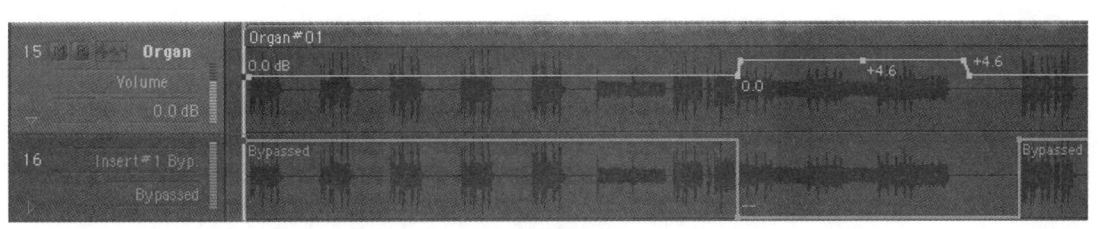

> **Info**
>
> The record button does not have to be activated when recording real time automation data – just play the track.

As with most functions in Logic there are several ways of doing things. Automating the bypass was done in the Arrange window by:

1 Selecting the organ track (15/16) and choosing track automation [View > Track Automation]. The selected track expanded to reveal three panels.
2 In the lower, left hand panel, Touch was selected (Figure P7.43). This is the most commonly used Automation Mode. Automation was now active and ready to record regardless of whether the piece was playing or not.

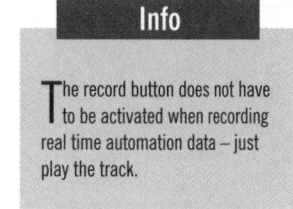

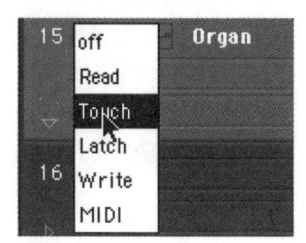

Figure P7.43
Touch selected.

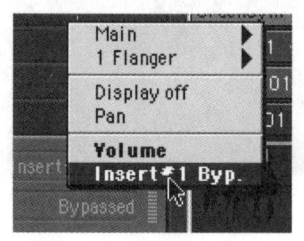

Figure P7.44
Insert#1 Byp. selected.

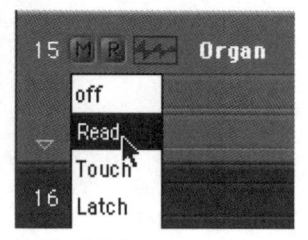

Figure P7.45
Read selected.

3 In the drop-down menu of the top panel (right hand corner) Main > Insert#1 Byp. was selected (Figure P7.44). A horizontal line appeared which ran the bottom length of the audio region.
4 By clicking in the panel directly below on the two hyphens (- -), the word Bypass appeared and the horizontal line jumped to the top of the audio region.
5 The Bypass was de-activated by scrolling to bar 15 and clicking in the bottom of the audio region. The horizontal line jumped to the bottom and the hyphens (- -) re-appeared.
6 After scrolling to bar 23, clicking at the top of the audio region re-activated the Bypass.
7 When finished Read was selected (Figure P7.45) in the lower left panel. This ensured nothing was accidentally over-written.

Automating the volume was done a different way, in the Track Mixer, by:

1 Selecting the organ audio object.
2 In the drop-down menu, just above the pan-pot, selecting Touch as the Automation Mode (Figure P7.46). Automation was now active and ready to record regardless of whether the piece was playing or not.
3 Pressed play on the Transport bar and when the music reached bar 15, raised the volume fader a little. On reaching bar 21, the fader was returned to it's previous position, 0.0db.
4 After playing back the piece and checking the volume (much fun had watching the magic fader and insert button) Read was selected as the Automation Mode, to protect the data.

Figure P7.46
Automation Mode – Touch.

Automating the volume could, of course, have been done using Hyper Draw in the Arrange page, just as with the flanger bypass data.

Right, that's it. As usual, there's always another way to mix things. I'm happy, but please feel free to experiment with it further.

Minimalism   9

Minimalism, as a musical art movement began in the early 1960s and was brought to prominence by Terry Riley with his enormously influential piece entitled 'In C'. It has been growing steadily ever since and composers such as Philip Glass, Steve Reich, John Adams and Michael Nieman, are all very successful in this genre, writing music for film and theatre as well as concert works. Indeed the music of Glass and Reich is now so frequently imitated that the style can be heard on all manner of television commercials and incidental music.

The cyclic and repetitive techniques used in minimalism often produce music of a static nature ideally suited for use with the moving image in the form of atmospheric soundtracks. These same techniques also make it ideal music for composing within sequencers such as Logic. However because the music is essentially repetitive, many people mistakenly believe that all they have to do is compose a few measures and apply the Create Repeat function. This inevitably leads to very boring music indeed. To make it interesting, just as in all other forms of music, repetition must be combined with variation.

There are many techniques used in minimalism, and the repetitive nature of the music often belies it's complexity. I have chosen two techniques used by minimalist composers for us to examine.

- Load minimal1

A gradual cumulative process of adding notes is used here (Figures 9.1, 9.2 and 9.3). It's a simple technique which quickly leads to very complex structures. Bar 1 contains a group of seven notes of equal length (1/8 notes) which are repeated three times in succession. In bar 5 an extra note is

> **Info**
>
> To examine the Logic files for this chapter, copy the folder named 'minimal' from the CD to your computer.

Figures 9.1 and **9.2**
minimal1, Arrange view.and Matrix view.

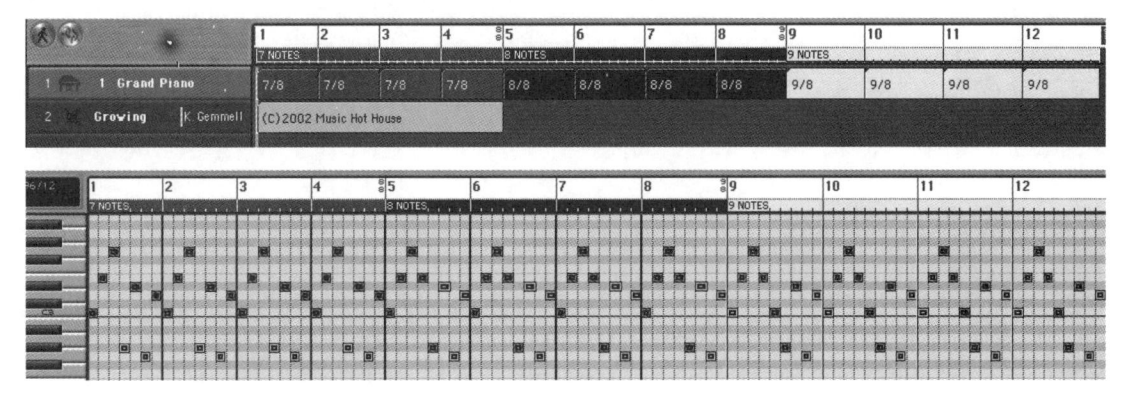

Figure 9.3
minimal1, Score view.

added to the group and another at bar 9. If these 12 bars are cycled round we hear first an expanding effect and then as the cycle begins again a contracting one. The general melodic structure remains the same whilst quite different rhythmic structures emerge.

- Load minimal2

Figures 9.4 and 9.5
minimal2, Arrange view and Matrix view.

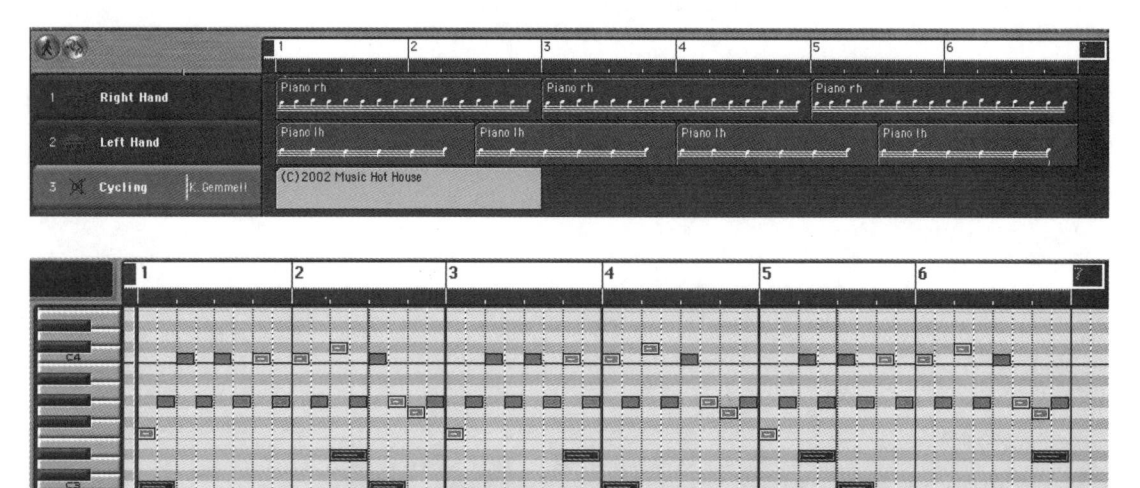

Repeating two or more rhythmic patterns of different lengths simultaneously is another technique. In minimal2 (Figures 9.4, 9.5 and 9.6) the first right hand piano part is two bars long and is repeated twice making a total of six bars. The left hand part however is only one and a half bars long and has to be repeated three times to finish along with the right hand part. When both parts are viewed together in the Score editor we see seven bars of music in 4/4. The result is rather hypnotic and although the music is repetitive no two measures are the same.

In the next chapter we will use similar techniques to those above and combine them with pre-recorded audio parts to produce a minimalist piece of music.

Figure 9.6
minimal2, Score view.

Project 8 – a minimalist soundtrack

Tip

When loading example files containing MIDI settings its quite likely that you will initially hear the wrong sounds (very likely those from a previous project or song). Use [Options > Song Settings > Used Instrument MIDI Settings] to correct them. A faster way – quickly cursor up or down the tracks using the arrow keys on your computer keyboard.

Musical objectives

- Use a pentatonic scale to construct a simple ostinato, oriental in character and suitable for manipulation in a minimalist fashion.
- Decide upon instrumentation to create an atmosphere for film clip depicting an oriental landscape.
- Create 'cycles' using repetitive techniques to generate new patterns.
- Introduce new musical elements that coincide with, and enhance the addition of a procession in the landscape film.

Logic skills

- Setting up a Looped Object.
- Inserting an RPN (Registered Parameter Number) message in the Event List.
- Drawing Pitch Bend data in Hyper Edit or Hyper Draw.
- Importing Audio files.
- Using EQ.
- Using track automation.

Preparation

1 From the CD, copy the folder named 'project8' to your computer.
2 On your computer, create a folder called 'mywork8' or something similar in which to save your work.
3 From the project8 folder, open the template – templt8.
4 In your new 'mywork8' folder, save the template as mywork8 or something similar.

The assignment

Using minimalist techniques, compose a piece of music about one and a half minutes long minutes long for use as a soundtrack with an oriental landscape scene. The scene first opens with an empty landscape. After about 20 seconds we see the beginnings of a procession of people appear on the horizon. The procession winds its way into the foreground. After about 55 seconds we can see that the procession contains not only marching figures but acrobats and elephants. After about a minute and a half, the procession has passed and gradually disappears from view.

As with previous projects, you may prefer to listen to the finished article before going further. To do this, open either project8/11 or project8/8.mix and play it through a few times.

Take 1

Track 1: Guitar 1

Follow these steps:

1 Ensure the Song Position Line is at 1.1.1, and from the project8 folder, import the audio file named guitar.aif This is a pre-recorded audio file, containing a very simple ostinato which is repeated throughout this composition. It actually consists of an acoustic guitar and a harp sample. A one bar, stereo audio region containing a reference to the audio file itself is created. On playing it, you will notice the guitar begins on the first beat of the bar. Well, we need it to begin on the second eighth note of the bar so:
2 In the Parameter box, use the drop-down menu to set a Delay of 1/ 8 (Figure P8.1). Play it through. Checking it against the metronome click will illustrate the parameter change. Now, we need this one bar audio region to repeat continuously throughout the piece. Setting up a loop is the easiest and most convenient way to do this.
3 Select the audio object, and in the Parameter box, turn on the loop function (Figure P8.2). A seires of repeated grey objects appear, all named after the original (Figure P8.3).
4 Save Song – compare with project8/8.1.

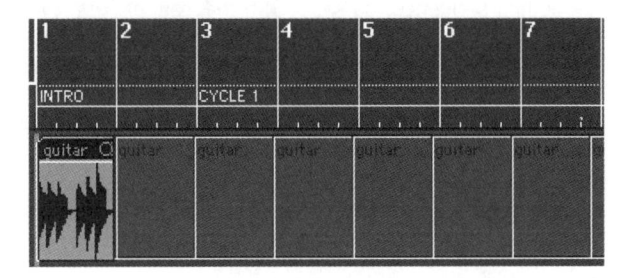

Figure P8.1
Setting the delay.

Figure P8.2
Loop switched on.

Figure P8.3
Looped objects will continue until stopped either by another object, or in our case the song end marker (bar 75).

Take 2

Track 2: (Ch 2) Pizzicato Str
Sequence Parameters box: Qua1/8 – Note
Instrument Parameter box: Cha 2, Prg 45
Transport Bar: (L) 3.1.1 (R) 5.1.1

The brief requires something oriental in character and the most obvious thing that comes to mind is the pentatonic scale E G A B D. However the guitar is only playing two notes and it would be nice to keep things simple. So let's drop the G and A. That leaves E B and D with which to build another ostinato. A light texture is required. How about pizzicato strings? Violins are not oriental instruments as such, but when plucked strings are used they provide that kind of flavour.

Follow these steps:

1 Record the pizzicato strings (Figures 8.4 and P8.5). Minimalism, as we know, is about repetition. We also know that variation is needed to stimulate interest so we are now going to duplicate the sequence just recorded and then work on each resulting sequence individually.

Figures P8.4 and **P8.5**
Pizzicato strings, Score and Matrix view.

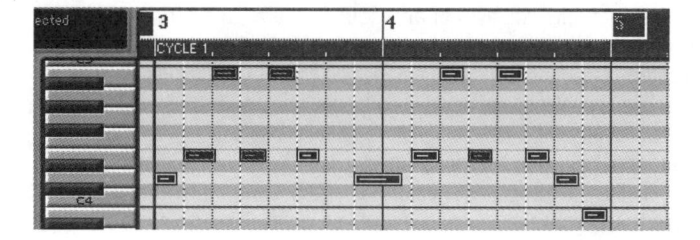

2 Repeat the pizzicato strings (bars 3 – 5) five times as far as bar 15 [Functions > Objects > Repeat Objects... (x5)].
3 Now here's what we are going to do. Each Part will keep it's rhythmic structure but the notes will be changed according to a few simple rules:

- The first sequence (bars 1 – 3) remains unaltered. We'll refer to this as the 'Original Sequence.'
- The second sequence (bars 3 – 5) begins on the second note of the Original Sequence.
- The third sequence (bars 5 – 7) begins on the third note of the original sequence.

4 Repeat the process on the remaining sequences until we have a 12 bar ostinato, named 'Cycle 1' in the Marker (Figure P8.6).
5 Save Song – compare with project8/8.2.

Figure P8.6
Cycle 1.

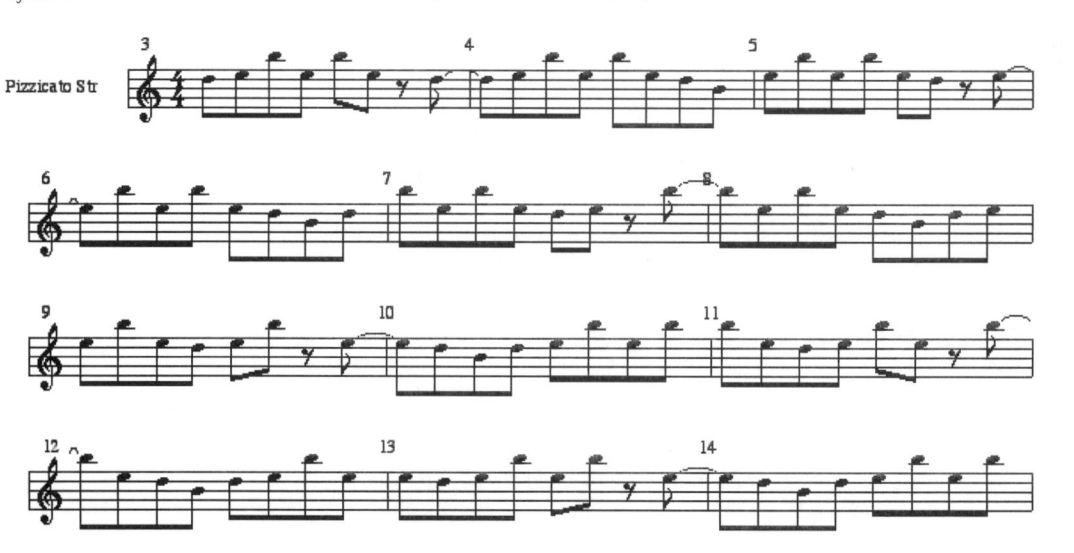

Take 3

Track 3: (Ch 3) Viola
Sequence Parameters box: Qua 1/8 – note
Instrument Parameter box: Cha 3, Prg 41, Transpose 12

> **Info**
>
> A canon contains musical imitation. A melodic strand is repeated after a certain interval, in our case after one and a half bars. There are many forms of canon. The imitation may be at the octave, or another interval such as a fifth. Simple canons take the form of a round such as 'London's Burning' or 'Frere Jacques'.

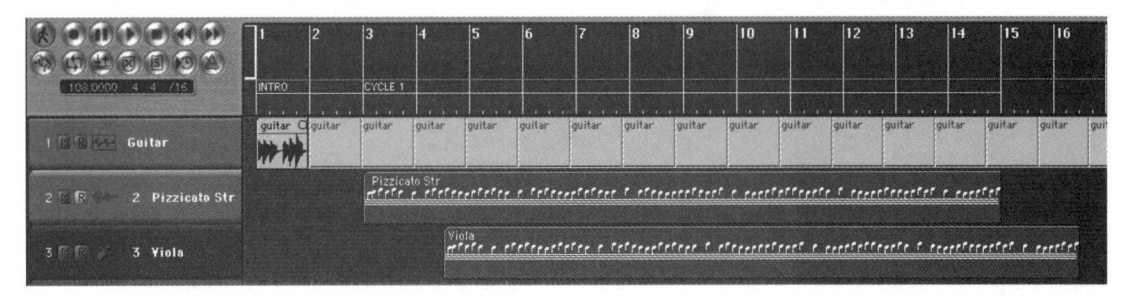

Follow these steps:

1 Return to the pizzicato string track and glue the pizzicato string objects together as one.
2 Drag a copy of the pizzicato string sequence to 4. 3. 1 on the viola track. Ensure that Transpose is set to –12 in the Instrument Parameter box.
3 Rename the copied sequence 'Viola' and play back the piece. The 12 bar ostinato 'Cycle 1' begins with the pizzicato strings and is echoed as a Canon, one and a half bars later by the Viola (Figure P8.7). Things are becoming interesting even though only three notes have so far been used. Already we have the oriental backdrop required.
4 Open the Track Mixer and, depending on how you played, adjust the volume levels of the pizzicato strings and the viola. Because they are both playing essentially the same thing, and to avoid confusion, pan the viola to the right and pizzicato strings to the left.
5 Save Song – compare with project8/8.3.

Figure P8.7
Pizzicato string and viola canon.

Take 4

Track 4: Oboe

Follow these steps:

1 Place the Song Line at 3.1.1, and from the project8 folder import the audio file named oboe.aif [Audio > Import Audio File...]. This is a pre-recorded mono audio file which contains a four bar ostinato melody.
2 Select the oboe audio object and, as with the guitar audio object, turn on the loop function. Once again we have a continuous repetition of the audio region as far as bar 75.
3 Save Song – compare with project8/8.4a.

4 Select the pizzicato strings sequence (bars 3 – 15) and repeat them three times as far as bar 51.
5 Select the viola sequence (4.3.1 – 16.3.1) and repeat it three times as far as 52. 3. 1.
6 Save Song – compare with project8/8.4b.

We have reached the point where the beginning of a procession appears.

Take 5

Track 5: (Ch 5) Strings | Strings 1
Sequence Parameters box: Qua 1/8 – note
Instrument Parameter box: Cha 5, Prg 48
Transport Bar: (L) 11.1.1 (R) 17.1.1

Info

Part of the GM specification RPN (Registered Parameter Numbers) messages are MIDI controller numbers that allow us to change the parameters of tones such as: Pitch Bend Sensitivity, Master Fine Tuning etc. Each RPN is made up of a Controller Number and value.

Figure P8.8
Hand wheel symbol.

A glance at the strings 1 part (Figure P8.12) will reveal a glissando from D down to G.

We can achieve this by just playing the note D2 and using the pitch bend controller on our MIDI keyboard for the slide down of seven semitones. But first we have to ensure that our GM sound source will receive the information. To do this, we will insert a RPN (Registered Parameter Number) message in the Event List window to define the pitch bend sensitivity. Follow these steps:

1 Position the Song Line at bar 11, and with the Pencil tool, create an object by clicking at bar 11. Extend it as far as bar 17 (grab the lower right corner and drag).
2 With the new object selected, open the Event List window [Windows > Open Event List].
3 Select the Pencil tool and click on the hand wheel symbol (Figure P8.8) to enter a control change event. This could be anything! On my version of Logic the default controller entered is Number 7 – Volume.
4 If not already there, scroll the newly created event's position to 11.1.1.1.
5 Click on the contoller number, and from the drop-down menu, choose 101 [101 = Reg.Par. MSB] (Figure 8.9). Scroll its value to 0.
6 Enter another event and change the controller number to 100 [100 = Reg.Par. LSB] and the value number to 0.
7 Enter another event and change the controller number to 6 [6 = Data MSB] and the value to 7. Seven represents the pitch bend range. Compare with Figure P8.10.

Figure P8.9
Choosing controller numbers.

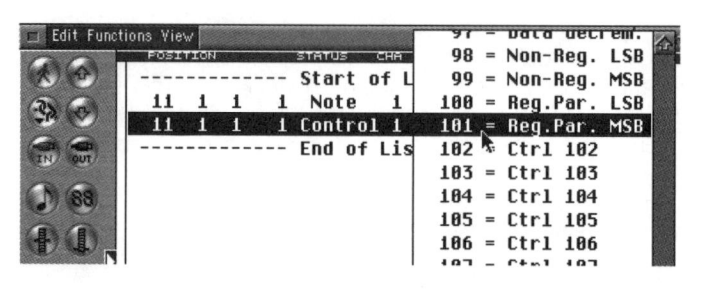

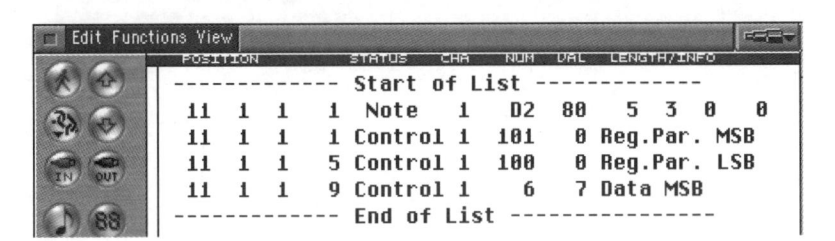

```
  Edit Functions View
         POSITION       STATUS   CHA   NUM   UAL  LENGTH/INFO
         -------------- Start of List --------------
         11  1   1    1 Note      1    D2    80     5  3  0   0
         11  1   1    1 Control 1      101    0 Reg.Par. MSB
         11  1   1    5 Control 1      100    0 Reg.Par. LSB
         11  1   1    9 Control 1        6    7 Data MSB
         -------------- End of List ----------------
```

Figure P8.10
Pitch bend sensitivity data.

Phew! That's the complicated stuff over. The General MIDI sound module will now have a pitch bend range, up or down, of seven semitones. On with the music.

1 Record the strings 1 part (Figure P8.11). To achieve the descending glissando from D down to G just play the note D2 and use the pitch bend controller on your MIDI keyboard for the slide down.

Another way to do it is to record the note first, or draw it in the Matrix Edit window, and add the glissando afterwards, either in the Hyper Edit window (Figure P8.12) or directly into the sequence in the Arrange window with Hyper Draw (Figure P8.13). However, in my experience it is usually best to record it as you play. Less of a fiddle! It's also worth checking to see that pitch bend has been reset at the end of the note. If not the next note on that channel will sound terribly wrong! Do this in the Event List (Figure P8.14).

2 Save Song – compare with project8/8.5a

> **Tip**
>
> Danger! Selecting objects with Hyper Edit turned on will alter any recorded data. Turn it off in the menu for safety.

Figure P8.11
Strings 1.

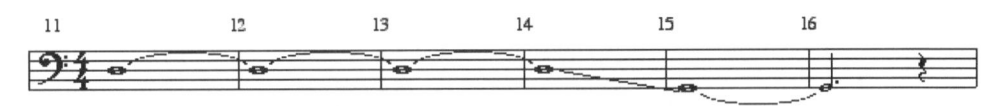

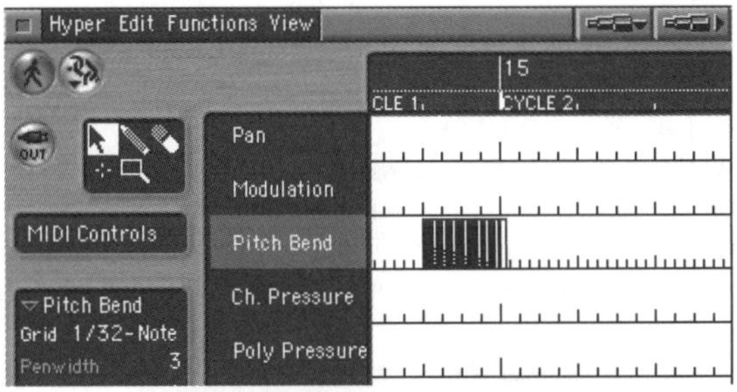

Figure P8.12
Pitch bend data – Hyper Edit view.

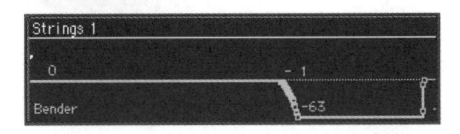

Figure P8.13
Pitch bend data – Hyper Draw.

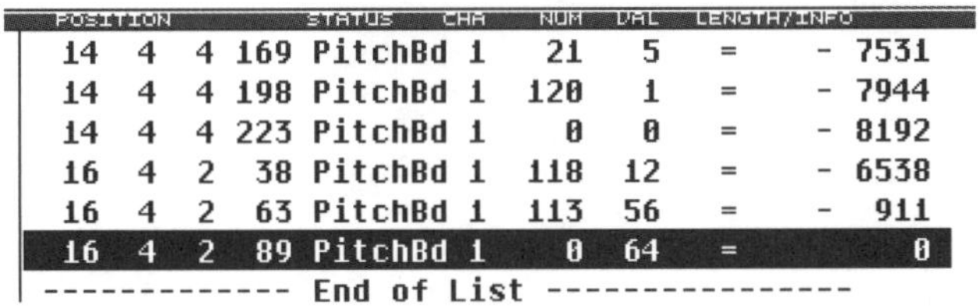

```
  POSITION       STATUS   CHA   NUM   UAL  LENGTH/INFO
    14  4   4  169 PitchBd  1    21    5    =    - 7531
    14  4   4  198 PitchBd  1   120    1    =    - 7944
    14  4   4  223 PitchBd  1     0    0    =    - 8192
    16  4   2   38 PitchBd  1   118   12    =    - 6538
    16  4   2   63 PitchBd  1   113   56    =    -  911
    16  4   2   89 PitchBd  1     0   64    =          0
    ------------- End of List -------------
```

Figure P8.14
Pitch bend reset data – Event List view.

The strings could be stronger. How about doubling them one octave lower? Follow these steps:

1 Select the Strings 1 sequence and drag a copy to track 6. Ensure that it starts at bar 11.
2 In the Sequence Parameter box, transpose the new string part down an octave (–12). It will help identification if you rename the new object Strings 2.
3 In the Track Mixer adjust the volume for Strings 1 and 2. Avoid having them too loud. I panned them hard left and right for separation. The effect is more dramatic too.
4 Save Song – compare with project8/8.5b.

Take 6

1 Return to the Strings 1 track, set the Locators at (L) 17.1.1 (R) 23.1.1 and record a second glissando in the same manner as the first. This time play C2 and glide down to F (Figure P8.15). Again, copy the resulting sequence to the Strings 2 track. Transpose it down one octave (–12) and rename it Strings 2.
2 Save Song – compare with project8/8.6.

Figure P8.15
More strings.

We have now reached the point where the full procession including the acrobats and animals is in view.

Take 7

1 Return to the String 1 track.
2 Set Locators at (L) 27. 1. 1 (R) 31. 1. 1 and record the strings (Figure P8.16 and P8.17).
3 Copy the resulting sequence to the String 2 track and rename it. Transpose it an octave lower.
4 Select both the String 1 and 2 sequences between bars 27 – 32 and repeat them three times as far as bar 43 [Functions > Object > Repeat Objects... (x3)].
5 Save Song – compare with project8/8.7.

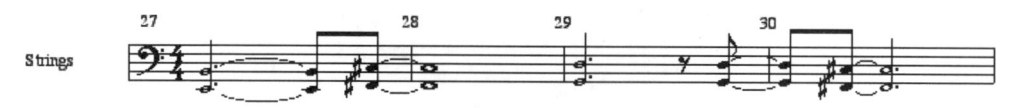

Figure P8.16
Strings.

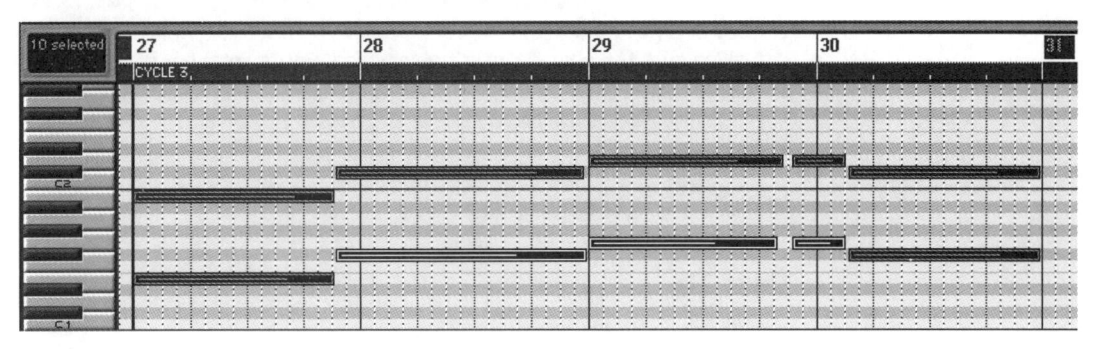

Figure P8.17
Strings, Matrix view..

Take 8

1 Return to the String 1 track.
2 Set the Locators at (L) 43. 1. 1 (R) 53. 1. 1 and record the strings in Figures P8.18 and P8.19.
3 Copy the resulting sequence to the String 2 track, transpose it down one octave (−12) and rename it.
4 Save Song – compare with project8/8.8.

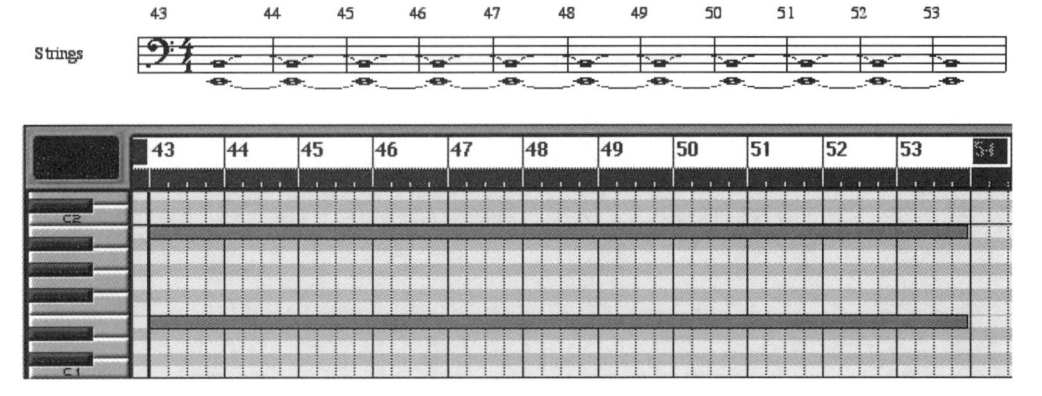

Figures P8.18 and **P8.19**
More strings, Score and Matrix view.

We now have strings, one octave apart, playing a moving line and creating a contrast with the repeating ostinatos above. Something more is needed to add extra weight and bass and drums are the obvious choice. However I think a slap bass is needed to give the edge needed to cut through those low strings.

Take 9

Track 7: Bass Guitar

1 Ensure the Song Position Line is at 27.1.1 and from the project8 folder import the audio file bass1.aif [Audio > Import Audio File...]. This is a pre-recorded audio file containing a four bar riff derived from the ostinatos playing above it but also follows the harmonic progression of the string line.

2 Copy and paste the resulting audio region to bars 31, 35 and 39, making sure the object always begins dead on the first beat of the bar.
3 Set the Song Position Line to 43.1.1 and from the project8 folder import the audio file bass2.aif to complete the bass line.
4 Save Song – compare with project8/8.9.

All that's needed are the drums.

Take 10

Track 8: Standard Drums | Kit
Sequence Parameters box: Qua 1/16 – Note
Instrument Parameter box: Cha 10, Prg 0
Transport Bar: (L) 26. 1. 1 (R) 44. 1. 1

1 Record the drum part (Figure P8.20). Bar 26 is an intro fill (Figure P8.21). 27 to 43 is a two bar pattern, repeated using Bass Drum 1 (C1) and Electric Snare (E1) (Figure P8.22). Bar 43 is a Cymbal Crash (C#2) (Figure P8.23). It can all be played quite easily in one pass on a keyboard but break it down if need be. I used the Extended Sequence Parameter box to loosen things a little, Q-Strength 90%.
2 Save Song – compare with project8/8.10.

Figure P8.20
Drum part.

Figure P8.21
Intro fill, Hyper view.

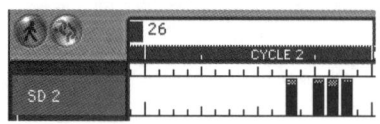

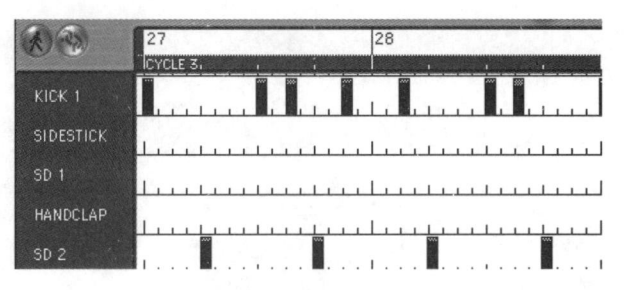

Figure P8.22
Two bar pattern, Hyper view.

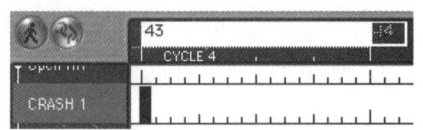

Figure P8.23
Cymbal crash, Hyper view.

Take 11

Track 9: Standard Drums | Tambourine
Sequence Parameters box: Qua 1/8 – Note
Instrument Parameter box: Cha 10, Prg 0
Transport Bar: (L) 27.1.1 (R) 43.1.1

1 The tambourine (F#2) plays a one bar pattern (Figures P8.24 and P8.25) repeatedly between the Locators. I used the Extended Sequence Parameter box to loosen things – Q-Strength 90%. If the result is too loud, smooth the velocities using Dynamics. I applied 75% compression.
2 Save Song – compare with project8/8.11.

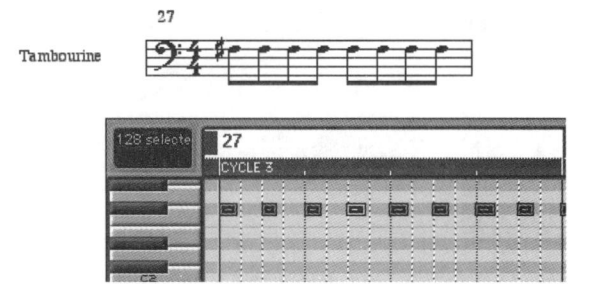

Figure P8.24
Tambourine.

Figure P8.25
Tambourine, Matrix view.

The final mix

A final mix can be seen and heard in 8silvmix, 8goldmix and 8platmix (Figure P8.26). Where have all the MIDI tracks gone? I re-recorded them as audio files and deleted them. It's not a particularly easy mix and this way allows more control by using EQ, inserts and send effects. Another reason? You can hear things exactly as they are because we are not relying on different GM tone generators. Open the Track Mixer, have a look around and play it through. The EQ has been left blank for you to experiment.

> **Info**
>
> There are three mixes on the CD, Platinum, Gold and Silver, each using slightly different plug-ins. However, should a plug-in not be found, just replace it with the equivalent included with your particular version.

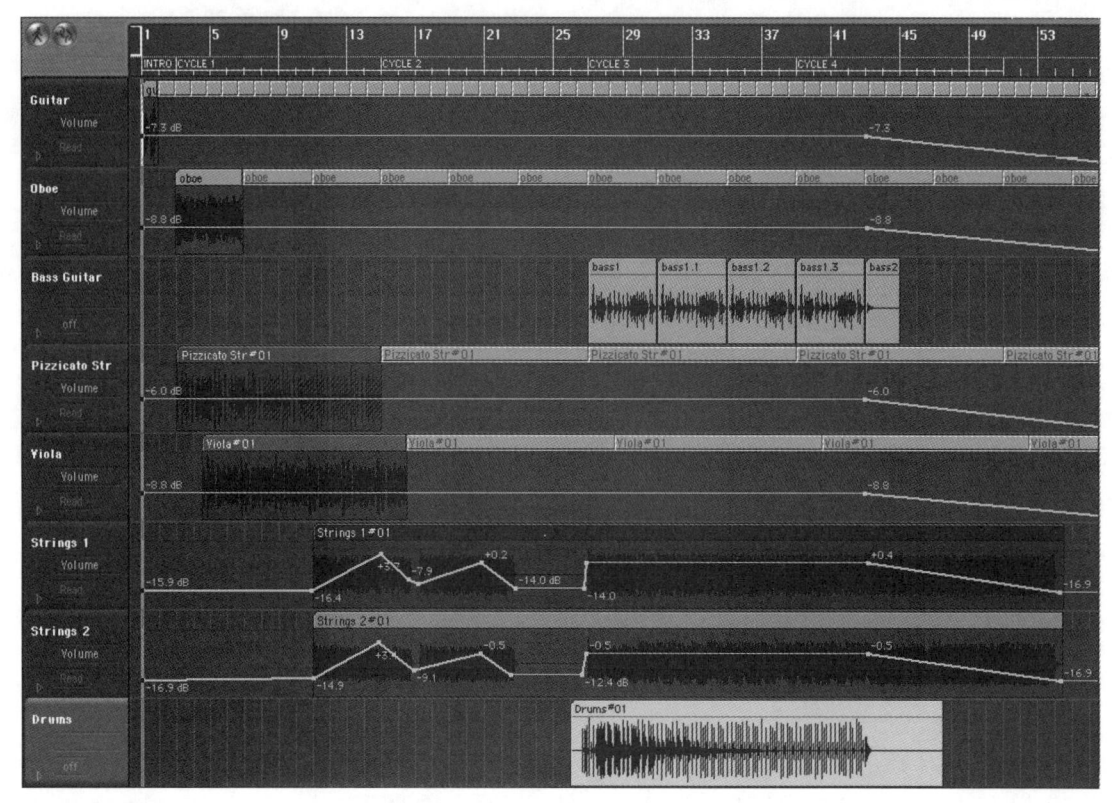

Figure P8.26
The final mix.

Figures P8.27a and b
Low Shelf EQ and Low Shelf EQ plug-in.

> **Tip**
>
> If you prefer a more intuitive approach to EQ, experiment with the plug-ins. They are identical to the track object EQs. Low Shelf EQ (Figure P8.27a) is shown as a plug-in in Figure P8.27b. When happy, note the settings and use them with the track object EQ instead.

There's a lot going on, particularly from bar 27 onwards, and the guitar needed to be just a bit lighter. Rather than boost the higher frequencies – always tempting, but rarely the right decision – try cutting those below 100Hz (Figures P8.27a and P8.27b). The bass benefits from some soft limiting (Figure P8.28). Bypass the Limiter to hear the difference. EQ, this time parametric (Figure P8.29), could be used to boost the rather lifeless snare (courtesy of my old Roland Sound Canvas, which is incidently resposible for all the MIDI derived sounds on this track). PlatinumVerb (Figure P8.30), has been inserted on Bus 1 and the WoodenVerb pre-set is used to 'float' the oboe above the general racket!

By now you've probably spotted those magic faders, moving all by themselves between bars 12 and 23. This automation data can be viewed in the Arrange window (Figure P8.26). Nodes were inserted with the Arrow tool to create crecsendos and decrecsendos on the strings. The strings are panned

Figure P8.28
Soft limiting.

Figure P8.29
Parametric EQ.

hard right and left. Finally, a complete fade-out is achieved using Hyper Draw and track automation.

Have a mess with it (project8/8.mix). If your system can take it, try inserting more plug-ins. Go easy on the reverb though. This tune gets very messy, very quickly!

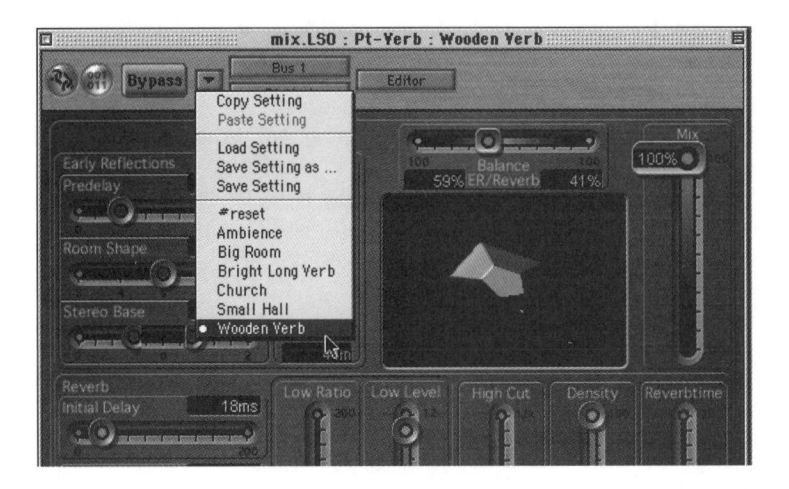

Figure P8.30
PlatinumVerb – WoodenVerb pre-set.

10
Dance music

> **Info**
>
> To examine the Logic files for this chapter, copy the folder named 'loops' from the CD to your computer.

Dance music started in the mid 1980s and nobody thought it would last. Here we are in the twenty-first century and it's still with us and getting stronger. Why is it so popular? Because people love dancing to it. More to the point, young people love dancing to it, and that's why it is being featured more and more in radio and TV commercials targeted specifically at the young. It also forms a backdrop to many sports, motoring, even wildlife programs on TV as well as frequent use in drama, soaps and films.

Styles and loops

Of course, there are many styles within this genre – House, Garage, Trance, Drum & Bass, Hip Hop and Ambient to name just a few – but when used as background music the actual style is not so important. What is important is the general impression that the product being plugged, or the program being watched, is cool and up to date! Unlike most dance music there is sometimes a strong melodic line and more harmonic movement involved but the key ingredient is always rhythm. Drum & Bass loops being the most prominent features.

There are many excellent loops available from companies such as PocketFuel, and these can often make a good starting point. I have made use of a PocketFuel loop myself in Project 9. Trawling through hundreds of loops can be time consuming and often it is quicker to make your own, particularly if you have a specific brief to work to. This is after all, far more creative. And where's an ideal place to construct loops? Emagic Logic for one! Once you have made one or two, confidence grows, and before you know it you may well have a large library of your own original loops.

Constructing a Drum & Bass loop

Realism gives way to creativity when making loops, although it cannot be disregarded altogether. The most popular drum machines, such as the TR808 started life emulating acoustic kits, even though they are chosen for different reasons today. Bass drum, snare drum, toms and hi-hats are all present on acoustic kits and function the same way on virtual kits. The beauty of using them in dance music is the knowledge that they do not necessarily have to sound anything like a real drummer. We are limited only by our imagination. Having said that, control is needed. As in most creative forms, no matter how complicated, simplicity lies at the heart of things.

Here's a four-bar loop to examine.

Dance music

- Load loops/latloop and have a listen.

It's fast, frenetic and Latin in style. It doesn't belong to any particular Dance Music genre but would be a suitable starting point for a number of uses – a carnival scene maybe. All percussion work was done in the Hyper Edit window using the Pencil tool to enter the notes with a mouse. This how I built it up.

1 Decided on a tempo – fast, frantic, Latin – 140 bpm seemed appropriate.
2 In the Arrange window, on track 1, created an object between bar 1 and 5.
3 Opened the Hyper Editor [Windows > Open Hyper Edit] and chose a General MIDI Drum Set from the drop-down menu, just above the Parameter box (right). GM drum sets can also be created using [Hyper > Create GM Drum Set].

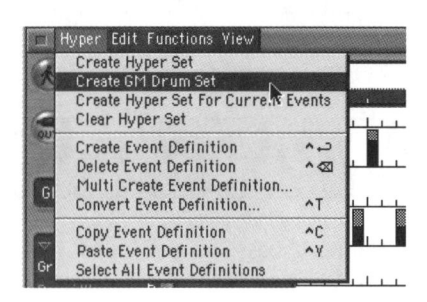

4 On the Kick 1 line placed an event on every beat of each bar.

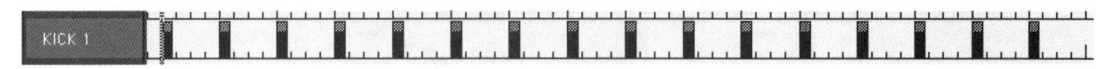

5 On the Ped HH line, entered a beat on every other eighth-note. Placing them between the bass drum adds a sense of urgency.

6 On the O Surdo line, entered a simple back-beat pattern.

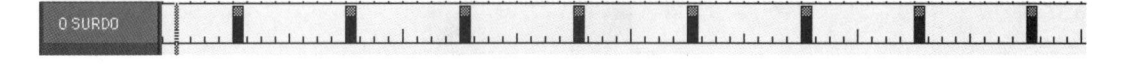

7 On the SD 1 line, entered a pattern between bars 1 and 3, then copied it between bars 3 and 5. It's the snare that brings this pattern alive. I kept it simple to begin with and…
8 …changed the Grid value to 32 and created snare rolls. For realism, drew a velocity ramp with the Crosshair tool.

9 On the H Agogo line, entered a pattern in bar 1 and copied it throughout the loop.

10 On the Vibra line entered a beat on the last sixteenth of Bar 4. As each new cycle begins this has the effect of anticipating the first beat and adds to the urgency.

11 On the Splash line placed an event on the third beat of bar 2.

12 On the H Bongo and L Bongo line added some, er ... bongos!

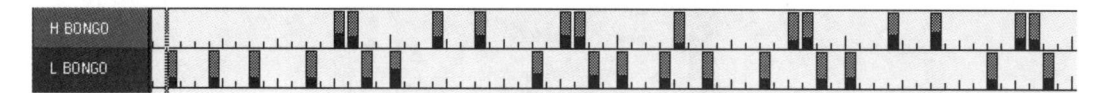

13 A meaty bass line was added. This was not entered with the mouse, but played in real time and left unquantized. Logic's ES M was used.

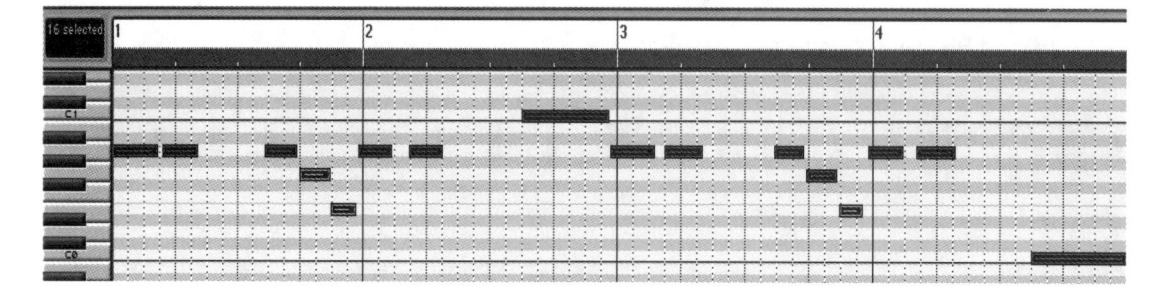

More could be done. Experiment with it yourself if you like. Congas, whistles ... anything you fancy really!

Project 9 – Get Creative with Logic jingle

Musical objectives

- To construct a jingle in dance music style.
- Improvise a vocal line using the phrase 'Get Creative with Logic'.

Logic skills

- Import and use a Recycle File.
- Utilize the ES M and ES E Audio Instruments.
- Apply EQ.
- Insert plug-ins: Pitch Shift II, Stereo Delay and Limiter.

Preparation

1 From the CD, copy the folder named 'project9' to your computer.
2 On your computer, create a folder called 'mywork9' or something similar in which to save your work.
3 From the project9 folder, open the template – templt9.
4 In your new 'mywork9' folder, save the template as mywork9 or something similar.

The assignment

Using a combination of audio loops and sequenced audio instruments compose a short jingle suitable for use with the Get Creative Web Site. Record a vocal track chanting or singing the words 'Get Creative With Logic'.

If you want to listen through the finished song file and find out how it goes load 9platmix or 9goldmix or 9silvermix.

If you have read Chapter 3 – all about getting ideas and developing them – then you will understand the importance of knowing where you are heading. This is often best worked out away from the computer either in your head or sometimes as notes or sketches on paper.

Although the drum loop comes first in this project, it must be said that the idea for the vocal part came first. It was buzzing around in my head for weeks before I actually got around to recording it. Although it's the essence of the piece and everything else is built around it, for now, it can wait.

Info

If your version of Logic does not support ReCycle files, import the audio file 120bpm.aif instead.

Tip

Before importing ReCycle files, define a path and check the Store ReCycle Audio Song Folder panel in the Set Audio Record Path window [Audio > Set Audio Record Path...], otherwise Logic will probably save the created audio files within the Emagic folder on your hard drive instead of your current Song folder (Figure P9.2).

Take 1

Track 1: Drums (Mono Audio Object)

We are going to import a ReCycle File – donated by those fine purveyors of loops, Pocketfuel (www.pocketfuel.com).
Follow these steps:

1 Ensure that the Song Line is at 1.1.1, and from the project9 folder import, or drag to track 1, 89bpm.rex [Audio > Import Audio File...]. Because our tempo of 120bpm is faster than that of the ReCycle file you will be given various options on how Logic should deal with the overlapping regions – Don't Fix, Add tracks, Crossfade and Render into single file. Avoid Add tracks. In this instance I settled for Crossfade. Logic creates an audio file – 89bpm.aif – that's added to the Audio and Arrange windows (Figure P9.1).

The ReCycle file was exported from ReCycle at 89bpm. Our piece is set to 120 bpm. The ReCycle file will play back at any tempo within about minus or plus 30bpm. Try it!

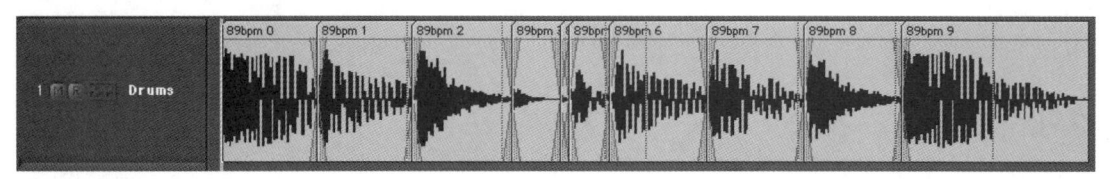

Figure P9.1
ReCycle file.

2 In the Sequence Parameter box – switch the Loop function to ON.
3 Save Song – compare with project9/9.1.

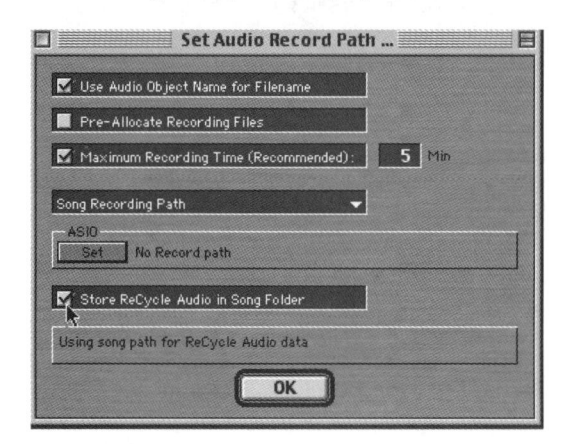

Figure P9.2
ReCycle audio path.

Take 2

Track 2: Bass – Audio Instrument 2 | ES M/Preset: tb_short
Sequence Parameters box: Qua 16F Swing
Transport Bar: (L) 1.1.1 (R) 5.1.1

The ES M synthesizer specializes in bass sounds and is just what we need here to underpin the drum loop. I've chosen the 'tb_short' pre-set. You may prefer another, or you may want to experiment and edit the chosen pre-set. A simple repetitive riff is all that's required.

Follow these steps:

1 Record the bass part between the Locators (Figures P9.3 and P9.4).
2 This riff will sound good in fifths. Drag a copy of the sequence to the next track down – track 3, Bass 2.
3 On track 3, Bass 2 – select the newly copied sequence and, in the Sequence Parameter box, enter a Transpose value of −7.
4 Make the transposition permanent [Functions > Sequence Parameter > Normalize Sequence Parameters].
5 In the Sequence Parameter box, switch Loop ON for both bass parts.
6 Save Song – compare with project9/9.2.

Figures P9.3 and **P9.4**
Bass part, Score and Matrix views

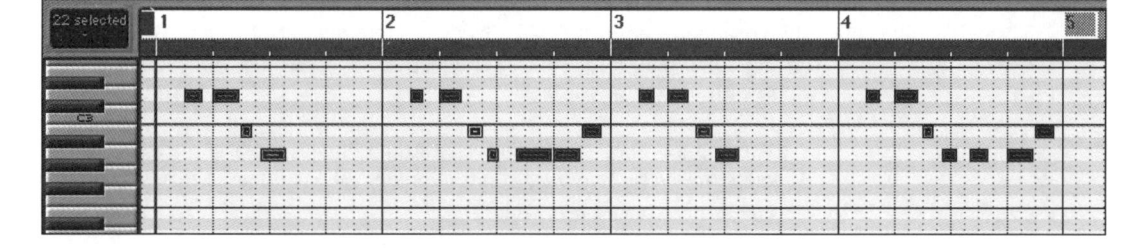

Start thinking about where in the piece to put the 'Get Creative With Logic' vocal line. Try improvising, either singing or chanting, along with the track. Even in this short space of four bars there are endless possibilities. I know how my mine goes, it's been driving me nuts for days! However, before my forthcoming virtuoso vocal performance, let's add another short loop. This time it's funky guitar.

Take 3

Track 4: Guitar (Stereo Audio Object)

Follow these steps:

1 Set the Song Line to 5.1.1, and from the project9 folder import guitar.aif [Audio > Import Audio File...].

2 Repeat the new Audio Region (bars 5 – 6) between bars 7 – 8.
3 Save Song – compare with project9/9.3.

OK, we have a nice funky background as a basis for the vocal, bars 1 – 5 serving as an introduction. At this point in the project you have the choice of recording your own improvised vocal or loading the audio files provided. It may be better to continue with mine (if you can stand it!) and overdub yours later.

Take 4

> *Track 5:* Vocal (Mono Audio Object)

Follow these steps:

1 Set the Song Line at 5.1.1, and from the project9 folder import the vocal part, getcreat.aif. Play it through ... well, if you can do better, record your own! Obviously this piece has to move on, but quite how long is still unknown. The vocal can stand another repeat before boredom sets in and the same goes for the guitar so:
2 Select the guitar and vocal Audio Regions between bars 5 – 9 and repeat them at bars 9 – 13.
3 Save Song – compare with project9/9.4a.

The vocal between bars 5 – 13 has definitely run out of steam. Before introducing something new it may be effective to repeat just the second phrase along with the guitar so:

1 With Scissors tool, divide the vocal Audio Region at bar 11.
2 Select the guitar and vocal Audio Regions between bars 11 – 13 and repeat them once only.
3 Save Song – compare with project9/4b.

It's time for something new. Repetition and variation, remember. The drums and bass can chug on but we must introduce another element or two. We'll start with a moody synth line, something simple that first climbs and then descends.

Take 5

> *Track 6:* Pad – Audio Instrument | ES E/Preset: soft_solina
> *Sequence Parameters box:* Qua 1/2 – note
> *Transport Bar:* (L) 15.1.1 (R) 23.1.1

Follow these steps:

1 Record the synth part between the Locators (Figure P9.5 and P9.6).

2 Select the recorded data in the Matrix Edit window and Force Legato [Functions > Note Events > Force Note Legato]. Things have now taken a new direction with the synth creating a degree of tension.
3 Save Song – compare with project9/9.5.

Figures P9.5 and **P9.6**
Synth, Score and matrix views

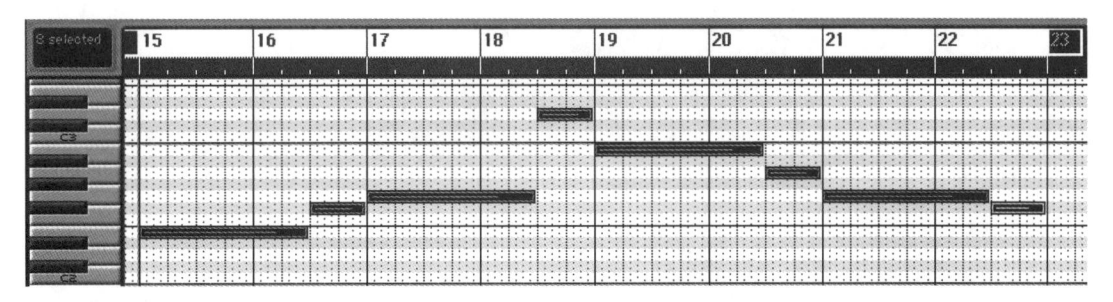

I'm rather fond of simple two note string pads for adding a touch of mystery. Placing one above the moving synth line will further establish the change of mood at measure 15.

Take 6

Track 7: Strings – Audio Instrument/ES E/Preset: bright_PWM_strings
Sequence Parameters box: Qua 1/8 – note
Transport Bar: (L) 15.1.1 (R) 23.1.1

Follow these steps:

1 Record the strings (Figures P9.7 and P9.8). Use a light touch and if need be, reduce the velocity of the notes in the Track Inspector.
2 Save Song – compare with project9/6.

Figures P9.7 and **P9.8**
Strings, Score and matrix views

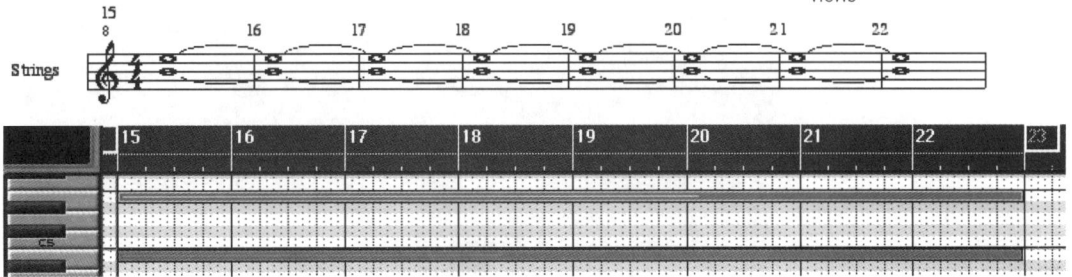

There's room for something else over those synth parts. Ask yourself what you can add. Sit back and listen. What comes to mind? You may well play guitar or some other instrument. If so it's time to 'Get Creative' and add something of your own. It is important though to try and hear what the piece needs first, before doodling commences. It need only be something very simple. What did I think of? Well I play saxophone and a very short jazz be-bop motif kept nagging away in my head. It refused to budge and so I recorded it.

As with the vocal part, at this point in the project you have the choice of recording your own instrument. You may prefer to continue with my soprano sax and overdub something of your own later.

Take 7

Track 8: Soprano Sax (Mono Audio Object)

Follow these steps:

1 Set the Song Line at 15.1.1, and from the project9 folder import the audio file soprano.aif.
2 Repeat the soprano Audio Region (bars 15.3.1 – 17.3.1) three times as far as bar 23.3.1.
3 Save Song – Compare with project9/7.arr
4 Set the Locators to (L) 1.1.1 (R) 23.1.1 and activate the Cycle button. That's long enough for our purposes. Each cycle lasts 44 seconds.

The mix

Load 9platmix or 9goldmix or 9silvmix to view and hear a mix of 'Get Creative With Logic'.

Only one send effect is used, PlatinumVerb/GoldVerb on Bus 1, and the vocal and soprano saxophone make use of it (Figures P9.9 and P9,10).

Info

There are three mixes on the CD, Platinum, Gold and Silver, each using slightly different plug-ins. However, should a plug-in not be found, just replace it with the equivalent included with your particular version.

Figure P9.9
Pt-Verb: WoodenVerb.

(right) Figure P9.10
GoldVerb : Short Reverb.

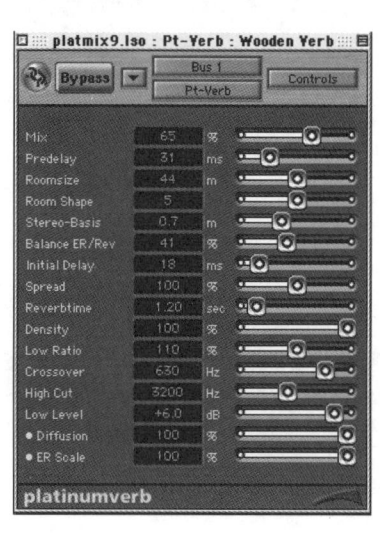

Inserts are used for the guitar: Stereo Delay (Figure P9.11) and Limiter (Figure P9.12) with a soft limiting pre-set. Pitch Shift II (Figure P9.13) is used on the vocal to create a 'shadow' a fourth below the original.

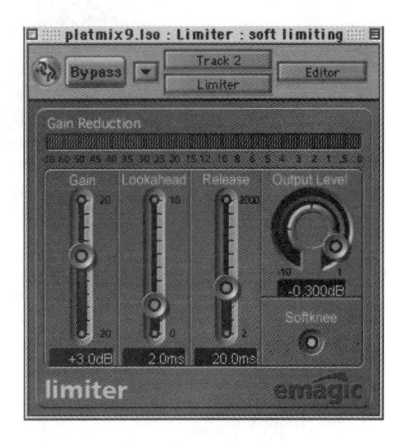

Figure P9.11
Stereo Delay.

(right) Figure P9.12
Limiter.

An EQ plug-in, Hi-Pass (Figure P9.14) has been inserted after Pitch Shft II to reduce some of the lower, muddier frequencies. The higher frequencies are allowed through. Solo the track in the Track Mixer and toggle By Bpass switch on and off to hear how this has affected the vocal signal.

The vocal was recorded with the aid of an outboard compressor with a fairly high compression ratio, about 6:1. Further compression in Logic seems, to me anyway, unecessary.

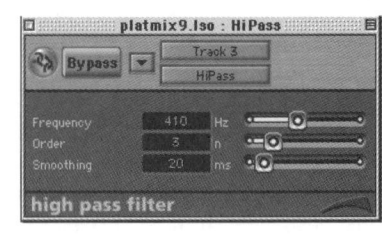

Figure P9.13
Pitch Shift II.

(right) Figure P9.14
Hi-Pass.

11 Knowing the score

> **Info**
>
> To examine the Logic files for this chapter, copy the folder named 'minimal' from the CD to your computer.

Rebecca's got the job. She's been sending demos and making follow up calls to a small independent TV production company in her area for some time now and they have finally given her a chance. They sent her a video. She composed some music using Logic, mastered it to DAT and dropped it off personally. 'Great', they said. 'How about a live version, played by real musicians?'

'No problem', replied Rebecca, I can print the score and parts direct from Logic. 'We'll book the studio and hire the session musicians', they said. Rebecca went home a very happy person indeed.

A week later Rebecca arrives at the studio and peers through the control room window at the motley bunch of musicians sitting around drinking cups of coffee and reading newspapers. Scraps of conversation can be heard through the studio monitors. 'My central heating has bust again ... I still haven't been paid for the last session we did here ...'

Rebecca hands out the printed parts and listens nervously as the band begins a run through. 'It doesn't sound too good', she thinks, 'I thought these guys could read and play anything that's put in front of them'. Pretty soon the band grinds to a halt. 'These parts are useless', exclaims a particularly belligerent trumpet player. 'My part hasn't even been transposed'. We've all got different note lengths', bemoans the trombonist. 'My dog could write better parts than this!' growls the drummer.

So what did she do wrong? Although Rebecca can play piano, compose tunes and arrange them in Logic, her music reading and writing skills lack professionalism. She made the all too common mistake of thinking that the notes she actually played into Logic would appear correctly in the score printing and layout section of the program. What she had not realised is that in order for the music to be readable by musicians some editing is required. She played the original sequenced version to the musicians and after correcting the parts, they played it perfectly. Of course this took up valuable studio time and the session over ran by fifteen minutes. Overtime had to be paid to the musicians and studio owners.

It is important to understand the relationship between the Score editor and the rest of the program. To begin with, it will not display the notes of recorded audio data. Not for the time being anyway. Maybe one day the technology will be able to handle it. No, Logic's Score interprets recorded MIDI data and according to the settings you make, displays the result as conventional music notation.

Before editing, every note recorded as MIDI data in Logic is faithfully displayed in the Score Edit window exactly as it was played. For example four

Figure 11.1
Before tweaking.

bars of Jingle Bells – score/jingle – captured in Logic displays like Figure 11.1. Looks wrong, doesn't it? But play it through and it sounds OK. The same data, after a little tweaking in the Score Display Parameter box yields a perfect display (Figure 11.2). The MIDI data hasn't changed, just the interpretation. A glance at the Score Display Parameter box will reveal:

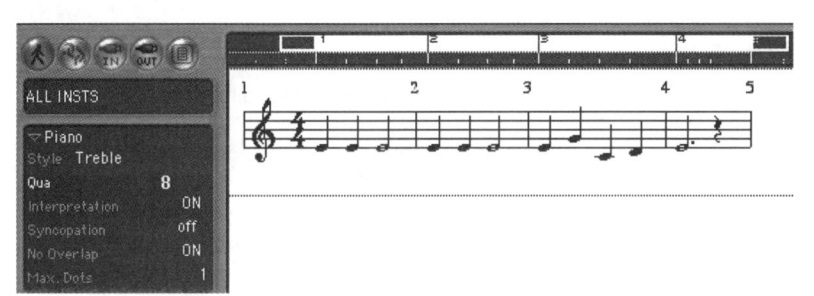

Figure 11.2
After tweaking.

- Quantization has been changed to 8. A setting of 4 would also have worked because that is the smallest note value actually needed for a correct note length display.
- Interpretation has been turned on.
- No Overlap has also been turned on and cleans up the overlapping note in bar 3.

Since this book is not a manual. I would advise at this point that those readers who are unfamiliar with Logic's Score to study the documentation shipped with the program and work through the tutorials contained on the CD. Afterwards, proceed to the next chapter in this book, where a good many of the commonly used Score editing features are used to format the music recorded in Project 6.

Info

To be fair to Logic, a reasonable score presentation is often initially displayed due to the default settings. These have a quantization value of 16,24 with Interpretation and No Overlap turned on. Even so, further editing is usually required.

Project 10 – Score clean-up

Musical objective

- To transform an intelligible mess into a readable score!

Logic skills

- Use the Page View icon to toggle between a linear and full page score view.
- Use the Score Display Parameter box for a readable interpretation of MIDI data as a music notation.
- Enter note and chord symbols from the Part box.
- Create Instrument Sets and brackets to seperate brass and rhythm sections on the score.
- Edit bar and page numbers using the Song Settings wndow.
- Select slurs from the Part box. Draw and edit them on the score.
- Automatically display a transposed trumpet part.
- Enter title and copyright information with the Text tool.

Preparation

- From the CD, copy the folder named 'project10' to your computer.
- Create a folder called 'mywork10' or something similar in which to save your work.

The assignment

The Football Theme, commissioned in Project 6, was a success. However, the program makers would like a studio version, played by real musicians. You need to prepare a score and printed parts for the session.

Because some of the work required to produce a presentable score may well involve some destructive editing we are going to work on a copy of the original. Use the example on the CD – project10/templt10 – as the basis for your work.

Follow these steps:

1 Load project10/templt10 and in your 'mywork10' folder, save as Logic Song File – myproj10 or something similar. If you have already worked through Project 6 – A Football Theme – you will remember that it contained an audio track featuring yours truly on tenor sax. This has been

deleted. It was an improvised overdub and will not need scoring anyway. Besides, the company commissioning the music prefer the alternative solo trumpet (there's no accounting for taste!).

2 In the Arrange window, select track 1, brass 1, and open the score [Windows > Open Score] (Figure P10.1).

Figure P10.1
Brass 1 score.

What do you think? Your answers will vary according to how much knowledge of music notation you possess. If you can't read music at all it will not make much sense. In this case some time studying music theory is the only course of action open to you if you want to work with Logic's Score.

If you have experience of reading music at an entry or intermediate level, your answer might be, 'Looks all right to me. The first note is F followed by Bb and C. Yes I can understand that'. In your case this project will help you display a decent, readable score.

If you are an experienced music reader your reaction will probably be something like, 'Well it is difficult to read because the key signature is missing and the note lengths are incorrectly displayed. There are no dynamic or articulation markings either.'

If you are a professional trumpet player your reaction may well be something like, 'Surely you don't expect me to read this rubbish! What's needed? A score clean-up.

Follow these steps:

1 In the Arrange window, select track 1 and glue all the sequences together. Open the score. Well, it's a start! All the extra clef signs and time signatures cluttering the staff have disappeared. What next?
2 The first thing to change is the Quantization setting in the Display Parameter box, on the left. Because the Global Display Value in the Transport window is set to 1/16, Logic has displayed 16,24 (binary – sixteenth notes, ternary – sixteenth note triplets) in the Score Display Parameter box. Our smallest note value in this brass part is an 1/8th note, so change it to 8. Scroll the staff and you'll notice that all the unecessary sixteenth notes and rests have disappeared. Much better!
3 Although accurate, the display in the last two bars will still remain ambiguous to our trumpet player so turn Interpretation ON. Better still. We're getting there! Still no key signature though.

Info

There are two ways of displaying the score: Linear view – with a faster re-draw for editing (Page Edit un-ticked) and Page view for layout. Use the Page view icon (Figure P10.2) to toggle between the two.

Figure P10.2
Page view icon.

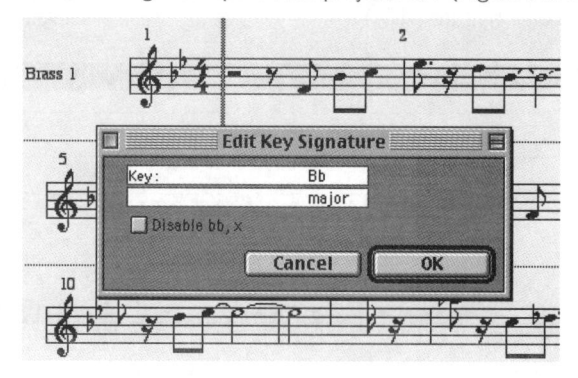

Figure P10.3
Editing the key signature.

Figure P10.4
Score parameters.

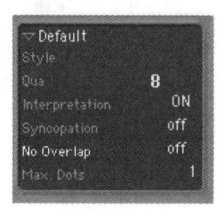

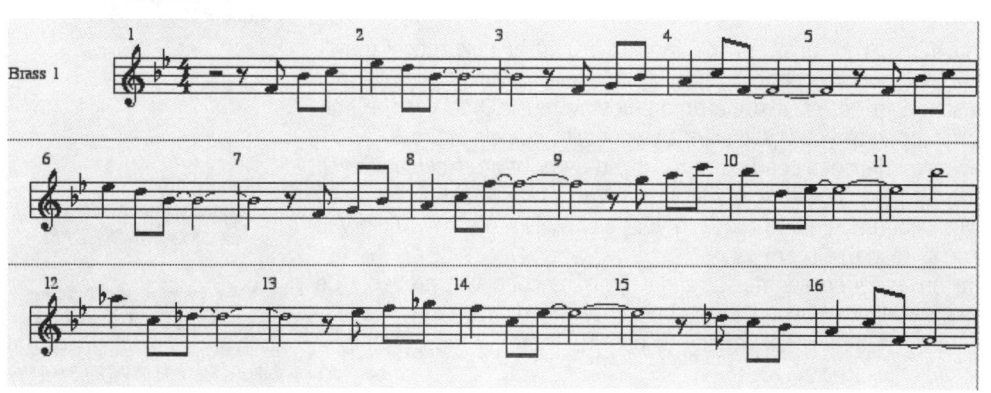

Figure P10.5
Project10/1.

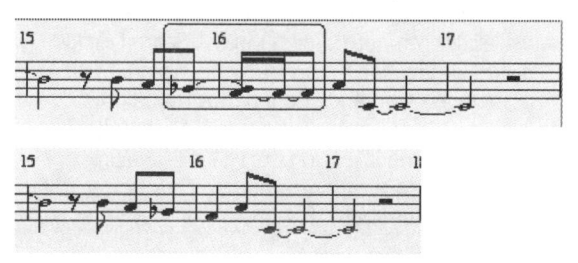

Figures P10.6a and **b**
Overlapping notes, before and after

4 Double click between the clef and time signatue, and in the resulting dialogue box, change the key to Bb major (two flats). All the unnecessary accidentals disappear. Wonderful! (Figure P10.3).

5 Save Song – compare with project10/1 (Figure P.10.5).

The score parameters should now look like those in Figure P10.4. Syncopation and No Overlap have been left off (they don't concern us here).

Let's move on. Follow these steps:

1 Select track 2, glue all the sequences together and open the Score Editor. In bars 15/16 and 31/32 we have a case of overlapping notes (Figure P10.6a). In the Display Parameters box, turn No Overlap ON. The overlapping notes are cured (Figure P10.6b). Turn Interpretation ON and change the Quantize Display to 8. Note (not strictly necessary because everything displays fine at 16,24). Note, Logic has changed the key signature to Bb major automatically.

Project 10 – Score clean up

2   Select track 3, glue all the sequences together and open the Score Editor. This time just turn on Interpretation in the Display Parameter box. Everything is cured, including the overlapped notes. Actually, using Interpretation alone would have sufficed on the other two brass tracks but I wanted to explain how the individual functions affect the display.
3   Select track 4, glue the sequences together and open the Score Editor. Again turning on Interpretation is all that's required for a readable display. That's the brass section done.
4   Save Song – compare with project10/2.

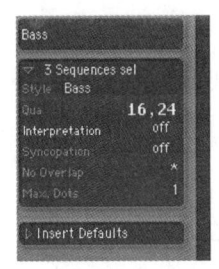

Figure P10.7
Bass staff.

1   Select track 6 (bass) and open the score. Oh dear! This is enough to drive any self respecting bass player completely crackers! It's a jumble. Parts like this have been handed out though, believe me! (Figure P10.7).
2   In the Arrange window, glue the sequences together, and in the Score Edit window turn on Interpretation in the Display Parameters box. Note that Bass has been selected as Style in the parameter box. This ensures the bass staff will display one octave higher than the bass actually sounds. The result is much improved (Figure P10.8).

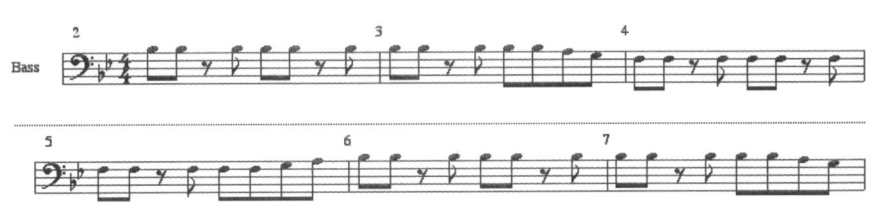

Figure P10.8
Bass staff, much improved.

3   Save Song – compare with project10/3.

Conventional scores do not have separate drum staves. We have two drum tracks (kick and snare) plus a whistle on the Referee track. Let's combine them.

1   In the Arrange window, Glue and merge the two drum tracks (kick and snare) sequences together to make a single track. Leave the Referee out of this for the moment. We'll deal with him later!
2   Open the Score Edit window and in the Display Parameter box, change the Style from Bass to #Drums. A drum clef appears and the drum beats are re-mapped on the staff. Turn on Interpretation and we have a very presentable drum part (Figure P10.9).
3   Close the score, and in the Arrange page delete the now empty, drum track. Be careful not to delete the Referee track.
4   Save Song – compare with project10/4.

Figure P10.9
Drum part.

On to the guitar. Follow these steps:

1 Select track 5 (guitar) and open the score (Figure P10.10a). Well we can't give that to a guitar player. He'll fall about laughing! Apart from it being a jumble, what he requires here is a chord sheet. How do we do that? There are various methods. Here's one way to do it.

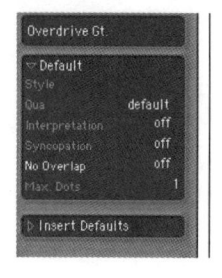

Figure P10.10a
Guitar score.

2 In the Arrange window, glue the sequences together, and in the Score Edit window turn on Interpretation in the Display Parameters box. That's the display fixed. Compare to Figure P10.10b.

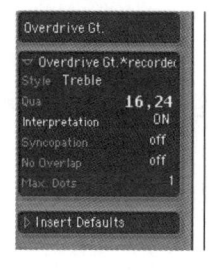

Figure P10.10b
A cleaner guitar score.

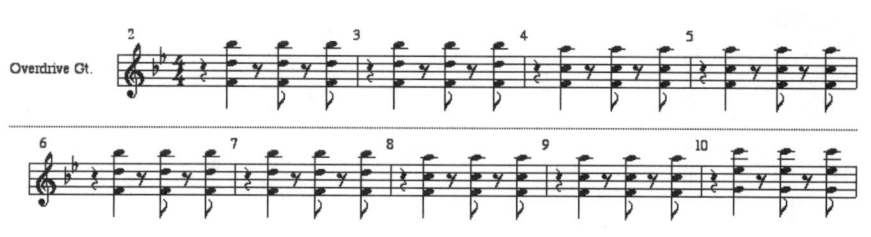

3 In the Part box click on 'A' to bring the Text Objects to the top of the menu (Figure P10.11). Drag the Chord object on to the staff and insert it at the beginning of bar 2 (2.1.1) beneath the staff. A text cursor appears.

4 Type Bb (upper case – lower case) and press 'Enter'. Logic redraws this as a B flat chord symbol (Figure P10.12).

Figure P10.11
Part box.

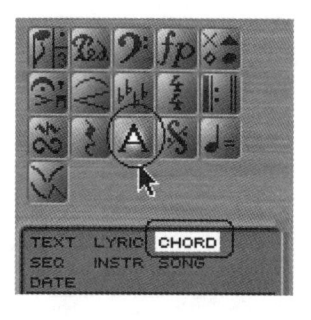

Figure P10.12
Bb chord symbol.

5 Enter the remaining chords. Type exactly as listed and Logic will automatically interpret the chord symbol.
Here's the full list.

(At bar 2 type Bb)
At bars 4 and 8 type F
At bar 6 type Bb
At bar 10 type Cm
At bar 12 type Db/Gb
At bar 14 type Gb
At bar 16 type F

Tip

When you insert chord symbols make sure they are at the correct bar position. Watch the Info Line above the staff.

6 When you reach bar 12, type the Db first then double-click on the chord symbol and up pops an edit window (Figure P10.13). Here you can enter the bass note – Gb.

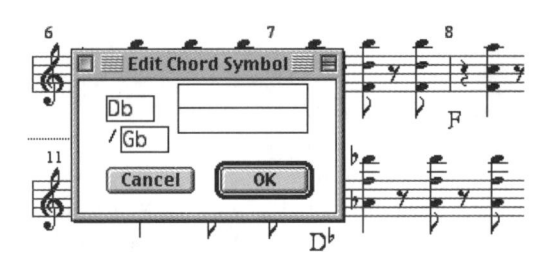

Figure P10.13
Chord Edit Window.

7 Select all the chord symbols – they will blink – and copy and paste them to bar 18.

Things are much clearer but we don't need the note display as well as chord symbols. We could leave them, it doesn't really matter. Although a little time consuming it's better to delete them.

1 Delete all the notes except the bottom note on each stem.
2 Open the Matrix Edit window [Windows > Open Matrix Edit] and use the keyboard to select all the G notes (Figure P10.14). Drag them down to F (bottom space on the staff). Do this with the other remaining notes until all the notes are F.
3 Back in the Score view, select all the notes – they blink – and from the Part box, drag a slash note-head symbol onto the first F. All the notes change to a slash symbol (Figure P10.15).

Tip

A quick way to alter notes of the same pitch in a sequence: In the Matrix Edit window, select the note(s) you wish to change on the keyboard. All the notes in the sequence will be selected. Simply drag them all to the new pitch.

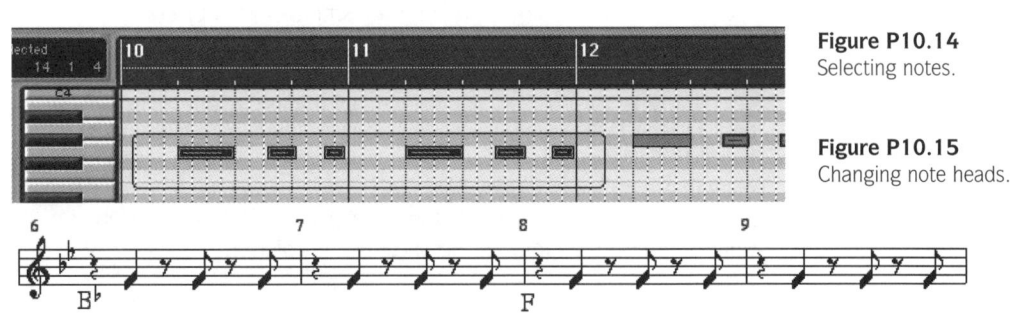

Figure P10.14
Selecting notes.

Figure P10.15
Changing note heads.

> **Info**
>
> To apply accents and other symbols to notes, drag them from the symbols group in the Part box onto the note-heads. Logic will snap them in place. The symbols will remain in position even if you move or transpose them.

4 Save Song – compare with project10/5.

Musicians need more than just notes on the staff to correctly interpret a written piece of music. Articulation markings are particularly important.

1 Return to track 1 – Brass 1 / Tpt 1, and open the score.
2 Click on the first note in bar 34 (Bb4). A glance at the Info line above will tell you that this note received more velocity than the note following. So did the notes at 34. 2. 3.1 (Ab4) and 34.1.1. (G). They were clearly accented and we need to point this out to the trumpet player, so:
3 Select an accent (>) from the symbols group in the Part box and drag it onto those notes (Figure P10.16).
4 Save Song – compare with project10/6.

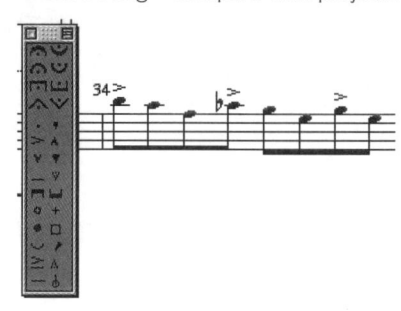

Figure P10.16
Applying accents.

1 Return to the drums – track 8 and open the score. In the treble clef, the whistle is represented as the note B. Changing the Style to #Drums will cause it to disappear altogether so drag it down to G, below the staff. Change the Style to #Drums and it changes to a cymbal note head. That's OK, we can indicate to the player that a whistle is required by entering text with the Text tool (Figure P10.17).

Figure P10.17
The whistle.

2 Merge the whistle sequence with the drums above on track 7.
3 Save Song – compare with project10/7.

It's time to do some layout work, so:

1 In the Arrange window, ensure that all the sequences are glued together. Make them start and end together too, otherwise bars will be missing on the full score. Do this by dragging the corners of the objects.
2 In the Arrange window, Select All [Edit> Select All]
3 Open the score. From the score, change the view to Page Edit. Double-click in the Instrument Set box, or use the menu [Layout > Instrument Sets...]. The Instrument Set window opens (Figure P10.18).
4 In the Instrument Set window, rename the set Full Score. In the Full Name column enter names for the brass section – Trumpet 1, 2, 3 and Solo Trumpet and names for the rhythm section – Guitar, Bass and Drums. Enter abbreviated names in the Short Name column.

Project 10 – Score clean up

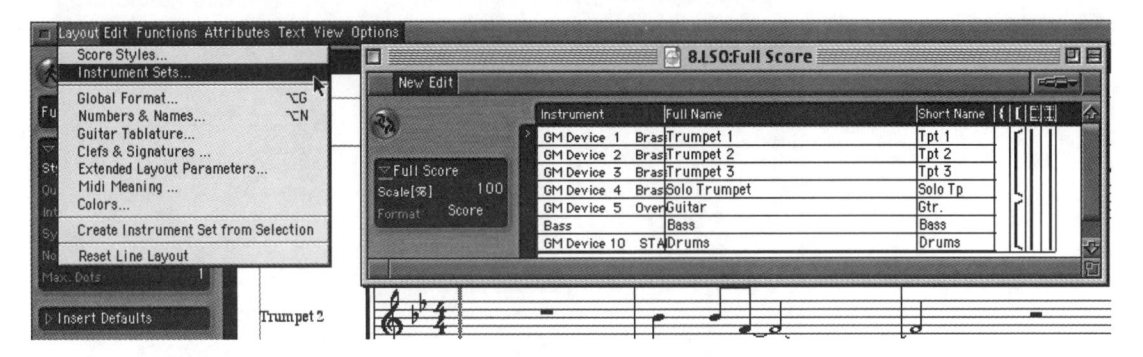

5 Use the Brackets and Bar Lines column to separate the brass section from the rhythm section. Drag the brackets with the mouse. This can also be done on the score itself.
6 Save Song – compare with project10/8.

Figure P10.18
Instrument Set box and Instrument Set window.

We are almost finished with the score. Just a few details to tidy up.

1 Using the Text tool enter the title – Football Theme – in the Header section, at the top of the page. When you have finished you will see an Event Parameter box appear on the left (Figure P10.19). Increase the Size parameter to 20 for a nice clear title. Change the font if you wish. I have left everything as Times. The text can be centred by choosing Text > Align > Page right.

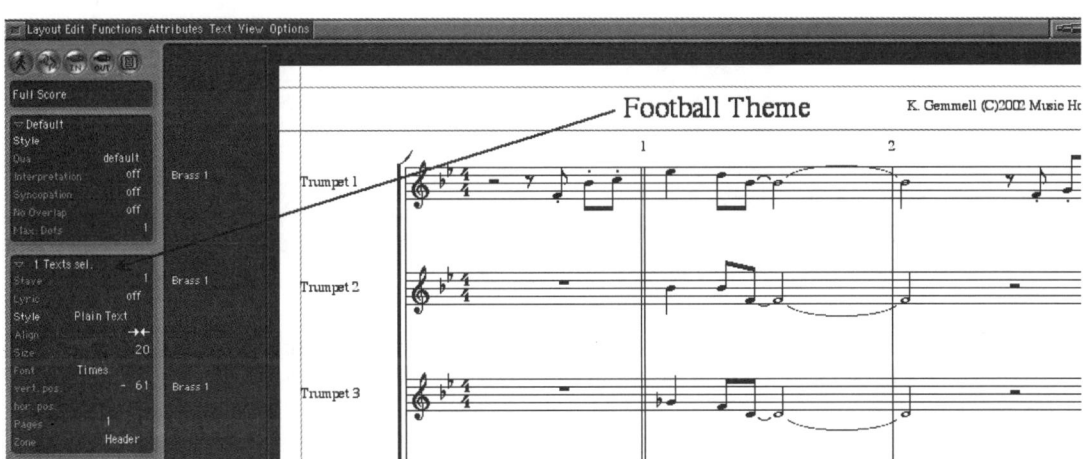

2 Save Song – compare with project10/9.arr.

Figure P10.19
Title and Text Event Parameter box.

On viewing project10/9 you will see that a number of other changes have taken place.

- The bar numbers have been offset – click on bar numbers to reveal the Song Settings dialogue (Figure P10.20) or use [Options > Settings > Score Numbers & Names...]. Bar and page number settings can be changed here as well as font and instrument name settings.

Figure P10.20
Song Settings dialogue.

Figure P10.21
Repeat Signs and Bar Lines.

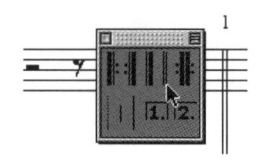

Figure P10.22
Slurs, Crescendi, Lines, Arrows.

Tip

Zoom in when inserting and positioning slurs. It's much easier.

Figure P10.23
Trumpet notation before and after alteration.

- Double bar lines have been inserted at bars 1 and 17 – use Repeat Signs and Bar Lines in the Part box (Figure P10.21).

- Slurs have been used in the brass parts at bar 33 – use Slurs, Crescendi, Lines, Arrows in the Part box (Figure P10.22). After insertion, use the 'handles' – small black squares – to change their shape.
- In bar 32 you'll see a change in the notation (Figures P10.23a and P10.23b). This was changed because, unlike a GM sound module, the leap from Bb to top C on a real trumpet may prove difficult!

- Staccato marks and accents have been inserted in the brass parts – use Symbols attached to Notes in the Part box (Figure P10.24).

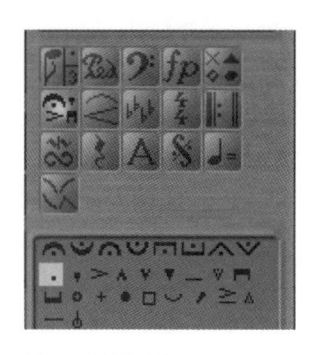

> **Tip**
>
> To enter multiple note symbols, select all the notes you wish to change and drag a symbol from the Part box to one of the notes. All the selected notes receive the same symbol.

Figure P10.24
Symbols attached to notes.

Change your version accordingly. A lot more can be done but by now I'm sure you've got the picture.

We will now prepare the Trumpet 1 part.

1 In the Arrange window, select track 1 and open the score. Use Page Edit view. Looks pretty good already doesn't it? However, if you read the previous chapter 'Knowing the Score,' you will remember the trumpet player complaining that his part had not been transposed. Our Trumpet 1 part is in Bb at the moment. It will have to be transposed up a tone for performance purposes.

2 From the drop-down menu In the Score Parameter box select Style > Trumpet in Bb (Figure P10.25).

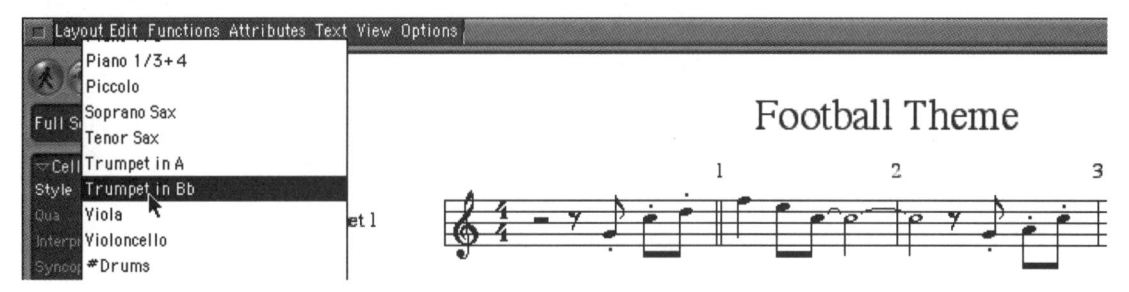

Hey presto! the Trumpet 1 score has been transposed to the key of C.

Figure 10.25

3 Save Song – compare with project10/10.

> **Tip**
>
> In real life, keep your players happy. Don't give them impossible things to play that may well sound good on a synthesizer. Use high notes sparingly (all the more effective). Big leaps, particularly on brass instruments are best avoided if you want a smooth session. Rule of thumb – keep it simple.

> **Tip**
>
> Transposing the Trumpet part will also transpose that part on the Full Score. To view the score at concert pitch, transpose it back again.

> **Info**
>
> Some writers prefer a transposed score, with all the instruments viewed in the keys that the actual players will read them. Others, myself included, prefer to view their scores in concert pitch.

12 Creative audio editing

Tim's frustrated. He's found the perfect drum loop for his latest project. Trouble is, for hours now he has been tearing his hair out trying to match the tempo of Logic with that of the loop. He's scrolled the tempo on Logic's transport bar with the mouse so many times that his arm is beginning to hurt. 'It's somewhere between 125 and 130 bpm', he mutters, 'but I'm dammed if I can nail it down'. Some time later (we'll not mention just exactly how long!) he finally settles on 127.2937bpm, but this is by no means certain. 'It'll have to do', he thinks.

Tim begins adding a bass line and a few keyboard licks to what seems a promising project. After a while he pauses to evaluate things and plays it through. Seems a bit slow', he thinks. 'It would be nice to move it up a notch or two'. He increases the tempo by several beats per minute. 'That's better. Wait a minute though, something sounds wrong. Of course, the audio doesn't fit now that I've altered the tempo. How am I going to fix it so that the audio follows my new tempo?', he asks himself. 'Oh well, back to the original tempo. What was it now? Oh no! I've forgotton. I think it was somewhere around 127 bpm'.

After much adjusting and re-adjusting, he finally settles on a tempo somewhere close to before but by now he's heard that drum loop dozens of times and he's rapidly going off it. 'That loop could do with a bit more swing', he mumbles. 'I wonder if it can be quantized, like the MIDI tracks? I seem to remember reading something about this in the Logic manual. Anyway, can't be bothered with all that'.

What has Tim done wrong? Well nothing really, apart from waste a lot of time fiddling about instead of fully reading the excellent documentation that's supplied with Logic. Had he done so he could have matched Logic's tempo to the drum loop in a fraction of the time it took him to do it manually, and far more accurately. He would also have discovered other useful and creative tools, such as the Time and Pitch machine, Groove Template, the Quantize Engine, the Audio to MIDI function and several more.

I tend to think of audio editing in two catagories, functional and creative. Functional editing might include the business of cleaning up noisy tracks, altering audio levels, normalizing and trimming regions. All this can be done in the Sample Edit window using the Functions menu. Creative audio editing may well include some of these features too, indeed functional and creative work constantly overlap. However you can be more creative and conjure up more powerful magic using the Digital Factory [Sample Edit Window > Factory]. Here you can do all manner of wonderful things including time stretching, altering pitch, and quantizing. There's even something called an

Audio to Score Streamer which will convert your audio creations into music notation (recommended only to those of you with unlimited patience and a very even temper!).

The following projects, 11 – 17, demonstrate just some of the wizardry possible when editing audio in Logic. The first five make use of a drum loop made from 'sample hits' supplied by top session drummer Keith Leblanc (www.keithleblanc.org).

For most audio editing work two windows are needed:

- The Audio window [Audio > Audio Window...], where you organize all the audio files used in a Logic song (Figure 12.1).
- The Sample Editor [Audio > Sample Editor...], where you can edit and process mono and stereo audio files (Figure 12.2).

Figure 12.1
The Audio window

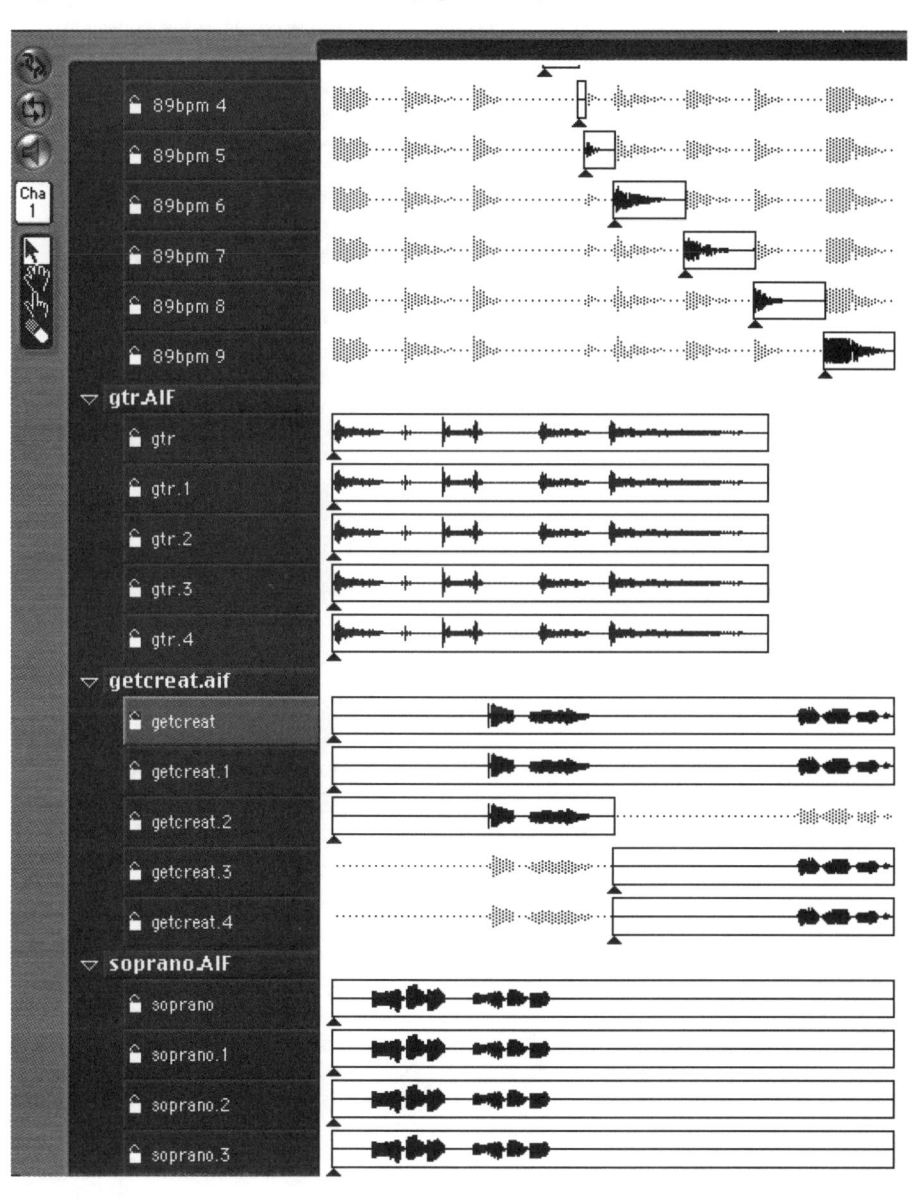

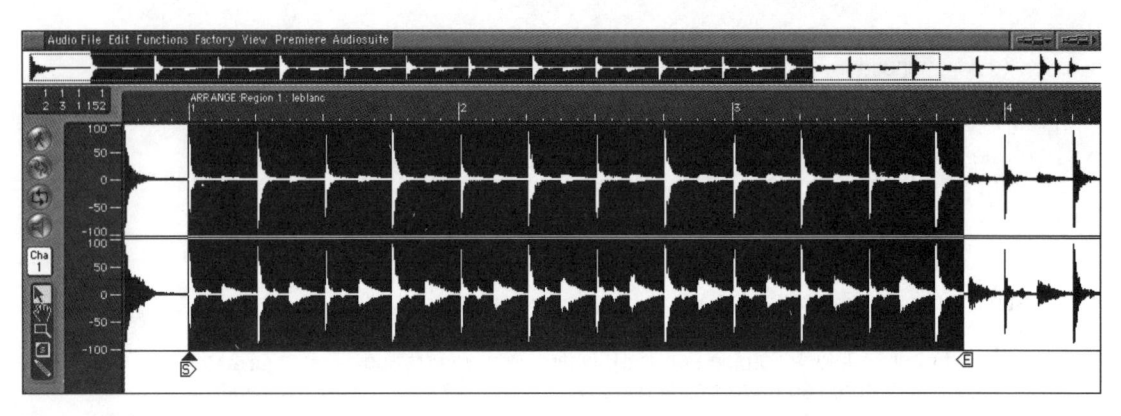

Figure 12.2
The Sample Editor

It's a good idea to save a screenset with three windows open containing the above plus the Arrange window. Much switching between the three often occurs.

Project 11 – matching Song tempo to audio

Objective

- Use the Sample Editor to match Logic's Song tempo with that of an imported audio file.

Preparation

1 From the CD, copy the folder named project11 to your computer.
2 On your computer, create a folder called mywork11 or something similar in which to save your work.
3 From the project11 folder, open the template – templt11
4 In your new mywork11 folder, re-save the template as myproj11 or something similar.

This template contains a mono audio file (drumkit.aif) that's just over four bars long. Take a glance in the Arrange window. 'That's odd. How is it that a four bar loop spans just over seven bars', I hear you mumble. Well, that's because we don't yet know the tempo of the loop itself. Our tempo on the Transport bar shows 120 bpm, but the loop's tempo is obviously slower. Before we record anything, MIDI or audio, it's best to determine the real tempo.

1 In the Sample Editor – select a one bar section (more if you want, a one or two bar section will do the trick). Click on the start of the area you want to select, hold down the mouse button and move it to approximately where you want the section to end. A shaded selection appears (Figure P11.1).

Figure P11.1
Audio selection.

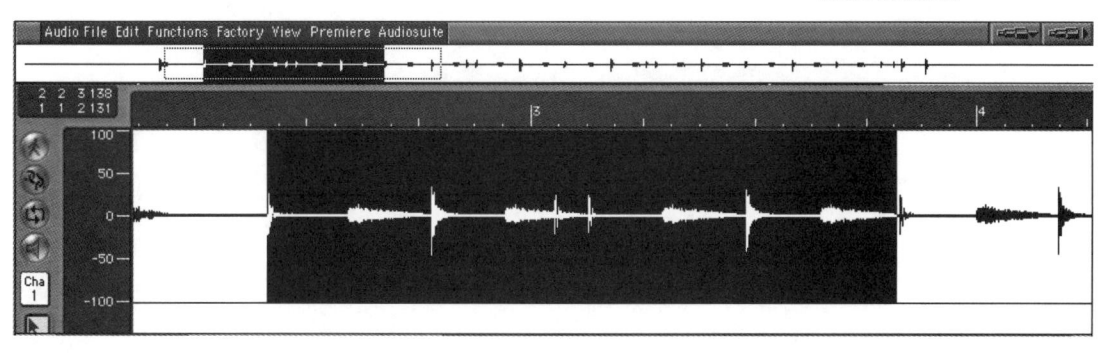

2 Activate the Cycle icon and press Play to audition the Selection. Fine tune the boundaries by holding down the shift key whilst adjusting the start and end points until the loop sounds accurate. Be sure that the Selection is cycling smoothly.
3 Turn the selected audio into a Region [Edit > Selection > Region]. New Start and End points are inserted. The audio regions in the Arrange and Audio windows are adjusted accordingly.
4 In the Arrange window – move the Region back to 1.1.1.
5 In the Arrange window – set up a one bar cycle (or more, depending on your choice in step 1).
6 In the Sample Editor – to find the real tempo use Functions > Adjust Tempo by Selection & Locators. A dialogue box appears giving you the option to adjust the tempo globally or just from the beginning of the region. Choose 'Globally'.
7 The tempo on my version changed to 84.8920. Yours, almost certainly, will be slightly different.
8 Save Song – compare to project11/11.1.

Now, although the tempo came out as 84.8920 bpm, I happen to know – because I recorded it! – that the original tempo was exactly 85 bpm. So, for the following projects that use this audio file I have adjusted the tempo to just that.

Project 12 – slicing audio for tempo adjustment

Objective

- In the Audio window, use the Strip Silence feature to slice up an audio file in multiple Regions and thereby facilitate the increase or decrease of its tempo.

Preparation

1 From the CD, copy the folder named project12 to your computer.
2 On your computer, create a folder called mywork12 or something similar in which to save your work.
3 From the project12 folder, open the template – templt12
4 In your new mywork12 folder, re-save the template as myproj12 or something similar.

This template picks up where the previous project left off. Logic's Song tempo has been adjusted to 85 bpm to match the audio file, now renamed drumkit2.aif. The Audio Region has been adjusted to exactly four bars in the Audio and Arrange windows. It would be nice, wouldn't it, if we could now adjust our tempo in the normal way and have the audio follow along with it? Well it can be done. Fiddly, yes, but possible. To begin with the audio has to be sliced up into segments of a suitable length. This process can be likened to that of Propellerheads' ReCycle program.
    Follow these steps:

1 In the Audio window – select drumkit2.aif and open the Strip Silence window [Options > Strip Silence]. You will most likely see the audio sliced into sections according to the default settings (Figure P12.1).

Figure P12.1
Strip Silence window.

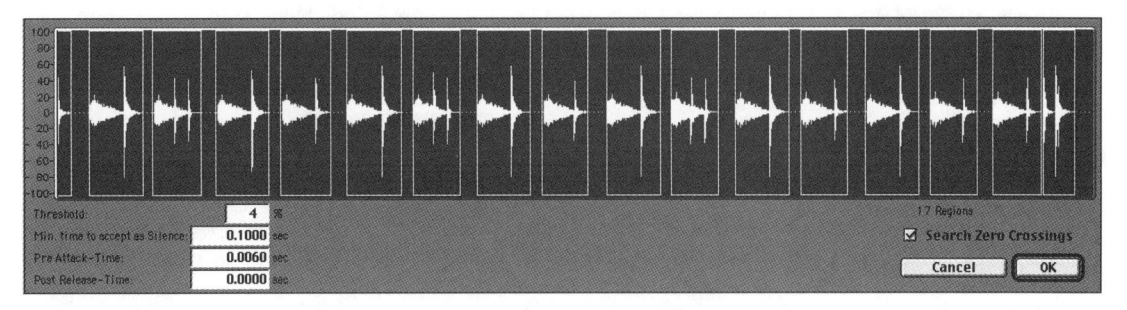

Now these settings will probably work, up to a point, but think ahead. The sliced audio is going to be speeded up and slowed down. We therefore need to find the smaller divisions of the beat. Where are they? The obvious ones are at the end of this loop. The sixteenth notes on the kick drum. So ...

2 In the Strip Silence window – gradually increase the Threshold percentage. How far? It's variable. I stopped at 14% (Figure P12.2).

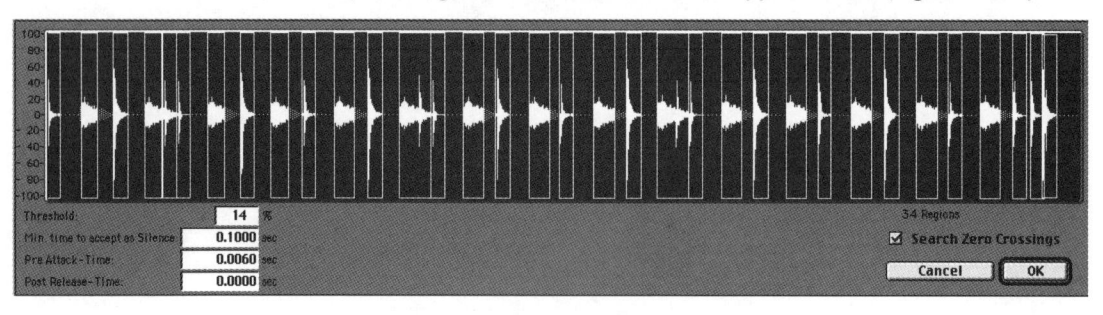

Figure P12.2
Increasing Threshold percentage.

Now, we don't really need any actual silence removed, if possible. We just want a nice set of Regions (slices) to manipulate. So ...

3 Reduce the Pre-Attack time to 0.0050 and increase the Post Release time 0.3000 (Figure P12.3). We now have a set of 34 Regions that should play pretty smoothly. Lets find out.

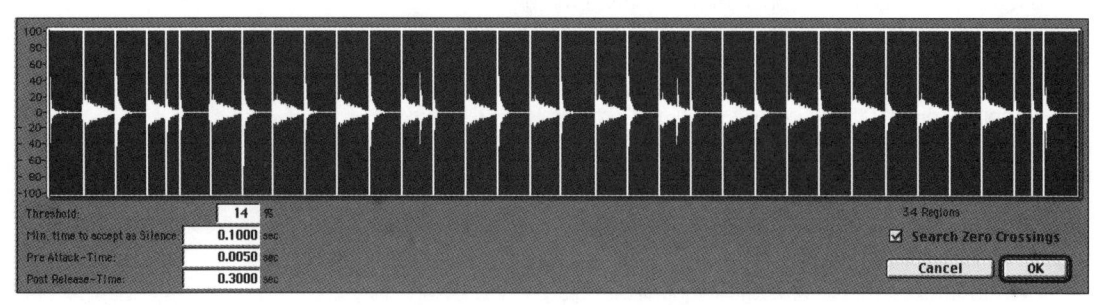

Figure P12.3
34 sliced Regions.

4 Ensure that Search Zero Crossings is checked and press the OK button. Logic will ask you whether or not you want to replace the regions in the Arrange window. Choose Replace. The Regions are now displayed in the Arrange window.
5 Save Song – compare to project12/12.1.

Experiment with the tempo and you will find that it sounds OK when sped up. Slow it down though and things don't sound so good. Clicks are sounding at the region boundaries. We'll fix it in project 13!

Tip

Another way to slice up the audio into ReCycle style regions is to use the Scissors from the toolbox (holding down the Option key – Alt on PC) and cutting the loop at 1.1.2.1 (the first sixteenth note division). The audio loop will be sliced into sixteenth note regions.

Info

The Strip Silence function allows you to create Audio Regions automatically. Silence is interpreted according to a variable threshold level and removed. New regions are created from the remaining passages. It has many uses, the most obvious as a noise gate. It can also be used for time compression or expansion (creating segments for drum loops) and multiple editing such as speech manipulation.

Project 13 – trimming regions and creating fade outs

Objectives

- Use the Fade tool to smooth clicks at audio region boundaries brought about by tempo changes.
- Adjust start points to remove audible clicks.

Preparation

1 From the CD, copy the folder named project13 to your computer.
2 On your computer, create a folder called mywork13 or something similar in which to save your work.
3 From the project13 folder, open the template - templt13
4 In your new mywork13 folder, re-save the template as myproj13 or something similar.

This template picks up where the previous project left off. After matching Logic's Song tempo to the audio file drumkit.aif and creating a four bar drum loop in project 11 the file was further processed in project 12 and sliced up, ReCycle style, into 34 separate regions. On speeding up the song we found that things sounded OK. However, on slowing the tempo down to 80 bpm nasty sounding clicks were appearing at region boundaries. How do we get shot of them?

Follow these steps:

1 In the Arrange window – set up a cycle for the first bar. At this tempo, 80 bpm, there are clicks all over the place! Double click on the first Region and the Sample Editor opens.
2 In the Sample Editor - Play the selected region. You'll notice that some of the hi-hat from the following region has been caught at the end (Figure P13.1).

Figure P13.1
Clipped hi-hat.

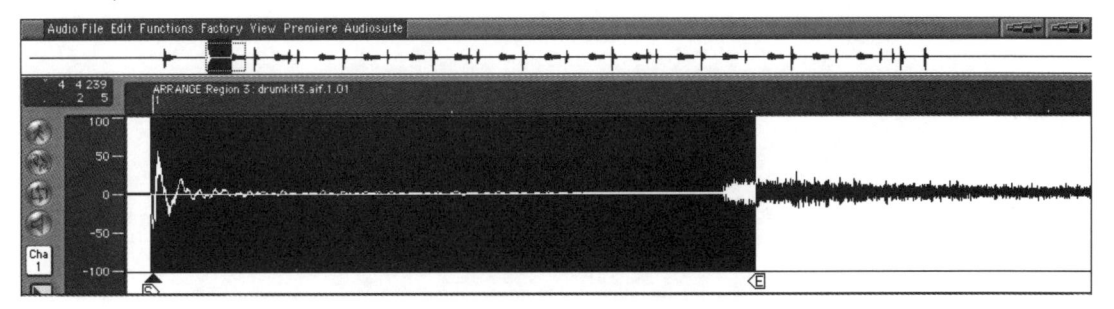

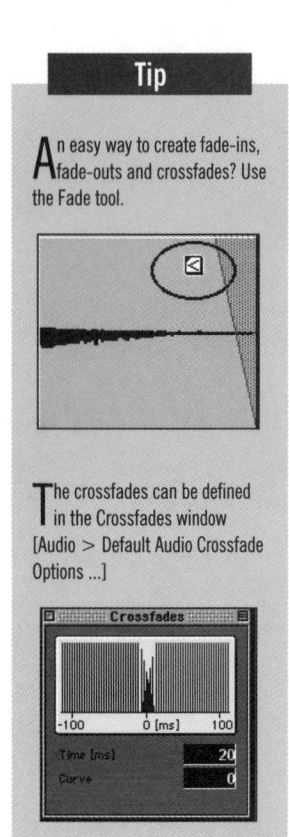

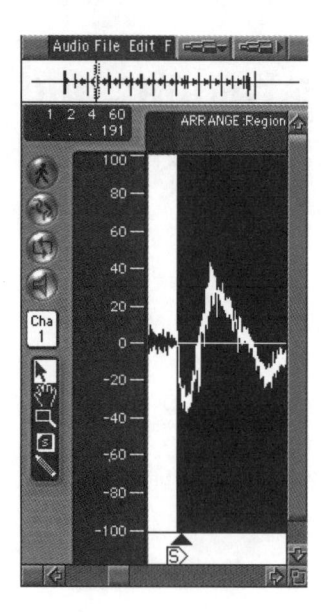

> **Tip**
>
> An easy way to create fade-ins, fade-outs and crossfades? Use the Fade tool.
>
> The crossfades can be defined in the Crossfades window [Audio > Default Audio Crossfade Options ...]

Figure P13.2
Start time adjusted.

3 Create a fade [Functions > Fade Out] to get rid of it. Alternatively, in the Arrange window use the Fade tool. I prefer the latter method.
4 Double click on the fifth Region. You'll see that a tiny bit of hi-hat, from the previous region, has been caught at the beginning. This time adjust the region's start time to cut it out (Figure P13.2).
5 Check each region in turn and make adjustments.
6 Save Song – compare to project13/13.1.

Project 14 – using Groove Machine

Objective

- Use Groove Machine to impose a swing quantize factor on an audio file.

Preparation

1 From the CD, copy the folder named project14 to your computer.
2 On your computer, create a folder called mywork14 or something similar in which to save your work.
3 From the project14 folder, open the template – templt14
4 In your new mywork14 folder, re-save the template as myproj14 or something similar.

This template picks up where the project 11 left off. Logic's Song tempo has been adjusted to 85.0658 bpm to match the audio file, now renamed drumkit5.aif. The Audio Region has been adjusted to exactly four bars in the Audio and Arrange windows.

It would be nice if we could alter the swing factor of the audio just as we do with MIDI. Of course, it's possible do this with Logic. The results are not always perfect but with patience a trial and error approach usually yields good results. Let's have a go!

Follow these steps:

1 In the Sample Editor – Open the Groove Machine window [Factory > Groove Machine ...] (Figure P14.1).
2 Choose a swing factor. A value of between 55% and 65% works best in most cases.

Info

The Groove Machine (Figure P14.1) is used to alter the swing, or groove of audio material, in percentage steps. These are based on parameters such as tempo and bar length. Down beats and off beats can also be raised and lowered to alter the feel of a particular groove.

Figure P14.1
Groove Machine.

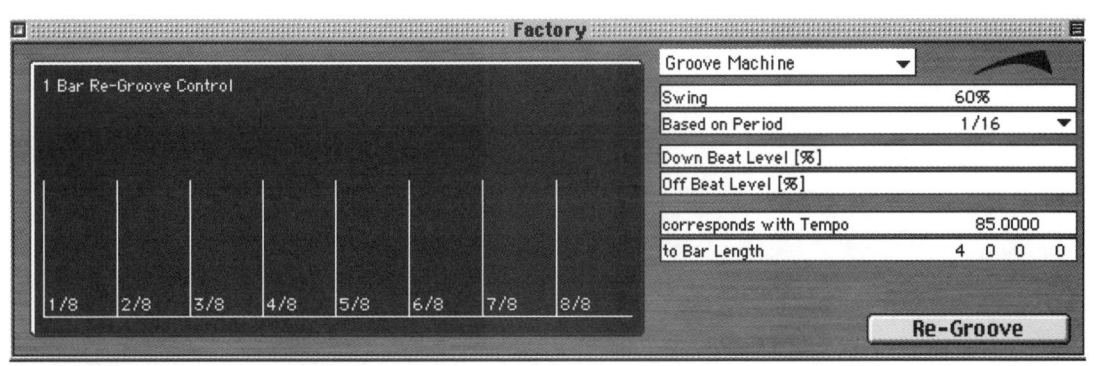

3 Choose a Based On Period parameter. In this case it will be 1/16 because of the sixteenth note kick drum fill near the end of the loop. Leave the Down Beat Level and Off Beat Level as it is. It's fine. Ensure that the Corresponds to Tempo parameter matches the song tempo and that the 'to Bar Length' box displays 4.0.0.0.
4 Press the Re-Groove button.
5 Play the result in Sample Editor. Notice how the kick drum beats have been affected. Experiment with different swing values yourself.
6 Save Song – compare with project14/14.1.

Project 15 – audio to MIDI Groove Templates

Objective

- Use Audio to MIDI Groove Template to extract a groove from an audio file and apply it a MIDI sequence.

Preparation

1 From the CD, copy the folder named project15 to your computer.
2 On your computer, create a folder called mywork15 or something similar in which to save your work.
3 From the project15 folder, open the template – templt15.
4 In your new mywork15 folder, re-save the template as myproj15 or something similar.

In the previous project we imposed a degree of swing onto an audio file. Can we now apply that same swing feel to our MIDI tracks? Yes, but first, we need to program a simple drum pattern similar to the one in the audio file.

Follow these steps:

1 On track 2, sequence this simple drum pattern (Figures P15.1, P15.2 and P15.3). Keep it straight and quantize to 16A if necessary.

Figure P15.1
Drum pattern, Score view.

2 Select the audio region on track one and in the Sample Editor open the Quantize window [Factory > Audio to MIDI Groove Template ...]. Two things happpen. The Quantize window opens and three new fields labeled Audio Qua, Basis Qua and Result Qua appear at the bottom of the Sample Editor (Figure P15.4).
3 Select Drums Mid from the Instrument Type flip menu. This gives us template parameters suitable for this particular loop.
4 In the Basis Qua box select 'off (3840)'. This is where you can add extra quantization points. Select one if you want, it will not alter the audio quantization points already selected. It just adds more.
5 Switch off the Search Zero Crossings option in the Edit menu.

Figure P15.2
Drum pattern, Hyper view.

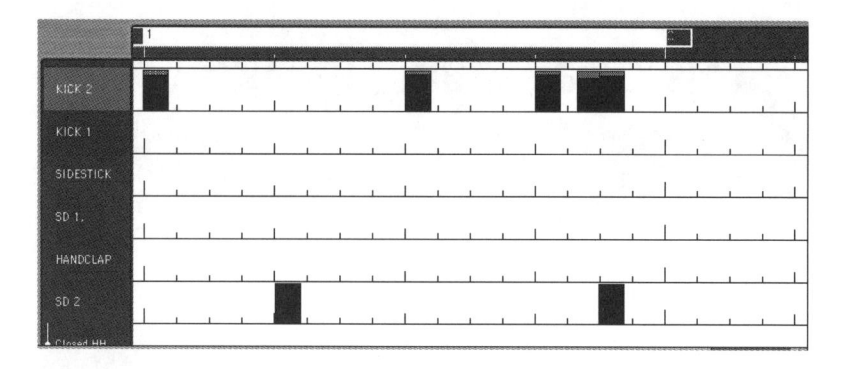

Figure P15.3
Drum pattern, Matrix view.

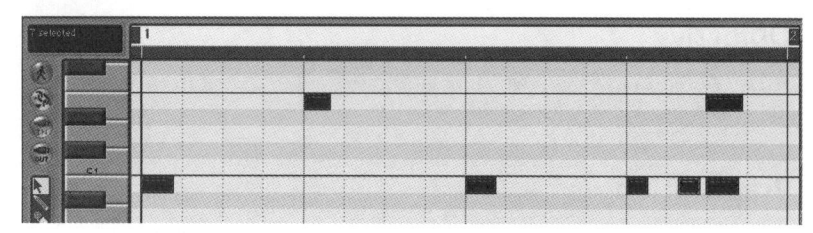

Figure P15.4
Sample editor, three new fields (encircled) and Quantize window.

Figure P15.5
Qua off and Qua drumkit.aif.

6 Click Try, to do just that. Click Use and the new template (drumkit6.aif) will appear, along with all the other quantize settings, in the Quantize flip menu. Only for this song though!

7 In the Sequence Parameter box, toggle between the new groove value, Qua drumkit.aif and Qua off (3840) to A B the result (Figures P15.5). There're quite different.

8 Save Song – compare to project15/15.1.

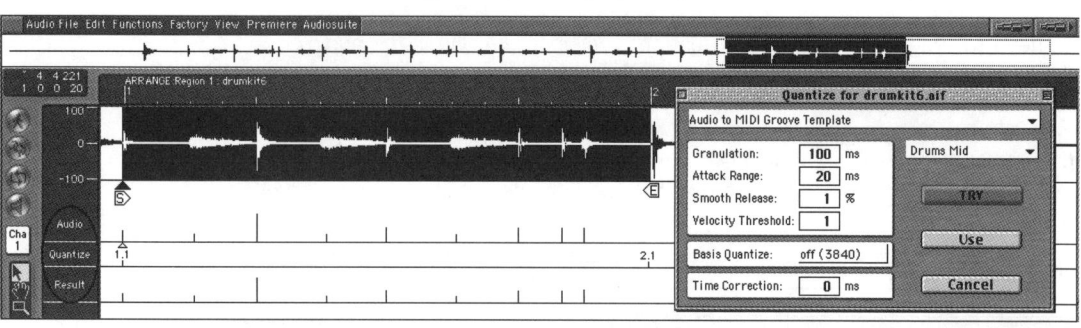

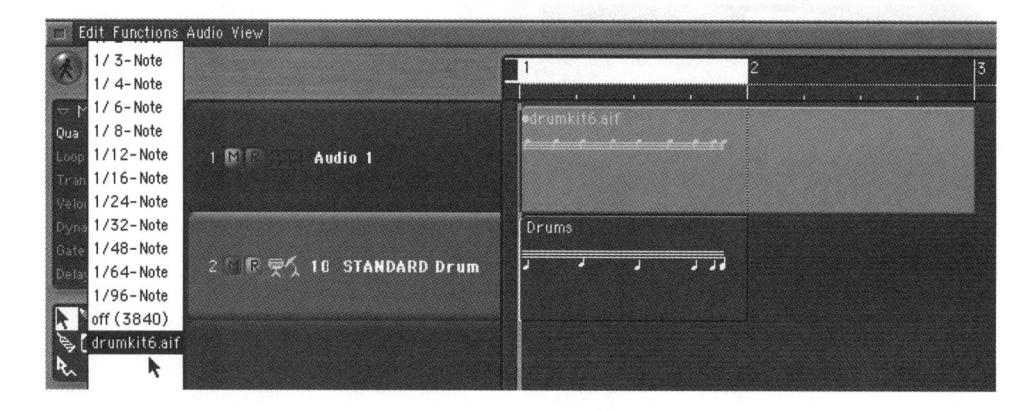

Project 16 – audio pitch shifting

Objective

- Use the Time and Pitch Machine to alter the pitch of audio files.

Preparation

1 From the CD, copy the folder named project16 to your computer.
2 On your computer, create a folder called mywork16 or something similar in which to save your work.
3 From the project16 folder, open the template – templt16.
4 In your new mywork16 folder, re-save the template as myproj16 or something similar.

This template contains three identical audio files, a few bars of alto sax playing a jazz waltz. How about turning this into a sax section with harmonies? It can be done quite quickly with Logic's Time and Pitch Machine. No extra players needed!
Follow these steps:

1 On Track 2 – select the audio region named altosax.2 and double click to open the Sample Editor.
2 In the Sample Editor – open the Time and Pitch Machine [Factory > Time and Pitch Machine …]. Now this looks interesting! For a start there's a picturesque graphic display with a ball that is moved with the mouse (Figure P16.1).

Figure P16.1
Time and Pitch Machine.

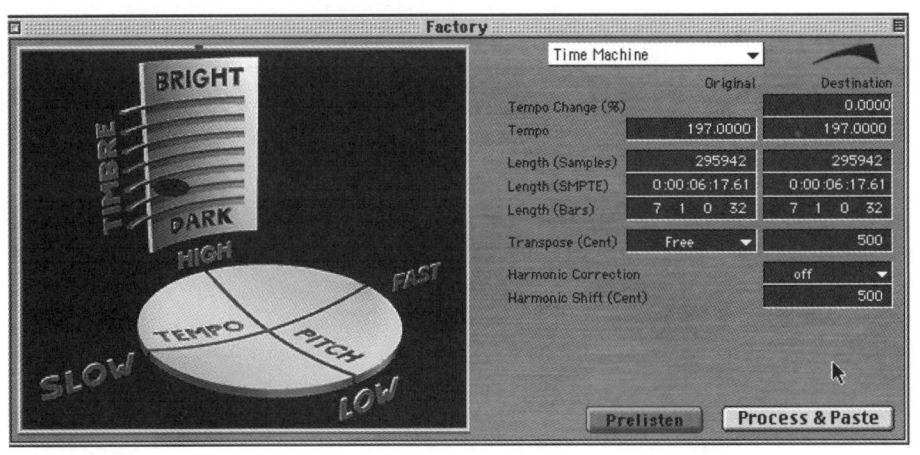

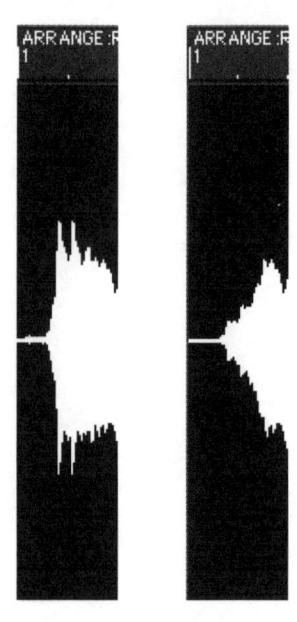

Figure P16.2 **Figure P16.3**
Before fade in. After fade in.

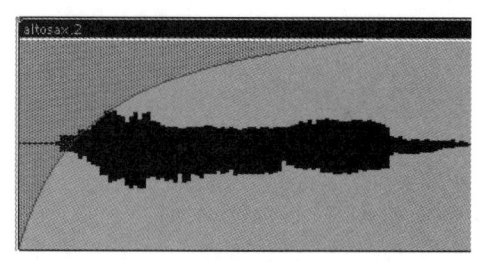

Figure P16.4
Curved fade in.

> **Info**
>
> In the Time and Pitch Machine transposition is measured in 1/100 semitone units (cents). In other words, one semitone is entered in the Transpose parameter box as 100. Raising pitch by a tone (two semitones) is therefore entered as 200 and so forth.

3 Experiment! Mess about with it and use the pre-listen button to hear the results. This will give you a fair indication of what it's about.
4 OK, you've had your fun! Let's get serious. The results we need are best obtained using the parameter menus. There are two columns, Original and Destination. We are going to transpose this file up a fourth. That's five semitones. So, enter 500 in the Destination Transpose parameter box. The Original should be set at 'Free'. Leave the Harmonic Correction set to 'off'. More on this shortly.
5 Hold down the Pre-listen button. You'll hear a speeded up version at a higher pitch. What do you think? Sounds a bit Mickey Mouse doesn't it? Well I don't mind. It'll not sound speeded up once processed and the altered tone sounds rather like that of a soprano saxophone. All the better in this case. Let's make a commitment. Press Process and Paste. The result? Well the original audio has altered a fair bit and the first note is now rather jagged looking and unpleasant to listen to. Apart from that, we can get away with it once it's played with the other saxophones.
6 How to clean up that entrance? There are various ways. Making a Fade In [Functions > Fade In] is easy and does the trick (Figures P16.2 and P16.3). Adjust the Settings [Functions > Settings] until it's right. Alternatively use the Fade tool and create a curved Fade In in the Arrange window (Figure P16.4).
7 In the Arrange window, on Track 3 – select the audio region named altosax.3 and double click to open the Sample Editor.
8 Open the Time and Pitch Machine, and this time set a Transpose parameter of –700. That's a fifth lower. This time turn the Harmonic Correction 'on.' Press the Pre-listen button. It sounds rather like a baritone sax to me, which is fine. Press the Process and Paste button.
9 Now play all three tracks together. Instant sax section!
10 Save Song – compare with project16/16.1.

Project 17 – time stretching audio

Objective

- Slow down a few bars of recorded saxophone (audio) without altering the pitch.

Preparation

1 From the CD, copy the folder named project17 to your computer.
2 On your computer, create a folder called mywork17 or something similar in which to save your work.
3 From the project17 folder, open the template – templt17
4 In your new mywork17 folder, re-save the template as myproj17 or something similar.

In the previous project we used the Time and Pitch Machine to alter the pitch of an audio file. In this project we will use the same file, but this time slow it down without altering the pitch. It's easy.

Follow these steps:

1 Double click on the audio region named altosax.1 to open the Sample Editor.
2 In the Sample Editor – open the Time and Pitch Machine [Factory > Time and Pitch Machine ...].
3 Scroll the Destination tempo down to 177bpm. That's a reduction of 20 bpm.
4 Press Process and Paste.
5 Save Song – compare to project17/17.1.

So simple! The new, stretched version is on track 2. Scroll the tempo to 177 bpm and it will shrink to size!

Appendix 1
Instrument ranges

Use these as a guide when emulating real instruments with MIDI. These are safe, practical ranges, used when writing for real players. For a realistic interpretation avoid the high and low extremes except perhaps for solo passages.

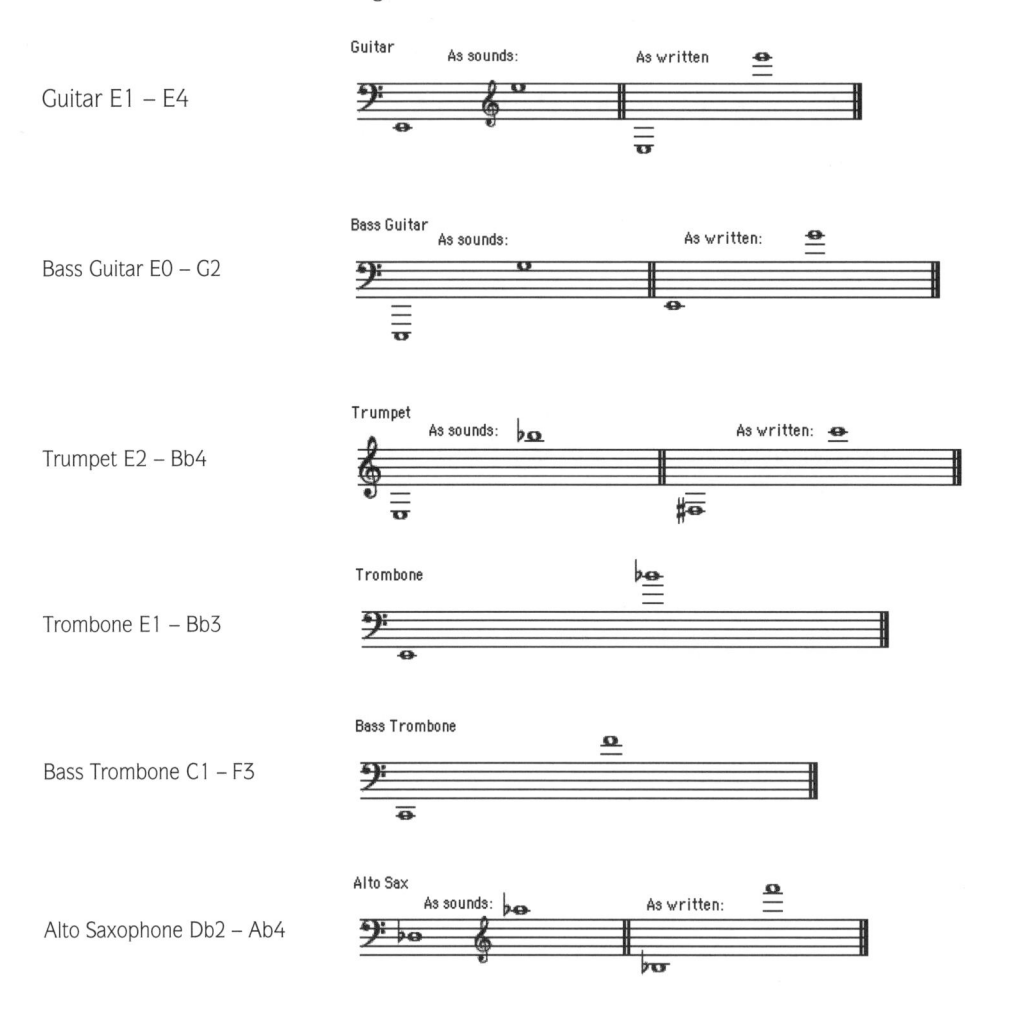

Guitar E1 – E4

Bass Guitar E0 – G2

Trumpet E2 – Bb4

Trombone E1 – Bb3

Bass Trombone C1 – F3

Alto Saxophone Db2 – Ab4

Tenor Saxophone Ab1 – Eb4

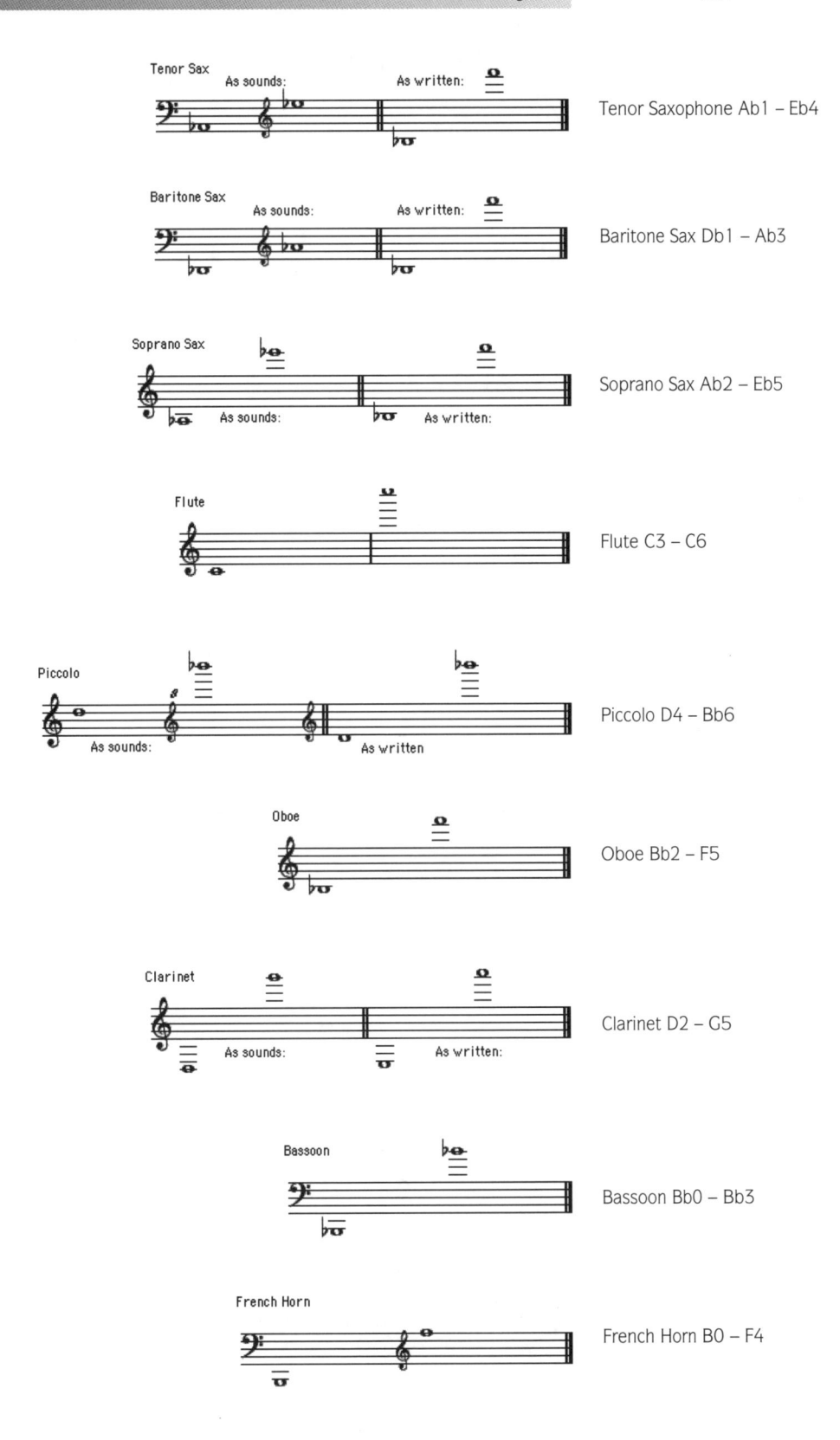

Baritone Sax Db1 – Ab3

Soprano Sax Ab2 – Eb5

Flute C3 – C6

Piccolo D4 – Bb6

Oboe Bb2 – F5

Clarinet D2 – G5

Bassoon Bb0 – Bb3

French Horn B0 – F4

Instrument	Range
Violin	G2 – C6
Viola	C2 – C5
Cello	C1 – G4
Double Bass	E0 – G2
Harp	Cb1 – Gb6
Glockenspiel	G4 – C7
Xylophone	B3 – C6
Celesta	C3 – C7
Marimba	C2 – C6
Vibraphone	F2 – F5

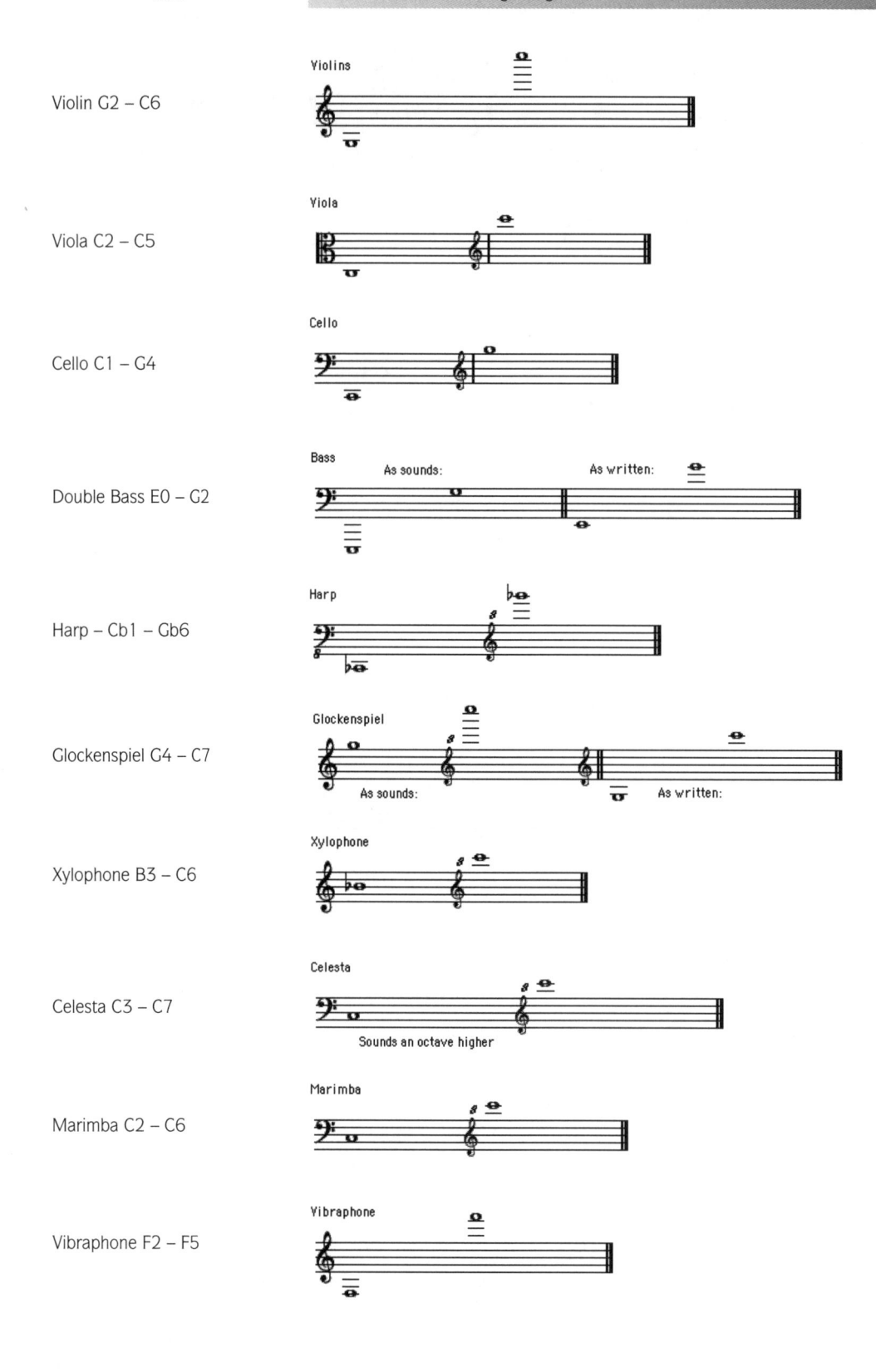

Appendix 2
Key Commands for Mac

Global Commands

*	Record	Shift L	Lock/Unlock Current Screenset
Shift *	Record Toggle	P	Extended Sequence Parameters...
Control *	Capture Last Take as Recording	Option O	Recording options...
Enter	Play	Option P	Preferences...
,	Pause	Command 2	Open Event Editor...
0	Stop	Command 1	Open Arrange Window...
Space	Play or Stop	Command M	Open Track Mixer...
Top	Rewind	Command 3	Open Score Editor...
Bottom	Forward	Command 4	Open Transform
Shift Top	Fast Rewind	Command 5	Open Hyper Editor...
ShiftBottom	Fast Forward	Command 6	Open Matrix Editor...
Return	Play from Beginning	Command 7	Open Transport...
G	goto Position...	Command 8	Open Environment...
B	Set rounded Locators by Objects	Command 9	Open Audio Window...
J	Swap Left and Right Locator	Command 0	Open Sample Editor...
Shift Enter	Play from Selection	F	Open Event Float...
C	Cycle	Option T	Open Tempo List...
D	Drop	Option K	Open Key Commands...
S	Solo	Option C	Open Object Colors...
Option S	Set Solo Lock Mode	Option M	Open Movie...
Shift Option S	Reselect Solo-locked Objects	A	Set Audio Record Path ...
Y	Sync intern/extern	Command W	Close Window or Song
K	MIDI/Monitor Metronome Click	Command N	New
Help	Send discrete Note Offs (Panic)	Command O	Open...
Z	Send Used Instruments MIDI Settings	Option Command W	Close
V	Send All Current Fader Values	Command S	Save
		Option Command S	Save Song as...

Command P	Print	Shift I	Select inside Locators
Command Q	Quit	Shift U	Select empty Objects
Command Z	Undo	Shift E	Select Equal Objects
Shift Command Z	Redo	Shift S	Select Similar Objects
Command X	Cut	Shift H	Select Equal Channels
Command C	Copy	Shift P	Select Equal Subpositions
Command V	Paste	Shift M	Select Muted Objects
Command A	Select All	Left	Select Previous Event
		Right	Select Next Event
		Shift Left	Toggle Previous Event

Various Windows

Esc	Show Tools	Shift Right	Toggle Next Event
Control Left	Zoom Horizontal Out	Q	Quantize Again
Control Right	Zoom Horizontal In	Tab	Note Overlap Correction
Control Up	Zoom Vertical Out	Shift Tab	Note Force Legato
Control Down	Zoom Vertical In	Command B	Paste Replace
Shift Control Up	Page Up	R	Repeat Objects…
Shift Control Down	Page Down	Control +	Merge Objects/Digital Mixdown
Shift Control Left	Page Left	Control /	Split Objects by rounded Song Position
Shift Control Right	Page Right		
H	Hide/Show Parameters	/	Split Objects by Song Position
.	Catch Clock Position	Control P	Pickup Clock (Move Event to SPL Position)
O	MIDI Out Toggle		
I	MIDI In Toggle	Shift Control P	Pickup Clock & Select Next Event
M	Mute Objects	Option Right	Nudge Event Position by Format +1
F4	Hyper Draw: Disable	Option Left	Nudge Event Position by Format -1
F1	Hyper Draw: Volume	Option Up	Event Transpose +1
F2	Hyper Draw: Pan	Option Down	Event Transpose -1
Shift F1	Hyper Draw: Modulation	U	Positions/Time Ruler in SMPTE units
Shift F3	Hyper Draw: Other…	PageUp	Unlock SMPTE Position
F3	Hyper Draw: Autodefine	PageDown	Lock SMPTE Position

Arrange and Various Sequence Editors

Arrange Window

Shift Command A	Deselect All	Up	Select previous Track
Shift T	Toggle Selection	Down	Select next Track
Shift F	Select All Following	Left	Select previous Object
		Right	Select next Object

Shift C	Select Equal Colored Objects	Tab	Remove Overlaps
Command F	Pack Folder	Shift Tab	Tie Objects by Length Change
Shift Command F	Unpack Folder	Option Tab	Tie Objects by Position Change
Control Return	Create Track	Control E	Erase outside Object Borders
Shift Control Return	Create Track with next Instrument	Control D	Delay in ms
		Control O	Object Content
X	Mute Track	Shift Option C	Instrument Colors To Objects
Control X	Mute All Tracks With Same Instrument of Song	Shift Option N	Tracknames To Objects

Environment Window

Control Option Down	Individual Track Zoom In		
Control Option Up	Individual Track Zoom Out	Control Backspace	Clear Cables only
Control Option Left	Individual Track Zoom Reset	Control C	Hide/Show Cables
Control Option Right	Individual Track Zoom Reset for All Tracks	Control P	Protect Cabling/Positions
Control A	Reassign Alias	Shift T	Toggle Selection
Shift O	Find Original of Alias	Shift U	Select Unused Instruments
Shift A	Select All Aliases of Object	Shift D	Select Cable Destination
Option +	Audio Crossfade Options for Merge...	Shift O	Select Cable Origin
		Control V	Send Selected Fader Values
<	Snip: Cut Time and Move by Locators	Control S	Cable serially

Score Window

Shift <	Insert Time and Move by Locators		
Command <	Splice: Insert snipped part at Song Position	Control P	Explode Polyphony
		Option Command V	Paste Multiple
Command D	Demix by Event Channel	Right	Next Event
Control Backspace	Delete Trackname	Left	Previous Event
T	Adjust Tempo using object length and Locators	Down	Next Staff
		Up	Previous Staff
Control R	Convert Regions to Individual Regions	Control S	Stems: default
		Control Top	Stems: up
Control F	Convert Regions to Individual Audio Files	Control Bottom	Stems: down
		Control Backspace	Stems: hide
N	Normalize	Control T	Ties: default
Option Q	Fix Quantize	Control PageUp	Ties: up
L	Toggle Loop	Control PageDown	Ties: down
Option L	Turn Loops to Real Copies	Control B	Beam Selected Notes
Shift Option L	Turn Loops to Aliases	Control U	Unbeam Selected Notes
E	Erase Duplicated Events		

Control D	Default Beams	Control Backspace	Delete File(s)
Control A	Default Accidentals	Control O	Optimize File(s)
Shift #	Enharmonic Shift: #	Control B	Backup File(s)
Shift B	Enharmonic Shift: b	Control C	Copy/Convert File(s)
Option Command A	Align Object Positions Vertically	Control M	Move File(s)
Option G	Settings: Global Format	Shift U	Select Unused
Option N	Settings: Numbers Names	PageDown	Show All Regions
Shift Control Top	Insert: Slur Up	PageUp	Hide All Regions
Shift Control Bottom	Insert: Slur Down	Control S	Strip Silence
Shift Control C	Insert: Crescendo	Control I	Import SDII Regions
Shift Control D	Insert: Decrescendo	Control E	Export SDII Regions

Event Window

Up	Scroll to Previous Event
Down	Scroll to Next Event
Control A	Length as Absolute Position
Control L	Local Position
Control E	Numerical Edit of Event Position
Control D	Duplicate Event and Numerical Edit
Control V	Copy value to all following events

Sample Edit Window

Space	Play/Stop Selection
Control Space	Play/Stop All
Control B	Create Backup
Shift Command S	Save Selection As...
Shift R	Region -> Selection
Shift Control R	Selection -> Region
Left	Goto Selection Start
Right	Goto Selection End
Down	Goto Region Anchor
Control R	Create New Region
Control N	Normalize
Control V	Change Gain...
Control I	Fade In
Control O	Fade Out
Control Backspace	Silence
Control <	Reverse
Control T	Time and Pitch Machine...
Control G	Groove Machine...
Control E	Audio Energizer...
Control C	Sample Rate Convert...
Control M	Audio to MIDI Groove Template...
Control A	Audio to Score...
Control Q	Quantize Engine...

Hyper Edit

Control Return	Create Event Definition
Control Backspace	Delete Event Definition
Control T	Convert Event Definition...
Control C	Copy Event Definition
Control V	Paste Event Definition
Control A	Auto define toggle

Audio Window

Up	Select Previous Audio File
Down	Select Next Audio File
Space	Play/Stop Region
Control F	Add Audio File...
Control R	Add Region

Appendix 3
Key Commands for PC

Global Commands

Num-*	Record	Alt Ctrl O	Recording options...
Shift Num-*	Record Toggle	Alt Ctrl P	Preferences...
Ctrl Num-*	Capture Last Take as Recording	F	Open Event Float...
Num Enter	Play	Ctrl 2	Open Event Editor...
Del	Pause	Ctrl 1	Open Arrange Window...
Num-0	Stop	Ctrl M	Open Track Mixer...
Space	Play or Stop	Ctrl 3	Open Score Editor...
Home	Rewind	Ctrl 4	Open Transform
End	Forward	Ctrl 5	Open Hyper Editor...
Shift Home	Fast Rewind	Ctrl 6	Open Matrix Editor...
Shift End	Fast Forward	Ctrl 7	Open Transport...
Alt Home	Rewind by format value	Ctrl 8	Open Environment...
Alt End	Forward by format value	Ctrl 9	Open Audio Window...
G	goto Position...	Ctrl 0	Open Sample Editor...
B	Set rounded Locators by Objects	Alt Ctrl T	Open Tempo List...
J	Swap Left and Right Locator	Alt Ctrl K	Open Key Commands...
Shift Num Enter	Play from Selection	Alt Ctrl C	Open Object Colors...
C	Cycle	Alt Ctrl M	Open Movie...
D	Drop	A	Set Audio Record Path ...
S	Solo	Ctrl N	New
Alt S	Set Solo Lock Mode	Ctrl O	Open...
Shift Alt S	Reselect Solo-locked Objects	Ctrl W	Close
Y	Sync intern/extern	Ctrl S	Save
K	MIDI/Monitor Metronome Click	Alt Ctrl S	Save Song as...
Ins	Send discrete Note Offs (Panic)	Ctrl P	Print
Z	Send Used Instruments MIDI Settings	Ctrl Q	Quit
V	Send All Current Fader Values	Ctrl Z	Undo
Shift L	Lock/Unlock Current Screenset	Ctrl X	Cut
P	Extended Sequence Parameters...	Ctrl C	Copy
		Ctrl V	Paste

Ctrl A	Select All	Shift Left	Toggle Previous Event
Ctrl Num—	Smaller View	Shift Right	Toggle Next Event
Ctrl Num-+	Larger View	Q	Quantize Again
\	Zoom Window	Tab	Note Overlap Correction
		Shift Tab	Note Force Legato
		Ctrl B	Paste Replace

Various Windows

Esc	Show Tools	R	Repeat Objects...
Ctrl Left	Zoom Horizontal Out	Scroll Lock	Pickup Clock (Move Event to SPL Position)
Ctrl Right	Zoom Horizontal In	Shift Scroll Lock	Pickup Clock & Select Next Event
Ctrl Up	Zoom Vertical Out	Alt Right	Nudge Event Position by Format +1
Ctrl Down	Zoom Vertical In	Alt Left	Nudge Event Position by Format –1
Shift Ctrl Up	Page Up	Alt Up	Event Transpose +1
Shift Ctrl Down	Page Down	Alt Down	Event Transpose –1
Shift Ctrl Left	Page Left	U	Positions/Time Ruler in SMPTE units
Shift Ctrl Right	Page Right	Page Up	Unlock SMPTE Position
H	Hide/Show Parameters	Page Down	Lock SMPTE Position
.	Catch Clock Position		
O	MIDI Out Toggle		
I	MIDI In Toggle		

Arrange Window

M	Mute Folders/Sequences	Up	Select previous Track
F4	Hyper Draw: Disable	Down	Select next Track
F1	Hyper Draw: Volume	Left	Select previous Object
F2	Hyper Draw: Pan	Right	Select next Object
Shift F1	Hyper Draw: Modulation	Shift M	Select Muted Objects
Shift F3	Hyper Draw: Other...	Shift C	Select Equal Colored Objects
F3	Hyper Draw: Autodefine	Ctrl	F Pack Folder
		Shift Ctrl F	Unpack Folder
		Ctrl Enter	Create Track
		Shift Ctrl Enter	Create Track with next Instrument

Arrange and Various Sequence Editors

Alt Ctrl A	Deselect All	X	Mute Track
Shift T	Toggle Selection	Alt X	Mute All Tracks With Same Instrument of Song
Shift F	Select All Following		
Shift I	Select inside Locators	Alt Ctrl Down	Individual Track Zoom In
Shift U	Select empty Objects	Alt Ctrl Up	Individual Track Zoom Reset
Shift E	Select Equal Objects	Alt Ctrl Right	Individual Track Zoom Reset for All Tracks
Shift S	Select Similar Objects		
Shift H	Select Equal Channels	Shift Ctrl A	Reassign Alias
Shift P	Select Equal Subpositions	Shift O	Find Original of Alias
Left	Select Previous Event	Shift A	Select All Aliases of Object
Right	Select Next Event	Ctrl +	Merge Objects/Digital Mixdown
		Alt Ctrl +	Audio Crossfade Options for Merge...

Shift Ctrl +	Merge Objects per Tracks		*Score Window*	
Alt Num-/	Split Objects by rounded Song Position		Shift Ctrl P	Explode Polyphony
			Alt Ctrl V	Paste Multiple
Num-/	Split Objects by Song Position		Right	Next Event
<	Snip: Cut Time and Move by Locators		Left	Previous Event
Shift <	Insert Time and Move by Locators		Down	Next Staff
Ctrl <	Splice: Insert snipped part at Song Position		Up	Previous Staff
			Shift Ctrl S	Stems: default
Ctrl D	Demix by Event Channel		Shift Ctrl Home	Stems: up
Ctrl Backspace	Delete Trackname		Shift Ctrl End	Stems: down
T	Adjust Tempo using object length and Locators		Shift Ctrl Backspace	Stems: hide
			Shift Ctrl T	Ties: default
Alt Ctrl R	Convert Regions to Individual Regions		Shift Ctrl Page Up	Ties: up
Alt Ctrl F	Convert Regions to Individual Audio Files		Shift Ctrl Page Down	Ties: down
			Shift Ctrl B	Beam Selected Notes
N	Normalize		Shift Ctrl U	Unbeam Selected Notes
Shift Ctrl Q	Fix Quantize		Shift Ctrl D	Default Beams
L	Toggle Loop		Shift Alt A	Default Accidentals
Ctrl L	Turn Loops to Real Copies		Shift #	Enharmonic Shift: #
Shift Ctrl L	Turn Loops to Aliases		Shift B	Enharmonic Shift: b
E	Erase Duplicated Events		Alt Ctrl A	Align Object Positions Vertically
Tab	Remove Overlaps		Alt Ctrl G	Settings: Global Format
Shift Tab	Tie Objects by Length Change		Alt Ctrl N	Settings: Numbers Names
Shift Alt Ctrl Tab	Tie Objects by Position Change		Shift Alt Ctrl Home	Insert: Slur Up
Ctrl E	Erase outside Object Borders		Shift Alt Ctrl End	Insert: Slur Down
Shift Ctrl D	Delay in ms		Shift Alt Ctrl C	Insert: Crescendo
Shift Ctrl O	Object Content		Shift Alt Ctrl D	Insert: Decrescendo
Shift Ctrl C	Instrument Colors To Objects			
Shift Ctrl N	Tracknames To Objects		*Event Window*	
			Up	Scroll to Previous Event
Environment Window			Down	Scroll to Next Event
Ctrl Backspace	Clear Cables only		Shift Ctrl A	Length as Absolute Position
Shift Ctrl C	Hide/Show Cables		Shift Ctrl L	Local Position
Shift Ctrl P	Protect Cabling/Positions		Shift Ctrl E	Numerical Edit of Event Position
Shift T	Toggle Selection		Shift Ctrl D	Duplicate Event and Numerical Edit
Shift U	Select Unused Instruments			
Shift D	Select Cable Destination		Shift Ctrl V	Copy value to all following events
Shift O	Select Cable Origin			
Shift Ctrl V	Send Selected Fader Values			
Shift Ctrl S	Cable serially			

Hyper Edit

Shift Ctrl Enter	Create Event Definition
Shift Ctrl Backspace	Delete Event Definition
Shift Ctrl C	Copy Event Definition
Shift Ctrl V	Paste Event Definition
Shift Ctrl A	Auto define toggle

Audio Window

Up	Select Previous Audio File
Down	Select Next Audio File
Space	Play/Stop Region
Shift Ctrl F	Add Audio File …
Shift Ctrl R	Add Region
Shift Ctrl Backspace	Delete File(s)
Shift Ctrl O	Optimize File(s)
Shift Ctrl B	Backup File(s)
Shift Ctrl C	Copy/Convert File(s)
Shift Ctrl M	Move File(s)
Shift U	Select Unused
Page Down	Show All Regions
Page Up	Hide All Regions
Shift Ctrl S	Strip Silence

Sample Edit Window

Space	Play/Stop Selection
Alt Space	Play/Stop All
Shift Ctrl B	Create Backup
Shift Ctrl S	Save Selection As…
Shift R	Region -> Selection
Shift Ctrl R	Selection -> Region
Left	Goto Selection Start
Right	Goto Selection End
Down	Goto Region Anchor
Ctrl R	Create New Region
Shift Ctrl N	Normalize
Shift Ctrl V	Change Gain…
Shift Ctrl I	Fade In
Shift Ctrl O	Fade Out
Shift Ctrl Backspace	Silence
Shift Ctrl <	Reverse
Shift Ctrl T	Time and Pitch Machine…
Shift Ctrl G	Groove Machine…
Shift Ctrl E	Audio Energizer…
Shift Ctrl C	Sample Rate Convert…
Shift Ctrl M	Audio to MIDI Groove Template…
Shift Ctrl A	Audio to Score…
Shift Ctrl Q	Quantize Engine…

Index

accents, 186, 189
acoustic guitar, 113
Adaptive Track Mixer, 82
adjust start points, 197
Adjust Tempo by Selection & Locators, 194
Aliases, 82, 93
altering pitch, 190
alto clef, 70
Arm and record enable an Audio object, 115
Arming an Audio Object, 129
arpeggios, 107
Arrow tool, 166
Arrows, 188
assignment, 3
audio device, 130
audio editing, 190
Audio files, 2, 114
Audio Instrument ES E, 115
Audio Instruments, 94, 121, 171
audio loops, 171
Audio Mixer, 5
Audio Objects, 5, 113, 114, 129
Audio Path, 113
audio pitch shifting, 203
Audio Region, 114, 130, 194, 199, 201
audio signal peaks, 137
Audio to MIDI function, 190
Audio to MIDI Groove Template, 201
Audio to Score Streamer, 191
audio track, 129
Audio window, 113, 131, 191
Autodrop, 8, 9
automate the Track Mixer, 65
automated mix, 74
Automation, 152
Automation – effects, 151
Automation Mode, 152
AVerb, 136

bar and page numbers, 180, 187
Bar Lines, 188
Bar Ruler, 8
Based On Period parameter, 200
bass guitar, 112
bass line, 107, 121
big band swing, 134

blues scale, 44, 57, 137 – 139, 146
Brackets and Bar Lines, 187
brass, 18, 113
bridge, 102, 103, 107
bus object, 97
bus send, 83
Bypass automation data, 151

canon, 159
cell construction, 109
changing note heads, 185
channel insert, 150, 151
channel number, 3
channel strip, 60
Chase Control 0 – 15, 76
choosing a pre-set, 121
Chord Edit Window, 185
Chord objects, 184
chord sheet, 184
chord symbols, 180, 185
chords, 106, 107
chorus, 60, 61, 82, 98, 103, 107
clarinet, 66, 67, 88
clef signs, 181
Click and Ports Layer, 4
clipping, 130
Close Events, 76
close voicing, 24, 123
colour palette, 72
colour, 72
Comparison Song file, 3
composition and arranging, 2
compressing velocities, 95
compression, 65, 66, 82, 132
compression ratio, 177
compressor, 115, 133
condenser mic, 113, 129
Controllers, 27
creative audio editing, 2
crescendos, 166, 188
crossfade, 172, 198
Crossfades window, 198
Crosshair tool, 169
cycle, 8
Cycle button, 8
Cycle icon, 194
cycle record, 8 – 10
cymbal note head, 186

dance music, 168, 171
deleting doubled notes, 10

Destination Transpose parameter box, 204
Digital Factory, 190
Direct Output Assignment, 6
Display Parameter box, 22, 181 – 184
display resolution, 85
Double bar lines, 188
drawing Pitch Bend data, 156
drop-in, 115
drop-out, 115
drum clef, 183
drum editor, 22, 28, 38, 39
drum loop, 171
drum machines, 168
drum notation, 22
drum part, 183
drum rolls, 22
drum sequences, 23
drum staves, 183
dynamic processors, 115
dynamic type, 129
dynamics, 26, 65, 66, 82, 95

effects, 96, 137
electric guitars, 112
Environment, 4, 5, 97, 129
Environment (Audio Layer), 113
EQ, 156, 165, 166, 171
EQ plug in, Hi-Pass, 177
Erase MIDI Events, 10
ES E, 82, 93, 94, 96, 97, 171
ES M, 121, 170, 171, 173
Event List, 20
Event List window, 59
Event Parameter box, 187
example Song file, 4
expression, 26, 27
Extended Sequence Parameters, 25
Extended Sequence Parameters box, 12 – 14, 22, 26
external mixer, 130

Fade in, 204
Fade tool, 197, 198, 204
fade-ins, 198
fade-out, 167, 197, 198
Flanger, 151
flute, 113
font and instrument name settings, 187
form, 100

General MIDI, 6
General MIDI Drum Set, 169
General MIDI Multi instrument, 4
General MIDI program number, 3
glissando, 160
glissando effects, 59
Global Display Value, 181
Global Recording Path, 129
GM device, 60
GM Drum, 39
GM Drum Set, 23, 38, 40
GM Multi Instrument, 6
GM tone generators, 165
GoldVerb, 132, 133, 176
Grand Piano, 30
Groove Machine, 199
Groove Template, 190
guitar, 24, 35, 83
Guitar Score, 184

Harmonic Correction, 204
harmonic structure, 107
harmony, 107
Hi-Pass, 177
Hide Unused Parameters box, 120
horns, 44
humanize, 44, 62
Humanize preset, 76
Hyper Draw, 20, 24, 59, 137, 156, 167
Hyper Edit, 22, 24, 28, 38, 39, 156
Hyper Edit window, 21
Hyper menu, 38

Import audio files, 156, 157
Increasing Threshold percentage, 196
index finder tool, 85
info line, 87, 185, 186
Input, 113
input level, 113, 130
input signal, 115, 130
inserting ES M, 121
inserts, 98, 165, 176
Instrument Colors to Objects, 72
Instrument Parameter box, 3, 28
Instrument ranges, 206
Instrument Sets, 180, 186
Instrument Set box, 186

217

internal instrument, 5
Interpretation, 179, 181 – 184
inversions, 107

key changes, 107
key signature, 181, 182
KlopfGeist, 6

legato, 21. 22, 65, 67, 82, 83
lengthening a note, 85
Limiter, 137, 150, 151, 166, 171, 176, 177
Lines, 188
List Edit window, 49
Locators, 3, 8
loop, 82, 168, 193
loop function, 159, 172
Loop ON, 173
looped object, 156, 157
Low Shelf EQ, 166
low shelving, 166

mapped drums, 28
Marker, 100, 102, 107
Marker Track, 102, 135
matching Song tempo to audio, 193
Matrix Edit window, 10
Matrix View, 11
melody, 106 – 110, 115
metronome, 6
microphone, 112
MIDI Channel and Port Connection, 6
MIDI controllers, 26, 60, 61, 75, 82, 160
MIDI file, 27
MIDI Instrument Layer, 4, 5
MIDI objects, 129
MIDI sequencing, 2, 7
MIDI to audio, 150
Mixing, 96
modulation, 19, 24, 107
Mono track, 130
motifs, 82, 110
musical statements, 110

No Overlap, 179, 182
Nodes, 166
noise gate, 196
Normalize Sequence Parameters, 82, 86, 173
normalizing and trimming regions, 190
note length, 82, 179
Note overlap Correction, 18
note-head symbol, 185

open spacing, 24
open voicing, 24
outboard compressor, 177
Overlapping notes, 18

Page Edit, 186, 189
Page View, 180, 181
pan, 28, 60, 82
pan contol, 75
pan settings, 90

Parameter Set box, 120
Parameter Sets, 119
Parametric EQ, 167
Part box, 180, 184 –186
passing notes, 107
pentatonic scale, 137, 156
phrase, 110, 111, 139, 195
piano, 31
pitch, 106, 109, 115, 117
pitch bend, 19, 20, 24, 59, 136, 161
Pitch Bend Sensitivity, 160
pitch shift, 2
Pitch Shift, 177
Pitch Shift II, 171, 176
PlatinumVerb, 115, 133, 150, 166, 167, 176
plug-ins, 131, 171
polyphony, 24
pop songs, 103
post fader, 97
Pre-listen button, 204
preparation, 3
Process and Paste, 204, 205
producing a readable score and parts, 2
projects, 2

Q-Range, 12, 14, 22, 25
Q-Strength, 12, 13, 14, 22, 25, 26
Q-Swing, 25
quantization, 2, 10, 25, 179
Quantize Display, 182
Quantize Engine, 190
quantize grid postition, 14
Quantize menu, 116
Quantize selected objects, 12
quantize value, 22
Quantize window, 201
Quicktime Musical Instruments, 1

randomize, 26, 63
Re-Groove button, 200
Re-record MIDI tracks as audio tracks, 137
Read, 152
record an audio track, 129
Record button, 9
Recording Options, 8, 9, 15
recording vocal tracks and acoustic instruments, 129
ReCycle File, 171, 172
reducing velocity, 57
reed instruments, 18
Registered Parameter Numbers, 160
repeat objects, 47, 85
repeat signs, 188
repetition, 80, 82, 115, 139
repetition and variation, 109
reverb, 60, 61, 82, 96, 132
rhythm, 108
rhythm section, 136
rhythmic design, 108
rhythmic framework, 117
rhythmic pattern, 111

rhythmic shape, 106
Rock rhythm, 107
Roland Sound Canvas, 1, 166
RPN, 160

Sample Edit window, 190
Sample Editor, 191, 192, 193, 197, 201, 203, 204, 205
Save Song, 3
saxophone section, 136
Score, 10
score – transposition, 189
Score and Layout section, 2
Score Display Parameter box, 179, 180, 181
Score editing features, 179
Score Editor, 178, 182, 183
Score Numbers and Names, 187
Score parameters, 182
Score view, 11
Search Zero Crossings, 196, 201
Select and Operate, 76, 118
Select by Condition, 118
Select slurs, 180
selecting notes, 185
send effects, 115, 165
Send full MIDI Reset before Chasing, 76
send knob, 97
Sends, 97
sends menu, 97
Sequence Parameter box, 3, 12, 13, 22,
set a Delay, 157
Set Audio Record Path, 129
Set audio Recording Path, 113
Set button, 130
setting Pitch Bend range, 160
setting up a loop, 157
setting up Your MIDI Hardware, 6
Short Reverb, 176
signal input levels, 115
signal processing, 96
Silver Compressor, 115, 132
SilverVerb, 83, 98, 115, 132
slash symbol, 185
sliced Regions, 196
slicing audio, 195
slurs, 188
soft limiting, 166, 167, 176
software GM, 5
Song Position Line, 15
Song Recording Path, 129, 130
Song Setting window, 180
Song Settings, 15, 76, 187, 188
soprano saxophone, 176
speech manipulation, 196
staccato marks, 189
staccato notes, 88
staff, 181
Stereo Delay, 171, 176, 177
stereo picture, 75, 96
stereo track, 130
strings, 21, 68, 113

Strip Silence feature, 195
Style, 183
swing groove, 44
swing quantize factor, 199
swing templates, 26, 49
symbols, 189
syncopation, 182
System Performance window, 6

takes, 3
template, 3
tempo, 7, 8, 193, 199
tenor sax, 44
Text Objects, 184
Text tool, 180, 186, 187
three part forms, 100
three part sectional harmony, 123
Time and Pitch Machine, 203, 204, 205, 190
time compression, 196
time expansion, 196
time signatures, 181
time stretch, 2, 190, 205
title and copyright information, 180
Title and Text Event Parameter box, 187
Touch, 152
TR808, 168
Track Automation, 137, 152, 156, 167
Track Mix, 65
Track Mixer, 44, 60, 61, 74, 97
Transform, 44, 119, 120
Transform Humanize preset, 62
Transform Parameter Set, 119
Transform window, 26, 63, 76, 118, 120
Transport bar, 8, 9
Transport window, 181
Transpose, 70, 82, 86, 146, 173
transposing instruments, 138
transposition, 28, 65, 36
treble clef, 50
trimming regions, 197
trombone, 44, 136
trumpet, 44, 136

Used Instrument MIDI Settings, 3

variation, 80, 82, 115, 139
velocity, 26, 27, 82, 186
velocity ramp, 169
Velocity tool, 87
verse, 103, 107
viola, 70
vocal, 112, 176, 177
volume, 26, 27, 60, 82, 96, 137

WoodenVerb, 166, 167, 176
woodwind, 18, 113